KIRMEN URIBE: LIFE, FICTION

Basque Literature Series No. 15

KIRMEN URIBE: LIFE, FICTION

Editors:
Amaia Elizalde, Mari Jose Olaziregi

Center for Basque Studies
University of Nevada, Reno
2022

Cover photo: Ricky Rubio

This book has been financed by the Provincial Council of Bizkaia and carried out as part of the IT 1047-16 (Basque Government) and FFI2017-84342-P (Ministry of Science and Innovation, Spain) research projects conducted by the MHLI (Historical Memory in Iberian Literatures) Research Group of the University of the Basque Country. A version of the work was published originally in Basque under the title Kirmen Uribe: Bizitza, Fikzioa by the EHU/UPV (University of the Basque Country) in the Laboa Katedra series.

Basque Literature Series No. 15

Series editor: Mari Jose Olaziregi

Library of Congress Cataloging-in-Publication Data

Names: Elizalde, Amaia, editor. | Olaziregi, Mari Jose, editor. | Watson, Cameron, 1967- translator.
Title: Kirmen Uribe: life, fiction / [editors, Amaia Elizalde, Mari Jose Olaziregi ; translation, Cameron Watson].
Other titles: Kirmen Uribe. English
Description: Reno: Center for Basque Studies Press, [2022] | Series: Basque literature series; no. 15 | A version of the work was published originally in Basque under the title Kirmen Uribe: Bizitza, Fikzioa by the EHU/UPV (University of the Basque Country) in the Laboa Katedra series. | Includes bibliographical references. | Summary: "This volume is a collective book on Kirmen Uribe's literary trajectory and includes research undertaken by university professors"-- Provided by publisher.
Identifiers: LCCN 2022034244 | ISBN 9781949805710 (paperback)
Subjects: LCSH: Uribe Urbieta, Kirmen, 1970---Criticism and interpretation. | LCGFT: Literary criticism. | Essays.
Classification: LCC PH5339.U55 Z7513 2022 | DDC 899/.928--dc23/eng/20220801
LC record available at https://lccn.loc.gov/2022034244

Contents

I

Prologue: Kirmen Uribe, an invitation to read

Mari Jose Olaziregi Alustiza and Amaia Elizalde Estenaga

They say that sailors and fishermen are thinking about their return when they set out to sea. Leaving in order to return safe and well, leaving in order to get lost in the azure of the sea. Kirmen Uribe (1970) is a writer that was born into a family of fishermen, specifically in Ondarroa, on the coast of Bizkaia, and one could say that he lives and breathes the saltiness of the sea. That is why embarkations and distancing are a constant in his work; like the sailors and fishermen in his town, going away implies the promise of return.

This volume is a collective book on Kirmen Uribe's literary trajectory and includes research undertaken by university professors. His excellent national and international reception includes diverse awards—Spain's National Prize for Narrative for *Bilbao-New York-Bilbao*, in 2009; the Critics' Prize for poetry in Basque, in 2002, for *Bitartean heldu eskutik*, 2001 (*Meanwhile Take My Hand*, 2007); and, in 2017, the Critics' Prize for narrative in Basque for *Elkarrekin esnatzeko ordua* (The Hour of Waking Together), 2016—as well as translations of his work into different languages (*Bilbao-New York-Bilbao*, for example, has been translated into fifteen languages). In addition, he has received prestigious grants such as that awarded by the Cullman Center at the New York Public Library in 2018, and invitations such as that by the University of Iowa in 2017 to be a writer-in-residence during the fall of 2017 within its International Writing Program.

Uribe's literary works have provoked diverse, critical reflections, and, like a kaleidoscope, we have attempted to include here a varied sampling of those. The chapters are organized into four main sections arranged around the genre or sphere they address: poetics, narrative, poetry, and children's and young adult literature. The chapters that make up each section do not follow any predetermined progression and can be read in any order.

Kirmen Uribe's own "Manual of disobedience" initiates the collection. It is a literary manifesto in which the author makes a declaration in favor of creative disobedience. For Uribe, freedom is, without any doubt, the primordial element that encourages creativity. Freedom to provoke innovations as a consequence of breaking literary norms and traditions. Among the novelesque elements on which the author reflects, comments referring to literary characters—a pillar of the genre since its beginnings—are prominent. Like the *nouveau romanciers*, who are considered the last representatives of modernism, Uribe favors a novel in which there are not necessarily any deep, essential main protagonists. That, in turn, gives prominence to novelesque form. Uribe states that he flees from the linear telling of events and favors what he terms "composite novels"—that is, narrations that encompass diverse narrative planes, points of view, and contexts. He tells us that he loves "the quest," to explore with new forms. And he believes in the contribution that Basque literature can make to world literature. For Uribe, as for Claudio Magris and many others, marginal voices carry great importance, given that Basque literature, independently of how we may define it (small, minority, or minoritized literature), has been on the fringes of the hegemonic literature of the "World Republic of Letters." Freedom, renovation of form, and giving a voice to those who have not had one, therefore, guide the author in his writing.

The section we have termed "Poetics" begins with the chapter titled "On scales, mirrors, and words: Intermediality and heterotopia in the work of Kirmen Uribe," by Professor Amaia Elizalde Estenaga (University of the Basque Country), in which the treatment of time in Uribe's artistic work is explored. Loss and the passage of time take on a special role in Uribe's narrative and poetic texts, as well as in other more hybrid creations. Elizalde underscores the importance of non-places and intermediality in Uribe's poetics—elements that have become more prominent in the course of his career and that are especially significant in regard to the manifest resistance against the modern notion of linear time. In a journey through Uribe's work, with a special emphasis on *Bilbao-New York-Bilbao*, *Bar Puerto*, *Elkarrekin esnatzeko ordua* (The Hour of Waking Together), *ABC. The Alphabet of the Bilbao Museum*, and *17 segundo* (17 Seconds), one can note a constant intermediality between image (stemming especially from techniques such as painting and film) and word (whether it be the written word, recitation, or radio emission). Through the combination of various media and the evocation of other spaces, Uribe's work expresses and constitutes—at both the artistic and meta-artistic levels—another time/space presented in simultaneous form, which atomizes and juxtaposes past, present, and future.

"The sea that connects us: The life and fiction of Kirmen Uribe," by professor Sally Perret (Salisbury University), addresses various articles written by the Basque author and a detailed reading of the novel *Mussche* in order to examine the worldview projected by Uribe's literary production. Perret speaks about the peaceful worldview that is projected in Uribe's works, an optimistic point of view that has not lost faith in humanity. Uribe explores universal themes such as love, heroism, and virtue, and uses non-teleological narrative techniques, such as continuous alternations in time and narrative planes in works like *Mussche*, with the aim of contributing an impolitically optimistic vision. However, this does not limit the treatment of controversial subjects, or the maintenance of a resistant attitude toward traditional powers. Monolithic and politically rigid traditional conceptions are excluded, avoiding any temptation toward prophesy. The world is, for the Basque author, the meeting point for cultures, languages, and dreams, and therein Uribe situates Basque culture, overcoming the links with tradition and the temptations toward isolation.

The second section, dedicated to the Basque author's narrative, begins with Hasier Arraiz's contribution, titled "Kirmen Uribe's literature: A way of looking at Basque society." Arraiz reflects on the finality that the Ondarroa writer's narrative texts pursue. He contends that these works are close to postmodern esthetics, but that they flee from philosophical and political relativism. Arraiz reads the novel *Bilbao-New York-Bilbao* (2008) in light of the characteristics associated with late postmodern narrative, both in its formal features (autofiction, fragmentation, metafictional writing, and the playing with the margins of literary genres) and in the philosophical approaches that underpin postmodernity (relativism, weak thought, etc.). In any event, Arraiz interprets Uribe's work within the framework of what he terms the postmodernism of *resistance*, and he points out, in relation to Uribe's last two novels, the relevance of, on the one hand, the author's own personal situation (*Mussche*, 2012), and, on the other, the importance for Uribe of reflecting on the consequences of political violence in Basque society in order thereby to be able to imagine what our future community will be like (*Elkarrekin esnatzeko ordua* (The Hour of WakingTogether, 2016).

The chapter by the historian Leyre Arrieta (University of Deusto), titled "Lehendakari Agirre and the Basque Government's cultural strategy (1936–1939) in *Elkarrekin esnatzeko ordua*," seeks to outline the historical context addressed by Uribe's third novel and, especially, its exemplification of the cultural policy of the Basque Government led by Lehendakari José Antonio Agirre (1930-1960). Arrieta begins by analyzing the work carried out by the Basque Government based in Bilbao for nine months and, in particular, by its Minister of Culture and Justice, Don Jesús María Leizaola, and explains how the foreign delegations that were created in different European and American cities were structured. In an era and context in which the Statute of Autonomy granted important competencies in educational and cultural matters, milestones are cited such as the co-official status of Euskara (the Basque language) and the creation of a Basque university. As regards the delegations, she highlights the importance of those in Paris and New York, which are both mentioned widely in Uribe's third novel. As Arrieta says, Agirre's government made use of culture to carry out political propaganda, and this strategy sought, above all, to obtain support to win the war. Film (featuring depictions of Basque culture), the Basque national soccer team, and the Basque choir Eresoinka would be some of the projects that underpinned the cultural diplomacy of the Basque Government. Indeed, Karmele Urresti and Txomin Letamendi, the protagonists of the novel *Elkarrekin esnatzeko ordua*, were members of Eresoinka.

In "Kirmen Uribe and translation: An endless journey," Miren Ibarluzea (University of the Basque Country) addresses the study of the translation habitus in Uribe's narrative texts. She starts with the approaches that underpin Pierre Bourdieu's theories, and comments on Uribe's ideas, perceptions, and attitudes toward translation, as well as his reflections on his experiences of translation. Ibarluzea embraces the "fictional turn" line of research in translation studies and analyzes how Uribe's habitus is represented by the translator-character in the novel *Mussche*, also making use of a questionnaire given to both the writer and his translators. Uribe is presented as a writer who is close to his translators, who appreciates and values their work, because for Uribe translation is a way to learn to write better. One could say that translation helps the Ondarroa writer to situate himself as a Basque writer to the world, and that the fact that many of his works have been translated directly from Euskara into other languages is significant for him. In sum, it is the human aspect of the writer-translator relationship that Uribe emphasizes in his literary production, especially in novels like *Mussche*.

As for the chapter by Jon Kortazar (University of the Basque Country), "Writing and the Internet in Kirmen Uribe's novel *Bilbao-New York-Bilbao*" transports us to Uribe's well-known, prizewinning novel. The goal of the chapter is to analyze the influence of the Internet on the writing of Uribe's novel, and in order to do so, Kortazar begins with contributions such as those of Irene Zoé Alameda (2007) and Vicente Luis Mora (2006 and 2007). Kortazar alludes to the characteristics of Uribe's texts, such as the incorporation of graphical material, typographical play, polyglossy, allusions to the creative process, and the mobility that provides the text with its fragmentary structure. Above all, he makes reference to the objective that Uribe pursues with his wish to innovate: to provoke emotion. In sum, as Kortazar says, the comings and goings between fiction and reality, the capricious movements of memory, the vicissitudes that emerge within the stories . . . all take the form in Uribe's work of the movements we carry out when we use the Internet: the act of *navigating*, or being in a continuous leap from one reality to another.

The chapter titled "The origins of what I am: Family, collective, and historical memory in the narrative of Kirmen Uribe," by the professor José Martínez Rubio (Universitat Jaume I), includes reflections on memory. As its author says, Uribe's first three novels, in the same way as many other works that have been published in recent decades in the Iberian Peninsula, demonstrate the writer's process of investigation throughout the text. He would contend that the three novels emphasize the narrative elements, techniques, and strategies that structure a space of representative ambiguity. And it is precisely that ambiguous space that the author/character in the novels makes use of in order to analyze the past and transfer it to his present identity. As Martínez Rubio stresses, these investigative novels pose ontological, epistemological, and deontological questions about the past, and are presented as an instrument of consciousness-raising or knowledge about this past. In sum, the analyzed texts by Uribe demonstrate that knowing the past and transforming it into an object of reflection could serve to redefine our identities and appreciate certain values (freedom, generosity, humanity) as well as to recognize the pain and injustice caused by the past.

In his chapter "Literature and displacement: Kirmen Uribe," Luis Martín Estudillo (University of Iowa) addresses one of the key ideas throughout Uribe's entire work: the idea of displacement. In order to carry out his analysis, he starts from the dual meaning of displacement in the first three novels by the Ondarroa writer. On the one hand, the ethical and historical dimension of displacement: Uribe develops this aspect by focusing on characters that are on the move, in transit, as a consequence of political and economic pressures. On the other, the aesthetic dimension of displacement, which triggers some formal options, such as the literary commitment to fragmentation or polyphony—characteristics which, related to form, provide an unlimited and non-dogmatic understanding of literature, and are also the expression of a kind of fiction published in the West during the last half of the twentieth century. Additionally, Martín Estudillo analyzes the importance of the idea of displacement for poststructuralist thought and defines the literary tradition that underpins Uribe's narrative. In the European context, this tradition was created by an artistic tendency opposed to discriminatory or reactionary discourses that emerged in the face of vitally important mobility phenomena in the human geography of the continent.

It is the academic study of memory that structures the chapter by María Jesús Nafría Fernández (Universidad Complutense de Madrid) in "The construction of memory in Kirmen Uribe's narrative." According to this author, the need to reconstruct and rewrite memory completely conditions Uribe's narrative, a rewriting that, moreover, seeks to overcome the limits (political, linguistic, and emotional) imposed on him. Nafría analyzes the themes and characteristics that are repeated in Uribe's work, especially the connections that give rise to topics like language, recollections/memory, and death. As regards the first of these, she highlights the importance of choosing Euskara, which does not just allow Uribe to locate himself within a specific frame of identity, but also as a Basque writer in the global market. Through the memory carried by this language, different historical, political, cultural, and familial elements are filtered in Uribe's universe. His novels are, therefore, memory novels seeking answers about past events that have not been overcome, undertaking a literary contribution toward a more egalitarian future, through stories led by "small heroes." Moreover, one should state that death—the death of a friend or family member—serves as the stimulus for the plot of these novels. These losses serve Uribe with the possibility of paying homage to his friends/relatives and of recovering his society´s conflictive past.

The section dedicated to Kirmen Uribe's narrative is concluded with the chapter by Mari Jose Olaziregi Alustiza (University of the Basque Country), "Kirmen Uribe's *Mussche*: A paper grave for Robert." The author begins her analysis contending that, in the same way as many other works that recall a conflictive historical past, Uribe's second novel seeks to recover the memory of those anonymous heroes who perished tragically and to alleviate to some extent the grief generated by their loss. It is precisely there, in the possibility of giving a voice and protagonism to unjustly forgotten individuals, that literature fulfills one of its most important functions. Indeed, Uribe's novel reflects on the function that the writer must have in politically convulsive contexts. *Mussche* also presents characteristics that are easily attributable to the postmemory generation, given that remembering the past is creative and only possible through the images, testimonies, and other elements compiled by Carmen Mussche throughout her life. Likewise, Olaziregi's study underscores the fragmentary nature of the novel and the hybrid character of historical documents as a consequence of the manipulation of narrative time. In sum, Uribe reminds us of the itinerant transcultural nature that all memory possesses and for that reason he does not hesitate to establish intertextual dialogs with W. G. Sebald or with works by contemporary writers in the Basque sphere such as Katixa Agirre.

The section dedicated to Uribe's poetry begins with a thought-provoking interpretation of his first book of poems,

Meanwhile Take My Hand. Authored by Estibalitz Ezkerra (University of California, Santa Barbara) and titled "Gestural poetry," it is based on the argument that the Basque author's first book of poems is an attempt to return to the "subject" and, in order to explain what that means, analyzes how it explores three aspects that influence human existence and experience: the body, affect, and gesture. In regards to the body, Ezkerra highlights the importance of body vulnerability, given that death and pain are important in many of Uribe's poems (with the poem "Visit" serving as an example). Alongside that, as Judith Butler emphasizes in *Frames of War* (2009), Ezkerra reminds us that not all bodies have the same vulnerability. and, as regards the presence of war in Uribe's collection of poems, brings to light non-painful (awake) bodies that surface in various poems or the bodies consumed by Europe. What likewise stands out is Ezkerra's approach to several poems on the basis of what Sara Ahmed (2006) terms "emotional intentionality" in order to explain the object-affect-memory chain that follows the mechanism of memory in the poems, and the commentaries surrounding activism that, on the basis of small gestures, the collection of poems *Meanwhile Take My Hand* proposes. It is precisely those small gestures that have the capacity to make lives worthy of being lived or bodies grievable.

The contribution of Lourdes Otaegi (University of the Basque Country), titled "Kirmen Uribe's work and an interpretation of *Bar Puerto*," does not focus on Uribe's novels, but on his short format works and the multimedia shows that came out of those, such as the show *Bar Puerto: Voices from the Edge* (2001). Otaegi seeks to highlight from the start the literary importance that, in her opinion, this work possesses, given that therein she sees the characteristics that conditioned Uribe's later trajectory—both that relating to the intimate self-expression of being human in the abyss of a change, and that relating to the need to collect the testimony of marginal voices. She therefore considers *Bar Puerto* a creative work that is seminal to his literary essence, and compares it to the rest of the well-known multimedia projects in the author's trajectory. Likewise, Otaegi reflects on the place poetry occupies in the current Basque literary system, contrasting the fall in production in the genre with the statements of different literary critics about the possible crisis and, above all, reflecting on the impetus that multimedia contributions have given the lyrical genre during almost the last forty years. At the end of the day, performance has helped the lyrical genre to reach readers, and numerous examples are offered recalling the projects of artists predating Uribe's work, such as those of Xabier Lete or Pott Banda. The key to the success of Uribe's poetic works is not due solely, in Otaegi's view, to the appeal of the multimedia performances that he has produced, but also to the veracity and proximity that his form of communication transmits. Uribe achieves both effects through the auto-diegetic narrative voice and thanks to the testimonies of others, of marginal people. In sum, according to Otaegi, the reason for the success of works such as *Bar Puerto* is the emotional authenticity that emanates from the truth that testimonial language transmits.

The volume concludes with a section dedicated to a genre that is not central in the Basque literary system: children's and young adult literature. Olaziregi once again authors a study dedicated to Uribe's work, titled "Stories of a Basque sheepherder turned gunslinger: Kirmen Uribe's *Garmendia* series." It describes the *Garmendia* series of works (based on the adventures of a Basque sheepherder who emigrates to America and, eventually, becomes a gunslinger) while at the same time highlighting its intertextual nature. This series aimed at younger readers establishes a dialog, in terms of a counternarrative, both with the traditional representation of the Basque sheepherder who emigrated to the Americas in Basque literature and with the stereotype of the cold, cruel gunslinger of American Westerns. As the author points out, the series forms a part of Basque cultural production about that "Other" that has shaped the Basque diaspora in the Americas. What is more, the series contains constant references to—and even reappropriations or rewritings of—typical characters in stories of the Far West. In this way,

Uribe creates a hybrid Basque-American universe facilitated by the diasporic element, which deconstructs (in a humorous way) the archetypal male characters both of the good Basque sheepherder—typical of the *costumbrista* Basque novel—and the cold-blooded outlaw gunslinger of the American tradition. Like the characters, the very space of the Basque-American diaspora shifts, given that the story—far from being represented in a serious, solemn tone (in the traditional Basque style)—is presented as a comic scene full of adventure and fun.

In conclusion, the diversity of the works and perspectives included in this book is a sign of the interest that Uribe's work has awakened in different fields of research. These works form a polyhedral portrait of a literary oeuvre—that of Kirmen Uribe—in which, as the authors of this volume reiterate, life flows with all its contradictions and grandeurs. The book is finalized with the biobibliography of the contributors. It remains only for us to wish, as Uribe himself does in the text preceding the studies herein, that readers enjoy the reflections and emotions that his work has elicited among all of us.

II

Manual of disobedience

Kirmen Uribe

I have always been disobedient, since I was a child. And I think this detail is also important in order to understand my literary work. I read recently in an interview with the writer Rachel Cusk that she does not believe in characters. That readers nowadays do not need leading characters, that we already know them all. In nineteenth-century novels, yes, they were necessary, but since then many things have happened. Readers are not like they were then, they are not passive but active. After the Internet, readers (also) write; they have changed author-reader relations radically. In Cusk's opinion, what is important now is the voice.

At one time, painters were taught how to paint a horse. And this format was followed over and over again. But there came a day when painters went outside, when they began to look at real horses and paint them directly. They did not paint them according to the teacher's instructions, no, they began to paint what they saw with their own eyes. I think we writers have often been told what to say and how to say it, as if the laws of literature were everlasting, as if society had not changed in the last 150 years. Whoever paints according to what the teacher says will be "good"; whoever goes outside, "bad."

It may perhaps be a bad habit, but I have always said no to what I have been told to do. "One cannot write a novel without a main character." That is what we have always heard. Fine, in *Bilbao-New York-Bilbao* there is no main character. "Nor can one write a novel without a plot," others would say. Nor does it have a plot. The point is that the novel follows its own internal rules, and if readers accept the agreement, then who cares? *Bilbao-New York-Bilbao* is a proclamation in favor of total freedom. Everything that surrounds a novel appears in the book, but the novel as such does not exist. It is, in some ways, a sculpture by Oteiza which envelops the void that is the book.

Literature and art progress by transforming a no into a yes. Oteiza and Chillida created sculptures with noble materials. Steel, iron, wood, stone. What was left for the next generation? What did Txomin Badiola, Pello Irazu, or Ángel Bados do? Txomin Badiola creates sculptures with industrial composite chairs. With already fabricated objects. He just makes them his own and gives them another form. Should they have carried on with the noble materials of their predecessors? Why?

I also create composite novels. Instead of inventing characters, I have made use of people who already exist. In *Mussche*, for example. The structure of the novel—not the content, but the form—explains the sentimental situation of the writer. It is important to understand this. At the start, this form is broken, in pieces, just like the will of the writer, and insofar as the narration progresses so it appears that the grief of the writer himself also dissolves. Passages from my own life appear in the novel, but they are told through the flesh and blood of Robert Mussche or Herman Thiery or Vic Openbeck. I "make use of" the lives of Robert Mussche and the others to relate my own life. Although I narrate the life of certain historical figures, it is my most autobiographical novel. The third one, *Elkarrekin esnatzeko ordua* (The Hour of Waking Together), is ultimately a novel about identity, about a minority. What it meant to be Basque in the twentieth century. That is what I wanted to relate. Where we came from, in order to know where we can go. Why everything that happened took place. And understanding the past does not mean that I am justifying the violence, because seeking to understand it is always a step toward overcoming what has happened. Everything is true in this third novel. In contrast to the previous ones, here there is no literary game. I tried to reconstruct the life of Karmele Urresti, and it was important for readers to realize that what I was saying was true. Yes, literature can also be created like that. Narrating a real life. Did not Homer recount Odysseus's life as if it were real?

In my case, before the novel there is always an idea. Like Bruce Nauman's works of art, the idea is the beginning. Nauman would then transform that idea into a photo, a performance, a sculpture, or whatever. Depending on the moment, he would give it form in one way or another. But at its source there is always a general idea. And I also begin to write when I have a clear idea of the novel. The story line is never the start; the character, plot, all that comes later, they are the second or third steps. Behind all my books there is an idea and that idea is surrounded by a theoretical discourse. I like to play around with that. Every novel has a specific purpose. That purpose is often to break away from something, the desire to do things in another way, the desire to try out something, to seek out something.

Writing, for me, has to do with discomfort, with rebelliousness, with non-conformism. I have never wanted to write as one "normally does." The Japanese writer Haruki Murakami did not want to imitate the prose of Mishima, Tanizaki, or Kawabata. For that reason, he began to write in a language he did not master so well, English. In the new adopted language, the sentences were short; he wrote sharply, without employing any adornments or vices. He wrote the beginning of a novel in English, then translated it into Japanese. Thereafter, he continued in Japanese, but followed the sober style of his English. He found his voice, his own way of narrating. I try to explore other paths. I am not content with just trying to translate outside styles into Basque. I have a dream: Why not take the opposite route? Why not give birth to a new method of expression in Basque? Well, that demands a lot of work and searching, and not repeating anything that has been done previously.

Three impetuses rally me when it comes to creating. First is freedom. The writer must break with tradition in order to be part of it. They must write with freedom, without any pressure, without any fear. They must be disobedient. Second, illuminate terrains which have been silenced, give a voice to the voiceless. Reclaim stories that have not been told. Third, form. Because it is the form that changes the history of literature, and not content.

The book, once it is published, belongs to the reader; the writer forgets about it because their mind is already on the next project. Thus, it is then when the book makes its own way. The work of critics, in my opinion, illuminates that direction for readers and for the book itself, searching for connections with other texts, analyzing the influence of the book on its surroundings. Asking questions, questions which raise other questions. And that way continuously. Reading the book in a way nobody else has done, discovering in the book things that nobody else has seen. I have always thought that the work of a writer has three pillars: a robust work, an important number of readers, and a critical apparatus. If one of these three ingredients is missing, it is difficult for a writer to make any progress. For that reason, we writers should be grateful to critics, because they take the time to analyze our works, time that detracts from their own lives.

I am therefore grateful to all of the people that have taken part in this book. Without readers there are no books, and without criticism a book is a bird whose wings have been clipped. Many thanks, then, for multiplying my work.

Kirmen Uribe, New York, Winter 2019.

POETICS

1

On scales, mirrors, and words: Intermediality and heterotopia in the work of Kirmen Uribe[1]

Amaia Elizalde Estenaga

1 Introduction

It is no secret that the passage of time has always been an essential raw material in art, and with that, the loss it generates. For time implies space, and space implies matter and life. The most obvious, palpable form in which that constant—time—is demonstrated is in the subject matter of artistic works. But it is also true that artistic practice itself and its reception, whatever the content may be, constitute a spatial time, a time of creativity. Time unfolds through artifact, separate from empirical time, but real—because real time for humans can only be subjective, a time in which past, present, and future coexist. In the case of certain artists, this spatial-temporal condition runs through and infuses their whole work, both in artistic and meta-artistic form. This is the case of Kirmen Uribe, who, although not the first writer to demonstrate this feature with constancy in his poetics, is singular in how he conveys it.

Uribe's constant tendency toward recovering the past and what is found at the edge of loss is reflected both in his narrative and in his poetry, whether written or performed, and even in

1 Paper prepared within the projects IT 1047-16 (Basque Government) and FFI2017-84342-P (MINECO), developed by the level A consolidated research group MHLI (Memoria Historikoa Literatura Iberiarretan / Memoria Histórica en las Literaturas Ibéricas / Historical Memory in Iberian Literatures).

his children's and young adult literature or other intermedial productions (Wolf 1999). This has not gone unnoticed for many literary critics, who have already noted such memory work (Olaziregi Alustiza 2020; Martínez Rubio 2020; Nafría Fernández 2020). However, despite the fact that he may have studied from the perspective of memory studies, that search for reverberation in the work on a lost past, forgetting, and a present that seeks to be rescued is encompassed within a broader poetics, in some way of understanding artistic practice, art, and its reception in relation to time. In a century in which there is an increasingly obvious "pictorial shift" that has reoriented modern thought around visual paradigms that threaten and overwhelm any type of discursive control (Mitchell 2009), there should also be an "intermedial shift" (Wolf 2011) at the level of analyzing artistic productions, with which the boundary between languages may be blurred, placing the focus on the medium more than the linguistic text. Uribe's poetics is especially susceptible to analysis from this emerging perspective. Throughout his work, one observes how there is a persistent attempt to transcend the traditional duality and rivalry between word and image (Alberdi Soto 2015), merging both through different means, and creating mixed expressions that juxtapose, atomize, and organize different times simultaneously into heterotopias (Foucault 1984)—other places. Uribe's art rebels, once more, against conventions, and it disobeys, in this case, time as it is presented to us, thereby creating art as a mirror, as a real and unreal place in which all spaces and all times have a place.

2 The tradition of resistance against the modern notion of time

One of the characteristics of the literature associated with canonical modernism, was the preoccupation with time, with its nature (Matz 2006; Dettmar 2006; Banfield 2007; Gillies 2008)—a predicament that flourished in the literary movement and featured resistance as a reflection of nonconformity. However, one must specify why and how this preoccupation took form and flourished, given that, as noted, time has always been material for art. According to Mary Ann Gillies (2008, 101), the topic was widespread in twentieth-century modern Western culture:

> Few concepts so preoccupied the twentieth century as time. Whether it was Einstein's radical challenge to centuries-old notions about how we measure time or cubist representations of figures in motion, such as Marcel Duchamp's "Nude descending a staircase," how time is analyzed or represented was a cornerstone of modernist culture.

The centrality of this topic, and the anxiety it may have created during the era, is understandable bearing in mind the change implied by Modernity with regard to perspectives on the passage of time. As Mircea Eliade contended in *Le Mythe de l'éternel retour: archétypes et répétition* (1949), in anthropological terms, from the seventeenth century on, ideas of progress and linear time gained strength to the detriment of those of cyclical time; however, as the twentieth century approached, the opposite trend began to be noted among Western thinkers like Friedrich Nietzsche (1844–1900) and Oswald Spengler (1880–1936):

> We must wait until our own century to see the beginnings of certain new creations against this historical linearism and a certain revival of interest in the theory of cycles; so it is that, in the political economy, we are witnessing the rehabilitation of the notions of cycle, fluctuation, periodic oscillation; that in philosophy the myth of eternal return is revivified by Nietzsche; or that, in the philosophy of history, a Spengler or a Toynbee concern themselves with the problem of periodicity. (Eliade 1959 [1949], 146)

The unease caused by the modern linear historicist way of understanding time, which was increasingly widespread and imbued all aspects of life and society, was reflected in literature, including the influence of literary theories such as the ideas of

Henri Bergson (1859–1941). As Ann Banfield points out, Bergson was a harsh critic of the division that Modernity imposed between public/objective and private/subjective time and defended the notion of *durée* (duration). In his thought, real time would not be the scientific time that was spatialized and linear as well as being susceptible to being divided into segments and measured objectively, but, rather, the continuity of moments that were included in each other. In the words of Kevin J. H. Dettmar, from that perspective of duration our experienced time stems from the constant advance of the past, which pierces and devours the future. Thus, the past would be considered as something unlimited in constant growth.

Bergson's ideas were quite influential in the English-speaking world, and hitherto in France. The literature of Modernism reflected a conflict with the modern notion of time, and even resisted it in different ways. Simple examples of this are expressions such as *epiphany* by James Joyce (1882–1941), *spots of time* by William Wordsworth (1770–1850), and *moments of being* by Virginia Woolf (1882–1941). Authors used different designations to express these vital moments: the infinite condensed into an instant. Many authors, like Joyce, T. S. Elliot (1888–1965), and William Butler Yeats (1865–1939), demonstrated a clear tendency toward the myth of a temporal dimension that was also special, cyclical, and eternal. As a matter of fact, Eliade identified these twentieth-century reactions as an updating of the myth of the eternal return, the consequence of humans' "mythical thought," of the subjective experience of time, which was very distinct from the historicist-linear logic. In ancient civilizations in which time was perceived and also conceived as cyclical, humans would tend to abolish real concrete time, making use of different rites and archetypes in order to do so, and reproducing cosmogony over and over again in an eternal return to the *in illo tempore*.

In the context of Basque literature, the case of the Parisian-Basque writer Jon Mirande (1925–1972) inaugurated the influence of mythical thought, in a Modernist style, in literary representations themselves, and this was especially palpable and recurrent in the nouvelle *Haur besoetakoa* (The Goddaughter, 1970) (Elizalde 2016, 2018), a work that Uribe knows perfectly well from the perspective of a literary critic. There is a reference to Mirande's text in the novel *Elkarrekin esnatzeko ordua* (The Hour of Waking Together, 2016), although much more brief in the Spanish than in the Basque version. While in the former there is only a reference to the fact that Mirande was a heterodox writer who wrote something similar to Vladimir Nabokov's *Lolita* (1955), the Basque version specifies that Mirande's short novel constituted the first Modernist Basque novel (2016, 273). Furthermore, one should not forget that Uribe has also been a literary critic and a consequence of that experience is, among other works, the article "*Haur besoetakoa*-ren imaginarioa. Lehen hurbilpen bat" (The imaginary of *Haur besoetakoa*: An initial approach, 1998), which analyzes specifically Mirande's short novel. In his analysis, Uribe detects the importance of a preoccupation with the passage of time in the story Mirande narrates, and he realizes how the representation and achievement of a cyclical time is pursued (1998, 85). In the same way that this reality was evident to Uribe's critical eye, it also appears constantly in his own production, both at the artistic and the meta-artistic level (that is, of reflection). It comes as no surprise that Uribe would choose to analyze that work by Mirande, given that, on the one hand, he was a heterodox writer in line with the spirit of Uribe's disobedient writing and, on the other, the literary text analyzed possesses ingredients that share Uribe's obsessions, such as the formulation of another time/space.

In the same way as other Modernist writers, in his short novel Mirande used expressions like "*betikotasunaren memento*" (moment of eternity) and "*betikotasunaren zati bat izango den ereti bat*" (an instant that will be part of eternity) (Elizalde 2018, 113–114), and Uribe, in the title of his first book of poems, *Bitartean heldu eskutik* (2001; English-language version, 2007) already uses the word "*bitartean*," translated into English as "meanwhile." The literal translation of the expression in

Basque would be "between two" (between two times, but also spaces)—in sum, between two. This reference to that other time, a time of transition, signifies the passage between life and death in the poem "Bisita" (Visit), a moment in which all times intersect but without touching each other, without really being any one. Likewise, in the novel *Bilbao-New York-Bilbao* (2008; English-language version, 2014), Uribe begins the narration with a reflection on loss and the passage of time, bringing to life metaphorically those instants that encompass a whole time, which absorb and demarcate it: the growth rings on fish scales.

> The growth ring of a fish is microscopic, you can't see it with the naked eye, but there it is. As if it were a wound. A wound that hasn't healed up.
> And, with the growth rings of fishes, terrible events stay on in our memory, mark our life, until they become a measure of time. Happy days go fast, on the other hand —too fast—, and we forget them quickly.
> What Winter is for fish, loss is for humans. Loss makes our time specific for us, the end of a relationship, the death of a person we love.
> Each loss a dark growth ring deep down. (Uribe 2014, 7–8)

In the audiovisual montage of a markedly intermedial nature (Wolf 1999), *Bar Puerto, bazterreko ahotsak* (*Bar Puerto: Voices from the edge*, hereupon referred to as *BP*), a performance that was premiered in 2001 and enacted again in 2009, leading to the publication of a homonymous booklet-DVD in 2010, the narrative text that initiates the show begins with "time doesn't always stay the same size" (*BP*, 91). As Professor Otaegi (2020) has already remarked, the audiovisual show is impregnated with the memory of marginal groups, and also at a decisive moment: the demolition of a neighborhood, a loss. The cited text forms part of a diary that is the common thread of the performance, a "diary of a nameless filmmaker" (*BP*, 88), a diary that, although written in prose, does not lack poetic force. The abovementioned initial declaration is repeated, like a litany, in the second paragraph of the first text, but also later on, in another fragment of the diary, it is repeated at the beginning of two paragraphs as an anaphora. Uribe evokes over and over again that real subjective time, that time that has so little to do with linear, historical time, and so much to do with memory:

> There are other measures of time, and one morning we get out of bed and suddenly realize that not one day but ten years have passed and we don't, as we did just last night, see our whole life stretching out before us. Events put up fences between us and the days gone by, and those events turn into bitter memories. That's precisely when we realize that a certain period in our lives has irrevocably ended. (*BP*, 91)

The anonymous producer who is writing the diary expresses the need to relive the past in passages about his infancy, which return to the *in illo tempore* typical of the mythical tendency referred to by Eliade. Besides that, there is a clear reference to a problematic relationship with the idea of progress, which is mentioned ironically, in the same way the modernists and Mirande himself did:

> I catch the train. The train that goes to our town. See again landscapes I left long ago. Ones I didn't fill. Ones that never were. See childhood places for the last time. They're going to be razing the neighborhood. The new road will go through there. Questions of progress. On the train a song hatches into my mind, a folk tango our grandmother used to sing at Christmastime. (*BP*, 93)

In the fragment cited, one notes the resonance of the poem "Bultzi leihotik" (Through the Train's Window, 1927) by the Basque poet Xabier Lizardi (1896–1933), in which the poetic

I is in a train from whose window it observes elements from the traditional Basque past that are being left behind. Not in vain, Uribe published together with Jon Elordi an essay titled *Lizardi eta erotismoa* (Lizardi and eroticism, 1996), in which they carried out an interpretation of his poems. In fact, Lizardi was one of those writers who, under the influence of French symbolism, modernized Basque lyrical poetry, and one cannot overlook the symbolic value in his era of the train as a feature of modernity. The tone of the fragment in *Bar Puerto* and of Lizardi's poem is nostalgic, but the train is going in the opposite direction. Lizardi is leaving the countryside, the rural farm environment, in the direction of all things urban, while the fictional producer who is writing the diary in *Bar Puerto* is heading toward his past, his childhood. The symbolic value of the train has changed and, clearly, the plane now has that value the train once had in the literary tradition.

As the examples cited suggest, the main similarity in Uribe's poetics with the tradition that has been sketched out is the denial of a historicist linear approach to an irreversible time that is built on "real time," that way of understanding time that Modernity brought with it and that has permeated all spheres of humanity, with whom, paradoxically, it is not fully compatible. Artistic practice as resistance to and disobedience against that time, and the construction and representation of another time, runs through Uribe's work, a tendency that is part of a tradition. Nevertheless, bringing that tendency up to date is a singular feature of this writer, who makes use of thought and the tools his era offers him to challenge the established order of things: intermediality and heterotopia as a form of transgression, deconstructing the divisions between the word and the image, time and space, reclaiming the condition of reality of the subjective through his artistic calling, through his mirror.

3 "Poetry is stopping time": Words that paint words

In Uribe's poetics, time appears tied explicitly to space in different ways. Memory, which is no more than the presence of the past in the present, inhabits that space, in things, without any linear organization for the subjectivity of human beings. This perspective appears by way of reflection in *Elkarrekin esnatzeko ordua*, in which toward the end of the novel it is stated that reminiscence is tied more to space than to time, and that the brain does not understand the so-called "arrows of time." Thus, in the past, use was made of things, of the material, as a basis for memorization, for reminiscence: the furniture and its layout in a room, for example. Emotion, too, takes on special relevance for Uribe, in such a way that each recollection would be linked to an emotion, and, often, the road there is emotional, linked to the senses. The autofictional narrator-writer expresses it thus:

> Be that as it may, as far as I know, it appears that remembering is an act more linked to space than to time, because the brain pays no attention whatsoever to the so-called "arrow of time," and although our life may just be an uninterrupted succession of events, our memory does not register them like that; in other words, recollections are not recorded according to a temporal order . . . Centuries ago, in a time without printed books, much less the internet, the techniques of memorization were based on the association between recollections and objects . . .
>
> What is well known is that each recollection remains attached to an emotion. (*Elkarrekin...*, 325–326)[2]

It is no coincidence that two of the novels in which the writer journeys into the past and reflects on the passage of time, *Bilbao-New York-Bilbao* and *Elkarrekin esnatzeko ordua*, are connected to painting and the recourse to ekphrasis, that is, to literary

2 Translated by Cameron Watson.

exercise that is based on a pictorial work, an artistic object, and finding inspiration therein.

From an intermedial perspective (Wolf 2002), one could say that painting is the artistic medium that is most present in Uribe's work, both as *pluralmediality*, that is, as the mere blend of artistic media, and as an *intermedial reference*, in which a medium refers explicitly to another medium or takes on the expressive technique of another medium, as in the case of ekphrasis. As Otaegi (2020) points out, Uribe's poetry is often interpreted by musicians, but it does not always form part of the subject matter of the work. On the contrary, in the case of *Bar Puerto*, each medium contributes an ingredient to the piece that is irreplaceable: the word provides its fundamental content, yet so do the music and, especially, the visual projection. Ultimately, as it is presented, this artistic creation wants to be a documentary, but it also wants to be fiction, creating a totally hybrid language that transgresses the boundaries between media. Insofar as the music and also the visual document affects the expression of the word, transforming it into a poetic voice, now as a documentary voice one would have to speak in terms of *remediation*, given that the experimental fusion of media has given rise to a new way of expression, a new genre.

The case of painting in Uribe's work is especially remarkable because it is a medium that appears in quite a constant way, particularly in his narrative works and often in a reflexive meta-artistic form. In the preface to his latest publication, *17 segundo* (17 seconds, 2019), Uribe recounts how in the Metropolitan Museum of Art it was explained to him that the average time a visitor dedicates to contemplating a painting is seventeen seconds, and he laments that this is the limited time that we offer a painting in these "unhinged times." Immediately thereafter, he emphasizes that the rhythm of poetry is distinct: "It is detaining time, poetry is the gaze, it is placing attention on what is going to disappear," he says, "contemplating things, thinking that they have been there before, and that they will probably stay there in the same place later on."[3] Once again, time and loss, space and things, a critique of the speed of our times and two artistic expressions marking another time/pace: literature and painting.

The painting of Aurelio Arteta is the central work in *Bilbao-New York-Bilbao*, with ekphrasis on the mural in Bastida's house (Bastina being an architect from Ondarroa) at the beginning of the novel. The fictional author is in the Fine Arts Museum in Bilbao contemplating the mural, in the place to which his grandfather took his mother the same day he was told he only had a few months to live. The novel relates how, according to José Julián Bakedano's explanation to the protagonist, the picture "represents the leap from old world to new" (*B-NY-B*, 10). At the museum, among paintings and memories, the search begins for the protagonist into his grandfather Liborio's past. In this novel, the mural by Arteta that is referred to is inserted into the book as a copy, but the intermedial relationship goes much further, because the reference to the picture and prewar Basque painting is inserted into the story itself.

For its part, in the abovementioned novel by Mirande (1970), there is also a painter who has a special function: when the love story of the protagonists appears impossible and they decide to die, the man turns to his only friend, the painter. He tells him the story and he decides to write it, to paint it, so that it will be immortalized. Uribe also gives an account of that, of the important role of the painter when it comes to immortalizing and reincarnating the story of the couple. For the painter Balthasar Klossowski, "Balthus," as he recounted in his *Mémoires* (2001), art—in his case, painting—consists of stopping and trapping time:

> Un tableau ou une prière, c'est la même chose: une innocence enfin saisie, un temps arraché au désastre de temps qui passe. Une immortalité capturée. (20)

3 Translated by Cameron Watson.

> C'est le tableau qui m'apprend à refuser la roue frénétique du temps. Lui ne court pas après elle. Ce que je cherche à atteindre, c'est son secret. L'immobilité. (33)
> Se souvenir du travail artisanal des Anciens, des préparations rituelles qui savent rendre cet effet de suspension, d'attente surprise, de temps enfin vaincu.
> Le temps vaincu: n'est-ce pas peut-être la meilleure définition de l'art? (15)[4]

This painter, in the same way as Arteta, liked to capture moments in transition, which led to a whole series of portraits of girls, young girls on the brink of puberty who, by creating another dimension still within the dimension of the painting, were reading or looking at themselves in a mirror. In Uribe's case, the painting that is introduced into the literature opens up that infinite, which, although fictitious, is real insofar as it forms part of the subjectivity and takes material shape in a real object that is the work of art. In the same vein as what the philosopher Maurice Merleau-Ponty (1908–1961) stated in reference to painting, this art takes a portion of reality and creates a world out of it: "la peinture serait, donc, non pas une imitation du monde, mais un monde pour soi" (*the painting would be, therefore, not an imitation of the world, but a world for itself*) (*Causeries* 1948).

Likewise in Uribe's third novel, *Elkarrekin esnatzeko ordua* (The Hour of Waking Together, 2016), painting appears from the beginning of the story, even before that of *Bilbao-New York-Bilbao*, because there is a painting on the front cover of the book itself whose poetics match those of the novel. This is not

4 *A painting or a prayer, it is the same thing: an innocence finally seized, a time snatched from the disaster of time passing. A captured immortality. (20)*
It is the painting that teaches me to refuse the frenetic wheel of time. It does not run after it. What I seek to reach is its secret. The immobility. (33)
Remembering the handicraft work of the Ancients, the ritual preparations that know how to render this effect of suspension, of surprised waiting, of time finally overcome.
The defeated time: isn't it perhaps the best definition of art? (15)"
Translated by the editors.

the case in the Seix Barral Spanish-language edition, *La hora de despertarnos juntos*, but it is in the Basque-language version, published by Susa. The main painter in the novel is Antonio de Gezala (1889–1956), from Bilbao, and the picture on the front cover is a fragment from the painting *Puerta giratoria* (Revolving door, 1927), a work that also forms part of the *ABC. El alfabeto del museo de Bilbao* (ABC. The Alphabet of the Bilbao Museum) exhibition (October 6, 2018–December 30, 2020) that Uribe curated at the Fine Arts Museum in Bilbao. In the educational material prepared for the exhibition, the painting is related to the word "Mirror" and the following is mentioned:

> It could be that art is finally just that, relity´s reflection distorted. Distorted on purpose, since creativity begins with having transformed what´s seen, because that´s exactly where freedom lies. And that created thing turns into a new reality. . (Uribe 2018, 81)

Artists create a new reality on the basis of what they perceive, another reality with another time. In the chapter titled "Maitasuna Belloyko Jauregian" (Love in Belloy Palace) in the novel, a similar explanation is offered by Gezala, who is one of the characters, in reply to a question by Txomin Letamendia about why he did not define any faces in his painting *Noche de artistas en Ibaigane* (Artists' nights in Ibaigane), also in 1927. This picture represents a party that the de la Sota family organized in their Ibaigane palace before the coup d'état of 1936. Gezala answers that the important thing for him is not what took place in reality but how he perceived it, not what happened but what was perceived. Alongside that feature of Gezala's poetics there is another, when speaking about *Puerta giratoria* (Revolving Door), namely, the drive to capture the ephemeral, the transitory, the very moment in which something fades away:

> . . . thus the transience of the moment is highlighted . . . The image is of an overwhelming fragility; the spectator

> perceives that soon young Begoña will abandon that space, will leave the revolving door and go into the hotel lobby. Gezala tries to capture that elusive instant, the inexorable passage of time, the manner in which everything disappears without any remedy and vanishes with each step. (*Elkarrekin...*, 31)

It is precisely that technique or poetics of the painter Gezala that Uribe embraces for the novel, very much in line with the characteristics of his creative philosophy with regard to the passage of time and loss. The main character, the autofictional writer of the novel, explains how he observed and investigated the past through its protagonists, making use of witnesses and documents in order to later express all of that in his work, transforming it for the sake of credibility, but seeking to stay as close as possible to reality. Uribe takes fragments of that past era, that instant of hope in exile, that moment of transition, of a revolving door, observes it and, with the license of free transformation that art allows, captures it in his novel.

In reality, one can argue that, in one image, the front cover of the novel *Elkarrekin esnatzeko ordua* marks, defines, and synthesizes the content of the work, the instant of the era, its fragility and its compartmentalization. That revolving door, which divides and includes the distinct facets of the character represented and makes the fragility of the moment evident, could also well represent an open book because the mirrored panels resemble, quite remarkably, pages. In this context, the intermedial relationship that is established between Gezala's painting and the literary work is complex, given that, first, there is inverse ekphrasis, that is, a painting that refers to the work in one way or another and, later, from the "Noche de artistas en Ibaigane" chapter on, the novel becomes an exercise in ekphrasis based on Gezala's homonymous painting. The whole story of the novel unfolds on the basis of that painting and, what is more, there are also ekphrastic exercises on other pictures by Gezala, *Eresoinka 8.45* and *Eresoinka 20.45*, scenes that are included in the novel's story in which the characters appear. The initial painting, with that cheerful representation of the festive scene prior to the coup d'état of 1936, reappears frequently at distinct moments in the novel, always as a nostalgic element, as a lost paradise, an *in illo tempore* that is revisited constantly with longing.

Elkarrekin esnatzeko ordua (The Hour of Waking Together) is a hybrid literary work with regard to painting, to the point of embracing a philosophy of creativity stemming from the pictorial discipline. From the point of view of intermedial relationships (Wolf 2002, 2011), it is not simply a question of *plurimediality* or a blend of different media in the same artistic representation, but of the fact that painting permeates literature, so that it is a question of a relationship of *intermedial reference*, in which, above all, the literary work makes reference to pictorial artistic works through ekphrastic exercises, but it also appropriates the poetics of another discipline. It does so by paying special attention to the treatment of time in the poetics of the painter Gezala, and in painting in general, underscoring the absolute independent temporal universe that makes up artistic work, which is similar to but totally other than the real one.

4 "The whole world could conceivably exist in a port." And in a museum

In the same way as the preoccupation with the passage of time, the relationship among the different arts has been a constant in history, both characteristics that intertwine in Uribe's work. Furthermore, there is a third facet within the writer's literary labor in which the previous two interlink: the other spaces, or heterotopias, about which Michel Foucault (1926–1984) would theorize in his lecture *Des espaces autres* (Of Other Spaces), given in 1967 but not published until 1984. According to the philosopher, the twentieth century would be the era of space, but he speaks about that in relation to temporal experience.

With the second half of the twentieth century already underway, Foucault argued that, instead of experiencing the world and life as something that occurs over time, he was living in a period in which the simultaneous and juxtaposition ruled, in which the distant, the near, and the dispersed, all blended together and intermingled. In reality, that perspective is perfectly consistent with Bergson's theory or the already suggested problematic about resistance to the linear approach to time and the mythical thought of human beings, advocated by Eliade. The characteristic that makes Foucault's reasoning special is the fact that he transferred the gaze toward space, in that space-time relationship, toward the transformations in space or spatial constructions that resulted from that tendency to refute a certain temporal notion. As Foucault emphasized, the "spatial turn," to term it one way, did not imply a true denial of time as something existent, but rather of the way of treating what we term time and what we call history. That direct reference to history goes back to the problematic between linear-historical and circular-mythical time raised by Eliade in regard to humanity from the late nineteenth century on. Therefore, the temporal problematic, in sum, would be a space-time problematic.

A taste for heterotopia is one of the most striking features of Uribe's work, which, moreover, as we have been able to see to some extent, dovetails with intermediality. It is a question of places that are the result of cultural creation that, in some way, incorporate the whole variety of culture's locations, while representing them, questioning them, and turning them inside out at the same time. They are places that, despite being effectively accessible, are outside all other places and hence they are *other* places. Out of all the principles that Foucault developed with regard to heterotopias, one especially stands out in relation to Uribe's artistic labor: the fact that the heterotopias are related to time confines. The term "heterochrony" would refer to that special temporality that would take shape within the heterotopias.

In line with the tendency that has been described thus far, Uribe's poetics often work with heterotopias of time in which the latter accumulates to infinity, eternalizing places in which time keeps piling up, as if in a library or in a museum. There is a clear recurrence of the museum space in Uribe's work, but before exploring this more closely, one should highlight the fictional heterotopia that takes shape in *Bar Puerto*. In this work, as noted, there is a clear use of poetics that recognize and endorse another time, but also the place that he takes as the setting is an other place, a heterotopia. In the prologue itself, the author's words discover the central elements of space and time, as well as their nature in the artistic piece:

> I wanted to record how they demolished Grandmother's house, how the loss of a physical space brings a loss of memory, too.
> (...)
> Bar Puerto is an urban story set in a microcosm. (*BP*, 88)

The form in which the prologue ends is especially revealing: "We often don't know how close the treasures are. The whole world could conceivably exist in a port of ten thousand inhabitants" (*BP*, 89). That port in which a whole world meets takes material shape fictitiously in Bar Puerto, a heterochronous space that brings together present voices that collect the past of the inhabitants of Ondarroa, voices that, however, constitute a whole world in that space, because, as is repeated twice in the diary, "in all coastal towns there's a tavern called Bar Puerto" (*BP*, 96, 121). Precisely at that moment in which a building, a space disappears, and with it its time, Uribe looks for and creates a heterotopic space, giving it material form and immortalizing it in his work, making use of audiovisual intermediality, and producing a documentary work of art.

Besides that real-imaginary heterotopic space that constitutes Bar Puerto, the heterotopic spaces of a prison and a cemetery appear in this piece. There is an especially interesting fragment about the prison, given that the extraordinary nature of the space-time relationship in that space is expressed very explicitly:

> Time doesn't always stay the same size. There are weeks, there are months, there are years, but time often takes several other forms. Those who are prisoners, for instance, divide up their day according to the mail call, their week according to visiting hours, their month according to conjugal visits. (*BP*, 91)

The prison space also appears in Uribe's latest book of poems, *17 segundo*, combined with a special poetic form, the haiku. Despite the fact that this form is unusual with respect to the Basque tradition, it is not so in the writer's universe, who already in his first book of poems, *Meanwhile Take My Hand*, included a haiku. Nevertheless, in this case the Japanese poetic form is associated directly with the heterotopia of the prison, making up a complete section titled "Espetxeko Haikuak" (Prison haikus) (Uribe 2019, 41–53). In the same way, the cemetery and the places in which the dead reside that fulfill the same function form an important part of Uribe's work. That transit between life and death, the *bitartean* or "meanwhile," is a door that unites two worlds, that of the living and that of the dead, worlds that cross and intertwine and through which the writer's work enters and exits constantly. Thus, loss—the past that lives on in the present in the form of memory or nostalgia—is translated into multiple artistic forms that form monuments, commemorative cards, and tombs. These may be paper tombs, as Olaziregi Alustiza (2020) reminds us in the case of the novel *Mussche*, which could well be valid for his other two novels, but also for music, such as the song "Kideari," set to music by Mikel Urdangarin and written as a result of the death of the filmmaker and friend of both artists, Aitzol Aramaio (1971–2011). Likewise, *Bar Puerto* forms a grave. As Foucault explains, cemeteries have not always been structured in the same way, but they are spaces that always fulfill a function, a function that inhabits the writer's work.

Up to now it has been obvious that the intermedial relationship between words and painting runs to a great extent through Uribe's work, but the audiovisual element fulfills a special function in his poetics. In the case of *Bar Puerto*, beyond the aesthetic value that music-word *plurimediality* may confer on the work, in the prologue there is an explicit reference to the audiovisual medium, specifically to cinematographic technique as a medium. This technique acquires special significance as a way of generating material form for the creation and perpetration of those microcosms, that heterotopia in Bar Puerto in which all of those voices from the past are present. In effect, following the theoretical base of Mariniello (2009) in the work of Begoña Alberdi Soto (2015, 27), in this facet of Uribe's poetics it is especially obvious how, "through the influence of the media—radio, photography, film—and the blurring between the limits of the real and the imaginary, the media are thought of as forms of mediation, more than as instruments of representing the world." The same is true of *Bilbao-New York-Bilbao*, which, as well as the plurimedial presence of painting in the novel, also contains a cinematographic audiovisual production in which the blending of past-present-future is represented in a very complex form.

In the short film *Bilbao-New York-Bilbao* (2009) made by Arkaitz Basterra, one hears Uribe's voice reciting a part of the first chapter of the book. The fragments are different in the Basque- and Spanish-language versions of the film, given that in the former (2009), the first seven paragraphs of the novel are narrated, in which the simile is made between the rings in fish scales and the way loss marks the time of human beings; while in the latter (2010), it is the following five paragraphs that are narrated, in which it is recounted how Grandfather Liborio, upon receiving news of his impending death, took his daughter-in-law, the mother of the autofictional Uribe, to visit the Fine Arts Museum in Bilbao, the first time that she had entered a museum. It is important to remark that, as Kortazar states (2020, 87–89), Grandfather Liborio goes to the museum to see the painting because his late wife, Ana, the grandmother of the autofictional writer Uribe, is portrayed in the picture. While Uribe's voice narrates the fragments in each version of the film, the background images and music are the same. Two narrative planes intermix and later combine, ultimately, in the museum: on the one hand, one sees Uribe writing in a park while his mother takes her grandson to visit the museum, where they stop to contemplate Arteta's murals, where Uribe will meet them at the end of the short; on the other, a family meal is shown at Uribe's family home and the postures represented in Arteta's murals are clearly reproduced, merging the "real" cinematographic image with that of the picture, as if the past painting were being projected into the present that, in turn, was blending into the past. At the family gathering, the grandson is drawing one of the images in the mural, which precipitates the reality of the mural toward the future. In addition, the image of the women in the painting merges into an image of Nerea, Uribe´s wife, who is posing like a model for the picture, reincarnating the past. Different times that coexist in the same moment, materializing at the end of the short in the mother-son-grandson union in the museum observing Arteta's world, of which they also form part. Thus, by using cinematographic technique as a medium, there is a merging of word and image, reality and fiction, past, present, and future, evoking the experience itself linked to the heterotopia of the museum.

Besides constituting a heterotopia *per se*, the Fine Arts Museum in Bilbao has an added meaning for Uribe that is also tied to the passage of time and loss. In *Bilbao-New York-Bilbao*, the autofictional writer recounts how his grandfather took his daughter-in-law to the museum when he knew that he would die soon. The short film demonstrates how that same woman takes her grandson to visit the museum, or at least this is one of the interpretations triggered by the relationship between the novel and the short film. In reality, it is hardly surprising that Uribe's journey culminated recently in curating the exhibition titled *ABC. El Alfabeto del Museo de Bilbao*, which ran from October 6, 2018 to December 30, 2020. In the interview-report on the EITB show *Kultura Transit*, Uribe confesses that, since childhood, he has had a very close relationship with the museum and that his family taught him how to enjoy art. Therefore, the

Fine Arts Museum has for Uribe a special affective connotation linked to his childhood, so that both his visit and its representation permit the return of that *in illo tempore*, the updating of the past in the present.

The museum recently renovated its installations and, on the pretext of its 110th anniversary, sought to offer a renewed look at its collections as well. It is hardly surprising that Uribe should opt to organize the past in the heterotopic space of the museum in a totally atypical form that, as well as drawing from literature, was true to the heterochronic nature of the museum: the organization of the works on the basis of an alphabet. The works are not ordered alphabetically but, rather, Uribe established a list composed of words, one for each letter of a singular alphabet, made up of twenty-seven letters plus the digraphs <ll>, <tz>, <ts>, and <tx>. The list of signifiers was made up of Basque, Spanish, English, and French words: Arte, Bilbao, Citoyen, Desira, Espejo, Friendship, Grotte, Heriotza, Iron, Japon, Kirol, Lluvia, Letra, Mom, Noir, Ñabar, Otherness, Pietate, Quiet, Retrato, Sueño, Terre, UhTS, eTXe, bikoiTZ, Urdin, Vida, War, X, Yo, Zubi.

As a result of this exhibition he organized, the museum's department of education and cultural activity published the free content publication *ABC. El alfabeto del Museo de Bilbao* (2018) and the homonymous exhibition catalog, in the four languages. As one can read in Uribe's prologue, his approach brings up-to-date the *ABC* of Joanes Leizarraga (1506–1601) and Bernardo Atxaga's literary form of the alphabet, with the result that he makes literary poetics permeate the duty of the museum as regards pictorial matters, but also, true to his poetics, he breaks totally with the linear chronological organization of the works. If on other occasions visual poetics have permeated his work with words, in this case that movement was reversed. Moreover, alongside all the former, the intermedial commitment goes further and, through the exhibition, the museum has opened up to the public and multiplied its content with a transmedial proposal: radio stories. Between the exhibition's inauguration and June

2019, there was a short-story radio competition organized by the Radio Bilbao-Cadena SER station, the BBK bank (the sponsor of the exhibition), and the museum. On a weekly basis, listeners sent in stories inspired by one of the words in the alphabet, stories that were voiced and broadcasted on the radio. Thus, the exhibition and the writer's subjective experience at the root of it were extended to the radio medium in the form of a literary proposal that invited people to visit the exhibition and take part therein. Such interactivity broadened the exhibition itself, given that the radio stories have been preserved on the Cadena SER website, which can be accessed from the museum's own home page, thereby nourishing the experience of visitors in a transmedial way, observing works rescued from the past and updated in the present through stories.

5 Uribe's mirror: By way of conclusion

The passage of time is not always measured in the same way, and poetry is stopping time. These are the words of Uribe himself, as narrator, in the first case, and as a writer who is speaking about his work, his art in general, in the second. The objective time-space relationship is diluted in the artistic experience, in the exercise that neither pretends nor wants to be ordered according to any criteria beyond the purely subjective. As regards the preoccupation with the passage of time and loss, about the space-time experience itself, Uribe's poetics is part of a tradition that reacts against a historicist, linear, and irreversible notion of time. If Mirande's literature reflected that same anxiety in the second half of the twentieth century, one could argue that Uribe has brought this tradition up to date. With the same disobedience that the writer expresses in his prologue to this book, his poetics rejects an imposed time, oblivious to one's own experience. In the same way as Mirande, Uribe turns to the pictorial medium in that challenge to a time that is perceived as distant, but going further, the writer embraces the spirit of the poetics of certain Basque painters, including their artistic attitude. In *Bilbao-New York-Bilbao*, he describes Arteta as a painter who did not want to follow unquestioningly the school traditionally marked out, and in *Elkarrekin esnatzeko ordua* (43–44) he demonstrates a Gezala who, "freed from the requirements of the dealers or the whims of collectors, gave free reign to his wishes, his likes, and his concerns, without any interference." They are, most likely, a mirror in which Uribe sees and recognizes himself.

The mirror, said Foucault (1984), is the mixed experience between unreal places that make up utopias and more properly heterotopic real places that contain therein the representation of all the places in culture. The mirror opens up an unreal dimension, given that what it reflects is no more than that: an immaterial reflection. However, it also constitutes heterotopia insofar as the mirror is something real and material, which, in addition, represents that in a place in which it is not really in. Uribe's poetics contain an important mirror component, as he includes in the reflection on the word "*Espejo*" (mirror, in Spanish) in his *ABC*: "Maybe at the end of the day art is just that, a deformed reflection of reality. Deformed on purpose, given that creation begins with the transformation of what is contemplated: that is where freedom resides. And what is created becomes a new reality" (2018, 5). That poetics is materialized in a form that is extremely true through the constant combination of media, through which it constitutes a singular language. Image and word are not opposing in Uribe's work, but quite the contrary; by overcoming the traditional rivalry between both media languages, the writer formulates them as allies, interweaving them in his heterotopias through intermediality.

In Uribe's work, art is that mirror in which all places over time are reflected and take material form in the present, and also the medium through which they are projected into the future and the past, permitting the constant updating of the *in illo tempore* and leading to the cyclical experience of time.

Bibliography

Alberdi Soto, Begoña. 2015. Escribir la imagen: la literatura a través de la écfrasis. *Literatura y Lingüística* 33: 17–38.

Banfield, Ann. 2007. Remembrance and Tense Past. In *A Companion to the Modernist Novel*, Shiach, Morag (ed.), 48–64. Cambridge: Cambridge University Press.

Basterra, Arkaitz & Uribe, Kirmen (prod.). 2009. Short film "Bilbao-New York-Bilbao" (Basque-language version, English subtitled). Online: https://www.youtube.com/watch?v=EuwYnlYi9Pg [26/12/2020]

Dettmar, Kevin J. H. 2006. Introduction. In *A Companion to Modernist Literature and Culture*, David Bradshaw & Kevin J. H. Dettmar (ed.), 1–5. Oxford: Blackwell Publishing Ltd.

Eliade, Mircea (1949): *Cosmos and History: The Myth of the Eternal Return,* trans. R. Trask, Willard. New York: Harper & Brothers. [*Le Mythe de l'éternel retour: archétypes et répétition*. Paris: Librairie Gallimard]

Elizalde, Amaia. 2016. Malenkoniaren aurkako nostalgia: betiereko itzuleraren gorputz errepresentazio artistikoa konponbide gisa. Jon Mirande eta Balthasar Klossowski paristarren lanetan oinarritutako hurbilpen konparatiboa. *Euskera* 60: 617–643.

Elizalde, Amaia. 2018. *Jon Miranderen* (H)aur besoetakoa *(1970), modernitate ukatua*. Dissertation. Online: https://addi.ehu.es/handle/10810/32629 [26/12/2020]

Euskal Irrati Telebista. 2019. ABC: el alfabeto del Museo de BilbaoIn *Eitb Kultura Transit*, 01/11/2019. Online: https://www.eitb.eus/es/television/programas/eitb-kultura/videos/detalle/6120149/abc-alfabeto-museo-bilbao/ [26/12/2020]

Foucault, Michel. 1984. Des espaces autres. *Architecture, Mouvement, Continuité* 5: 46–49. Online: https://foucault.info/documents/heterotopia/foucault.heteroTopia.fr/ [24/12/2020]

Gillies, Mary Ann. 2008. Bergsonism: Time out of Mind. In *A Concise Companion to Modernism*, Bradshaw, David (ed.), 95–115. Oxford: Blackwell Publishing Ltd.

Klossowski, Balthasar. 2001. *Mémoires de Balthus*. Paris: Éditions du Rocher.

Kortazar, Jon. 2020. Idazkera eta Internet Kirmen Uriberen Bilbao-New York-Bilbao eleberrian. In Mari Jose Olaziregi Alustiza & Amaia Elizalde Estenaga eds. *Kirmen Uribe: Bizitza, Fikzioa*, Mari Jose Olaziregi Alustiza & Amaia Elizalde Estenaga (ed.), 85–100. Bilbao: Universidad del País Vasco/Euskal Herriko Unibertsitatea.

Martínez Rubio, José. 2020. Naizenaren jatorria. Memoria familiarra, kolektiboa eta historikoa Kirmen Uriberen narratiban. In *Kirmen Uribe: Bizitza, Fikzioa*, Mari Jose Olaziregi Alustiza & Amaia Elizalde Estenaga (ed.), 101–113. Bilbao: Universidad del País Vasco/Euskal Herriko Unibertsitatea.

Matz, Jesse. 2006. The Novel. In *A Companion to Modernist Literature and Culture*, Bradshaw, David & J. H. Dettmar, Kevin (ed.), 215–226. Oxford: Blackwell Publishing Ltd.

Merleau-Ponty, Maurice. 1948. L'art et le monde perçu. In Merleau-Ponty, Maurice. 2002. *Causeries*. Paris: Seuil. Online: http://vventresque.free.fr/IMG/pdf/Merleau-Ponty_Causeries.pdf [24/12/2020]

Mitchell, W. J. T. 2009. *Teoría de la imagen*. Madrid: Akal.

Museo de Bellas Artes de Bilbao. 2018. *ABC. Alfabeto del Museo de Bilbao*. Departamento de Educación y Acción cultural. Online: https://www.museobilbao.com/uploads/actividades_educacion/archivopdf_es-228.pdf [26/12/2020]

Museo de Bellas Artes de Bilbao. 2018. *ABC. Alfabeto del Museo de Bilbao*.

Nafría Fernández, María Jesús. 2020. Memoriaren eraikuntza Kirmen Uriberen narratiban. In *Kirmen Uribe: Bizitza, Fikzioa*, Mari Jose Olaziregi Alustiza & Amaia Elizalde

Estenaga (ed.), 133–143. Bilbao: Universidad del País Vasco/ Euskal Herriko Unibertsitatea.

Olaziregi, Mari Jose. 2020. Kirmen Uriberen Mussche, paperezko hilobi bat Robertentzat. In *Kirmen Uribe: Bizitza, Fikzioa*, Mari Jose Olaziregi Alustiza & Amaia Elizalde Estenaga (ed.), 145–158. Bilbao: Universidad del País Vasco/Euskal Herriko Unibertsitatea.

Otaegi, Lourdes. 2020. Kirmen Uriberen obraren irakurketa *Bar Puerto* proiektu multimediatik abiaturik. In *Kirmen Uribe: Bizitza, Fikzioa*, Mari Jose Olaziregi Alustiza & Amaia Elizalde Estenaga (ed.),159–182. Bilbao: Universidad del País Vasco/Euskal Herriko Unibertsitatea.

Uribe, Kirmen & Jon Elordi. 1996. *Lizardi eta erotismoa*. Irun: Alberdania.

Uribe, Kirmen. 1998. "Haur besoetakoa"-ren imaginarioa. Lehen hurbilpen bat. *Uztaro: giza eta gizarte-zientzien aldizkaria* 24. 77–87.

Uribe, Kirmen. 2014. *Bilbao-New York-Bilbao* (trans. Elizabeth Macklin). Bridgend: Seren Discoveries. (Original work published in 2008).

Uribe, Kirmen. 2010. *Bar Puerto, Voices from the Edge* (trans. Elizabeth Macklin). Donostia: Elkar. (Original work published in 2010).

Uribe, Kirmen. 2016. *Elkarrekin esnatzeko ordua*. Zarautz: Susa.

Uribe, Kirmen. 2018. *ABC. Bilbaoko Museoaren alfabetoa / El alfabeto del Museo de Bellas Artes / The Alphabet of the Bilbao Museum / L'alphabet du Musée de Bilbao*. Bilbao: Museo de Bellas Artes.

Uribe, Kirmen. 2019. *17 segundo*. Zarautz: Susa.

Wolf, Werner. 1999. *The Musicalization of Fiction: A Study in the Theory and History of Intermediality*. Amsterdam-Atlanta: Rodopi.

Wolf, Werner. 2002. Intermediality Revisited: Reflections on Word and Music Relations in Context of a General Typology of Intermediality. In *Word and Music Studies* vol. 4, 13–34. Amsterdam: Rodopi.

Wolf, Werner. 2011. (Inter)mediality and the Study of Literature. *CLC Web: Comparative Literature and Culture* 13, 3: 1–9.

2

The sea that connects us: The life and fiction of Kirmen Uribe[5]

Sally Perret

"Desde aquí se ve muy claro:
un tiempo espléndido
avanza aceleradamente, es como un mar-
azul-mahón el viento!"

-Blas de Otero, "Ellos" (1955)

1 A splendid time: An introduction to Uribe's work

As an American academic, it was a privilege to be part of the course on Kirmen Uribe's work at the University of the Basque Country during the summer of 2018. For me, Uribe is unique not just because of the stories he tells, but also because of the optimistic perspective that underpins his texts. As in the citation above of Blas de Otero's hopeful voice, what stands out in Uribe's works is his peaceful worldview and his faith in humanity. It is easy to be pessimistic in this world: governments are corrupt, businesses influence everything, and, in many ways, we form part of a global system that aims to manipulate us. Being cynical is the order of the day. It is easy to see the flaws in others, even obvious. The difficult thing is to figure out what to do with this information. In reading through Uribe's work—from his poetry to his novels and essays—one sees a constant attempt to emphasize the good in life, even at uncertain or dark times.

5 A previous version of this article was published as the prologue to the anthology of works written by Uribe in Spanish: "Un nuevo tiempo espléndido. Prólogo." in *Kirmen Uribe. Vidas y ficciones* (Iruñea: Pamiela, 2014), 7-13.

In what follows, I examine Uribe's essays, poems, and novels, followed by a more detailed interpretation of his second novel, *Mussche* (2012, translated into Spanish as *Lo que mueve el mundo* in 2013), to demonstrate the different forms in which Uribe's works address controversial topics from a new perspective, one that attempts to reinterpret how we understand reality.

In the 1950s, social poets like Blas de Otero and Gabriel Celaya wrote under the shadow of Francoism, however, they did not let that embitter their spirit. "I ask for words and peace," said the Basque poet, Blas de Otero. Instead of using art as an escape from the world in which they lived, the poets used it to imagine another, better one in their verses (even though they had to do so exclusively in Spanish). More than sixty years later, the situation is very different for Basque writers. As Uribe himself explains in his essay "El idioma de la Virgen María de la playa" (Beach Virgin Mary's Language): "In 25 years the number of speakers has grown by 150,000. There is a Basque-language press, media, a whole literary system" (Uribe 2009). He goes on to admit that there is still much to do, but as Uribe's literary career itself suggests, now people no longer must ask to use words. They have them and, in Uribe's case, they can use them to continue inspiring peace (now in Basque and in many translations at the same time).

Nevertheless, wanting to open oneself up to the world comes with certain challenges within the Basque Country. When I wrote my doctoral thesis, I was apprehensive about including Uribe's first novel, *Bilbao-New York-Bilbao* (Uribe 2008; English translation, 2014) in my study of novels that had won the Spanish National Prize for Narrative Literature from 1977 to 2012, which is awarded by the central Spanish Government. I was introduced to *Bilbao-New York-Bilbao* because it won the prize in 2009.[6] The basic question I wanted to examine was: Who produces the culture of a country? The government or the

6 For more information on the Spanish National Prize for Narrative Literature, see Perret, Sally, "In the Name of the Nation?: The National Award in Narrative Literature, and the Democratization of Art in Spain (1977-2013)," *Journal of Spanish Cultural Studies* 16.1 (2015): 77–93.

people? And in my research, I realized that both have played a pivotal role. For example, when the Spanish state changed the rules of its national prizes to include texts written in all the official languages of the country in 1984, the space of literature opened to include more voices at the national level. However, as it is a literary prize which includes the obligation to participate in various events, giving authors a visible platform from which to express themselves in total freedom, I also contended that the artists/citizens have the power to change how the reality of the country is perceived, depending on how they chose to represent the space of the prize. In other words, it is not just the government that has the power to do so.[7]

At the same time, I recognize that such labels awarded by the state, like that of the "*National* Prizes," also serve to augment the image of a multicultural, yet united, state. In their circulation and promotion, it is possible to argue that those who win the *National Prize* with texts written in Catalan, Galician, and Basque, inadvertently end up legitimizing the state and the oppressive policies it practices, by helping to create "the fantasy" of a democratic country, as argued by Luisa-Elena Delgado (Delgado 2014, 177). Others, such as Joseba Gabilondo, go even further, claiming that Uribe's works (as well as those by other internationally renowned Basque authors like Bernardo Atxaga) end up sustaining the Spanish state's neoliberal political agenda more than any Basque political agenda, almost implying that such works are bad for Basque culture.[8] In fact, Gabilondo once warned me in person to be mindful when writing about Uribe because the arguments I make and the fact that I am not a Basque speaker and I read in translation could also inadvertently contribute to discourses that diminish Basque political power.

---

7 For more on that interpretation of *Bilbao-New York-Bilbao*, see Perret, Sally, "Fish and Trees Are Alike: The Movement of Identity in Kirmen Uribe's *Bilbao-New York-Bilbao*," *Hispanic Review* 85.1 (2017): 23–45.

8 For an example of this perspective, see Gabilondo, Joseba, "Indifference as Terror: On State Politics and Basque Literature in Globalization," *Oihenart: Cuadernos de Lengua y Literatura* 25 (2010): 217–40.

The arguments of critics like Delgado and Gabilondo are important and, we could say, "true," but at the same time such interpretations, in my view, do not take into account the literary beauty that Uribe's works also represent. Nor do I think that such critiques consider the fact that Uribe's works do discuss controversial subjects. His literary productions are not so naïve, and they often challenge traditional ideas of power, just not in exclusively political terms. Instead, they adopt a way of seeing the political in a particular way, one that is neither anti-political (in contrast to a political position) nor apolitical (absent of a political position)—a perspective that Roberto Esposito terms "impolitical" (Esposito 2006, 23). In Uribe's work, what stands out is his desire to see Basque culture as part of the world and not as a culture exclusively rooted to perpetually isolated ancient traditions. As Joseba Zulaika explains, the traditional view of all things Basque is based on a very binary perspective of the world: Basque is Basque and not Spanish; it is ancient and not modern; it is local and not universal; it allows only the exclusive use of Basque and not Spanish; etc. In sum, Basqueness is often defined, then, by what it is not, more than (or as much as) by what it is (Zulaika 2004, 116). Writers like Uribe represent another perspective toward the Basque situation: one that takes into account how complicated it is to write from a small culture at the same time as it attempts to see beyond rigid versions of what that culture should be.

Indeed, such debates over what is or what is not Basque literature almost made me not include Uribe in my thesis. I asked myself if I had the right to study a Basque novel in translation. Would I contribute to the displacement of the original novel, as the linguist Lawrence Venuti has suggested when describing the various power hierarchies within the world of translations? One of the problems with translation is that it tends to conceptualize authority as an individual concept. Thus, when discussing a translation, often the translation circulates around the world as if it were an exact copy of the original—as if it were the same text, word for word—thereby erasing the efforts of the translator

(Venuti 2002, 7). It is also true that translations can domesticate literary texts, as Venuti contends, by occluding the original. Yet, as Sakai has argued, translations also have the power to include ideas and to alter or modify dominant perspectives; in this sense, too, one can interpret translation as a political act (2010, 26). In the end, I decided that I did have the right to study Uribe's novel. First, I rationalized that if most of the jury members that had awarded the prize to Uribe had also read his novel in translation (given that only two members were Basque speakers), then I did have the right to study it for my purposes and, in effect, both versions had won the National Prize that year. Furthermore, I realized that I have been introduced to several world authors through translations, from theoreticians like Karl Marx and Michel Foucault to novels that I read in my courses on world literature, such as those of Kafka, Sartre, and Dostoevsky. Why, then, should it be so different with a Basque work?

One reason studying the translation of a work written in Basque is different is because the literary system in the Basque Country is distinct. As Jon Kortazar has pointed out, instead of being a minority literature, Basque literature might best be described as a "small" literature, given that it is not only a literature produced in the periphery of the state, but it also refers to the small number of readers there are in comparison to the dominant literary world (Kortazar 2013, 12). From this perspective, one can understand why some think that Basque literature must always fulfil the political purpose of supporting a certain image of Basque culture and why many think that Basques must only write about Basque things, in Basque, and for Basques. Period. It is natural, then, that some scholars have criticized Uribe, given that he does not write just for Basques, but rather for everyone. Moreover, as we will see, in his works Basque literature is presented as a literature that circulates around the world (and not just in the Basque Country) and that is capable of inspiring others (and not just serving as a political vehicle for Basques). In other words, instead of presenting Basque literature as a closed space, it is shown as an open space, full of infinite possibilities.

Even though Kirmen Uribe's work is rooted in Basque culture, the themes he explores—love, death, family, and the power of fiction—are universal. In fact, what I most admire about Uribe's work and life is his passion for culture, his dedication to bringing Basque literature to the world, and his ability to communicate his refreshingly optimistic perspective to a global community. From the titles of his most prominent publications—*Meanwhile Take My Hand* (Uribe 2001; translated to English in 2007), *Bilbao-New York-Bilbao* (Uribe 2008; translated to English in 2014 and again in 2022), *Lo que mueve el mundo* (What Moves the World, Uribe 2013c), *Jainko txiki eta jostalari hura* (That Tiny Playful God, Uribe 2013b), and his third novel, *La hora de despertarnos juntos* (*The Hour of Waking Together*, Uribe 2018)—one can see an implicit wish to celebrate the beauty of life through fiction. The author often finds inspiration in his own life. In fact, the novel *Bilbao-New York-Bilbao* is told from the perspective of a narrator/author of the same name. He also discusses the lives of his relatives, his friends, historical figures, and people he meets on his many travels. Sometimes, as in life, there is tragedy in his fiction too, like the poem "Visit" in his first book of poems *Bitartean heldu eskutik* (2001, translated into English as *Meanwhile Take My Hand* by Elizabeth Macklin in 2007), in which there is a verse that repeats twice:

> Meanwhile take my hand, she implored us,
> I don't want promises, I don't want repentance,
> just some sign of love is all. (13)

The poem is about a woman who is dying of something related to heroin (either the drug itself or AIDS). In the cited verse, one sees the woman's wish to not worry too much about the past ("I don't want repentance") nor to think too much about the future ("I don't want promises"). All there is for her is the present and as it is a present without past or future, she just seeks "some sign of love."

In other works by Uribe, the funny side of life is highlighted, as in the short story "Berlin 2006," which is a humorous tale about a father taking his son to see a soccer match (Uribe 2010a). The author is also frequently invited to write for various newspapers and other literary outlets. For example, in 2013 the editor of the Lumen publishing house asked Uribe to write a prologue for a special edition of Virginia Woolf's *A Room of One's Own*. In it, the author expresses his own desire for a space, "like that drawing room of Mrs. Crowe, in which nobody feels excluded and everyone may take the floor. Even writers like me, who is concluding this prologue in a library, because, effectively, I lack my own room" (Uribe 2013a, 29). Even in his more intimate works, such as the poem dedicated to his wife, "Un dios pequeño y juguetón," from his third book of poems, *Jainko txiki eta hostalari hura* (*That Tiny Playful God*, Uribe 2013b), or the short story "Hierba alta" (Tall grass) published in *El País*[9] about his childhood sexual experiences (Uribe 2010b), there is always a desire to see the good in life in its various facets.

In addition to speaking about real lives in his fiction, there is also much reflection on the role of fiction can play in life. In his poem "The Gold Ring" (Uribe 2007, 111), for example, the lyrical voice speaks of a family story that fascinated him as a child, a story that would later inspire not just that poem, but also a video/poem of the same name produced by the director Jon Garaño (Garaño 2011), and an episode in the chapter "Frankfurt" from his first novel in which he links his family's version of the tale with similar stories from other cultures (Uribe 2008; English translation, 2014). In these and other works there is an emphasis on the role that art and stories affect how reality is perceived.

Upon reading Uribe's works, from an optimistic perspective, one could conclude that the author assumes his role as a public figure seriously. Not only do his works offer a conciliatory

9 Daily newspaper written in the Spanish language, based in Madrid.

worldview, but also Uribe's implicit aim to inspire a better world stands out. As the literary critic Paulo Kortazar Billelabeitia argues in his analysis of *Bilbao-New York-Bilbao*, "Uribe believes in another future, a literature that, although it portrays the current world in which humans live . . . does not shy away from a local collective identity present in humanism and ethics as a path to follow" (Kortazar Billelabeitia 2012, 76). This eagerness to promote a new, more humanistic ethics is one that the author also embodies. Indeed, he received his first important literary award—Becerro de Bengoa—for the book *El erotismo de Lizardi* (1996, original: *Lizardi eta erotismoa*, 1996 Lizardi's eroticism) while he was serving a prison sentence for refusing to serve in the military, which was obligatory at the time. Since then, Uribe has taken an active role in the Basque Country, helping to organize festivals, readings, and book fairs. On June 8, 2014, he participated in a human chain from Durango to Pamplona in which thousands of other participants sought to call attention to the situation and changing laws in the Basque Country (Sainz 2014). The movement, called Gure esku dago—it's in our hands—is different from past movements, such as those of ETA, for example, whose acts of violence before the recent ceasefire in 2011 no longer seem a viable solution to Basque Independence in the twenty-first century. Instead of attacking the state with violence, Gure esku dago declares that its goals are peaceful and inclusive, and it supports the right to decide. Although at first sight the slogan "it's in our hands" seems to be a political decision (albeit positive), it is also a posture which signals the limits of the category of politics in and of itself. In other words, while people hold hands, they physically represent the insignificance of the national position that tries to ignore the will of the people.

In the end, Uribe is someone who, like a machine, never stops. He is generous with his time, and he has his feet on the ground; he answers his own emails and is available to do interviews with students by Skype. He is a well-balanced and humble person, and upon meeting him, one sees that his desire to inspire peace, love, and tranquillity is palpable and contagious. More recently, Uribe was invited to take part in an exhibition at the Fine Arts Museum in Bilbao, for which he organized the space within the museum according to the poetic vision outlined in his book *Con la A de arte y la B de Bilbao* (With the *A* in art and the *B* in Bilbao), a book of art which includes various works from different cultures that are not presented chronologically, but instead in thematic alphabetical order (Seisdedos 2018). If this were not enough, in 2018, too, the author began a residency in New York, as the winner of a grant awarded by the New York Public Library, where he wrote his fourth novel about the life of Edith Wynner, a feminist from Hungary who lived in the United States from the 1920s until her death in 1948 (Redondo 2018).

Wanting to emphasize the beauty of life does not mean that Uribe's work avoids more controversial or ugly topics. On the contrary, in his poetic world there is also war, pain, and many losses that alternate with images of everyday life, the loneliness of the writer, and the uncertain future of all cultures, especially small ones like that of the Basque Country, whose future does not only depend on how it is presented from within but also on how it is understood and appreciated from the outside. Nor does being an optimist mean that his works are utopian or nostalgic, or *costumbrista* either. When read carefully, one sees a certain acceptance of the dark reality typically absent in *costumbrista* works. Life is taken as inspiration and, with eyes wide open, its imperfections are accepted to advance a new, more humanistic worldview.

Although Uribe is now more known as a novelist, the majority of his works are rooted in the world of poetry. Some of his first literary works—*Bar Puerto*, performed and recorded in 2001 and published as a book/CD in 2010 (Uribe 2010c), and the already mentioned *Meanwhile Take My Hand*—were poetry books performed live with music and visual projections, and both represent the author's intimate style and his ethical position. Finally, both are accompanied by multimedia: the former in the form of a documentary by the same name; and the latter with a CD of music composed by Bingen Mendizabal, Rafa Rueda, and Miguel Urdangarin, from a concert performed in the spring of 2018. In the latter, many of the poems speak about Uribe's vision of the world as a writer. The poem "Don't Make It a Choice" describes his desire to live between cultures (Uribe 2007, 109), a position he developed further in his essay "El idioma de la Virgen María de la playa" (The language of the Virgin Mary of the beach), in which the author describes himself as "a borderland author" (Uribe 2009). According to Uribe, blindly defending a predetermined rigid political ideology does not lead us to concrete solutions. As a result, he opts to present his particular experience of reality as a way of inspiring a new, more humanistic perspective, an idea which one also sees in the essay "Sobre el derecho a la individualidad" (On the right to individuality), winner of the *El Correo* Journalism Prize (Uribe 2011). In this and in other works, Uribe's lyrical voice teaches us the consequences of adhering to fixed ideas about how a culture should be in demonstrating the limits of social prejudices.

The yearning to examine the rigidity of Basque identity is the principal theme of Uribe's first novel, *Bilbao-New York-Bilbao*, in which he uses a flight as the narrative thread which connects several stories that allow us to perceive how much life has changed in the Basque Country between the early twentieth century and the present. The novel is narrated from the perspective of an author (who is also called Kirmen Uribe) while he thinks about the novel that he would like to write about the last three generations of his family. Instead of being linear, the novel is fragmentary and includes several intertextual references to other artistic creations, including literary works. For this reason, the critic Paulo Kortazar Billelabeitia has argued that it is postmodern, since it has the form of a network that, like the Internet, connects real and sometimes fictional people and things, thereby creating a world in which political and geographical borders are not so important (Kortazar Billelabeitia

2012, 73). Additionally, although it is a novel about the past, it is always tied to the present by the fact that it takes place in a plane from beginning to end, pointing out that the cultural identity of a place is something that is always being formed in the present (in this case, through the memories of the narrator during the flight); and with the many anecdotes recounted, it is demonstrated that a culture does not always change by choice, but also by necessity.

2 A royal-blue sea: An impolitical reading of *Lo que mueve el mundo*

The second of Uribe's novels, *Mussche* (*Lo que mueve el mundo*), also explores the limits of political categories. It narrates in its pages the story of the Belgian writer Robert Mussche before, during, and after adopting little Karmentxu, who, like many children of the time, had to leave the country after the bombing of Gernika on April 26, 1937, in search of refuge abroad. Instead of being a linear story, like *Bilbao-New York-Bilbao* the novel is fragmentary in the sense that it blends historical eras, characters, and adventures related to the plot in the same chapter. The first chapter, for example, begins with a description of the historical reality of what happened to the Basque children during the Spanish Civil War (1936–1939). It includes facts, dates, and narrative descriptions of the voyage by ship that many Basque children made without their parents. From the first sentence, the reader is located at a particular historical moment: "Following the bombing of Gernika, the *lehendakari*[10] José Antonio Agirre reaffirmed his decision to safeguard the children. That 1937, between May and June, nineteen thousand little ones left the Port of Bilbao toward different European countries" (Uribe 2013c, 13). With such a beginning, Uribe not only makes a reference to one of the worst catastrophes of the twentieth century, the bombing of Gernika, but he also attributes the saving of the children to the Basque leader at that time and connects all of it to a specific place, the Port of Bilbao.

10 President of the Basque Autonomous Community.

Whether or not it is true the leader did indeed play such an active direct role is not important to the start of the story, although it does demonstrate indirectly a general Basque (and male) political perspective. Nevertheless, in launching Robert's story in this way, the novel presents an angle which points to the limits of the political reality at that time—the children had to be saved—without criticizing anyone directly for what happened or explaining the motives behind the bombing. In other words, we can say that it is not necessarily a Basque perspective, or anti-Spanish/fascist, or simply apolitical (a novel lacking a political position). It is a novel which depicts without judging.

In the paragraphs that follow the historical tale, Uribe begins to elaborate with the details of a particular trip undertaken by little Karmentxu and her brother Ramón. Instead of offering a purely fictitious narration, however, the description of the trip includes historical information to contextualize the story of the children and the story of the ship:

> On 6 May the ship *Habana* left the Port of Santurce for the first time toward La Rochelle. 2,483 refugees were aboard. At another time, the *Habana* had been a luxury transatlantic liner that sailed the route Bilbao-Havana-Mexico-New York. The ship, constructed in the La Naval in Sestao, was the star of the company. In the 1930s it had been named *Alfonso XIII*, but with the coming of the Republic its name was changed.[11] (Uribe 2013c, 13–14)

Just as the impressive number of refugee children is mentioned casually at the beginning of the chapter, here the narrator calmly mentions how the name of the ship had changed depending on the different political climates. What was previously a symbol of international relations and national pride for Basques soon became emblematic of the sordid everyday life at another historical moment. In presenting the history of the ship this way, the novel points out indirectly how ephemeral all political ideologies

11 Translated by Cameron Watson.

are, as well as the high cost of pursuing a particular political perspective.

Although the novel begins at a specific historical moment—the fleeing of the children, the journey of the two siblings, and the image of Robert collecting Karmentxu at the train station in 1937—it jumps in the same chapter to another year, 1929, when Robert was young and spending time in the arms of his beloved friend Herman, thinking about the future of the world. While both are lying next to one another tenderly, Robert says: "There must be a way of making this world better, of organizing things in another form" (Uribe 2013c, 23), and before the chapter ends, the novel jumps in time again to 1945 with the image of Robert's biological daughter, Carmen, waiting for her father at the same train station in which he had picked up Karmentxu, but this time after the Second World War. Without any more information than a few gaps between paragraphs to indicate one temporal jump to another, the reader must put the pieces together to create a coherent narrative about what happened and when, thereby avoiding imposing any teleological perspective, which is typical of all political perspectives in the sense that in any political narrative there is a clear before and after. In Uribe's novel, however, reality is presented instead as disconnected fragments that are experienced, which are only linked by the broader narrative level, thereby avoiding promoting any particular political perspective.

Even when the principal characters, Robert and Herman, have ideological conversations about the future of the world, at the end of the day, their dreams are mere words on a page that stay in the philosophical realm. For example, the only conversation which is represented (and not just summarized) is when both speak openly about what moves the world, in a clear nod to the title of the novel.

> "Robert, in your opinion, what moves the world?" Herman asked him on one occasion "according to Nietzsche, that

> obscure force is power; for Marx, it's a question of the economy; and according to Freud, it's love." [...]
> "I agree with Nietzsche" Herman decided, with conviction. "It is power that moves the world."
> "I have my doubts" Robert dared to refute. "At first I thought that that secret force was the economy . . . What's more, you know how much I admire Marx." [...]
> "But no, Herman. What brings us to life is love! That profound force is love. Or that's what I want to think at least." (Uribe 2013c, 36)[12]

Throughout the novel, one begins to understand how true that idea was for Robert, although he was a proud Belgian socialist who, ultimately, went to Spain as a journalist to cover the Spanish Civil War, and then enlisted to fight the Axis powers in the Second World War in Belgium and France. Despite all that, the reader realizes that behind Robert's every political motive there was always an emotional motive—the desire to protect his loved ones against all evil. Love, for Robert, however, is not permanent at all, but rather something that is renewed each passing day. As Robert says, "I don't believe so much in perpetuity, as I do in a love renewed at every instant. Transcendence doesn't impress me. It even scares me . . ." (Uribe 2013c, 144)—a sentiment which one can also interpret as a commentary on the constructed side of all metanarratives, including the political.

In effect, Robert's story has more to do with personal motives and desires even in the most repressive environments than with explicit political motives. In one passage, Robert and Herman speak about their love for Beethoven and start to imagine how hard his life must have been while at the same time they imagine him defending himself in the following manner: "Anyone can have anything made: ships, palaces, weapons, but not our minds; that cannot be made" (Uribe 2013c, 42). It is no coincidence that the list of things they imagine Beethoven mentioning could all be metaphors for political power and war

12 Translated by Cameron Watson.

(ships, palaces, weapons); however, what the musician feels, thinks, and dreams comes from him and only him.

In addition to Beethoven, the novel mentions various other artists, musicians, and writers whose works Robert would have known, including texts of different origins and political perspectives. When the narrator goes to Robert's daughter's house to interview her for his book, he comes across several Basque texts in Robert's personal library. In particular, the narrator describes a book of popular poems and songs from the Civil War that Robert possessed. Later, his daughter Carmen tells the narrator about a song that was sung on the ship to raise spirits:

> Las palomas huyen despavoridas
> y la montaña guarda silencio
> ¡La gallardía de los muchachos
> yace sin vida en el suelo
>
> The doves flee in fright
> and the mountain falls silent
> The bravery of the kids
> remains lifeless on the ground.

Although the poem was originally published as propaganda during the war, its content echoes the experience of many: that of having lived through something many people do not speak about. Moreover, the fact that the copy of poems Carmen has also includes a note which explains how the poet Estepan Urkiaga "Lauaxeta" was killed during the war and buried in Vitoria-Gasteiz represents the futility of war and how difficult it was to fight fascism.

The novel also includes poems by Robert Mussche, who, as well as being a soldier, was also a poet. By including his poems in Flemish, the novel does not just commemorate Robert's work, but it also puts Flemish on a global stage. Toward the end of the novel, the narrator also tells us why he decided to write it:

first, because of a promise he made to a friend, who was on the verge of dying, to write something about an everyday hero. Second, he tells us that he identified a lot with Robert, a poet, new father, and humanist, and for that reason wanted to leave "a small paper tomb for Robert. That tomb which Carmen has never been able to visit" (Uribe 2013c, 213). In ending the novel with his personal motives for writing it in the first place, the narrator makes the reader reconsider the whole book from a different perspective: one of a contemporary writer who is looking for a way to reconcile his emotions of happiness and sadness about the birth of his daughter in 2010 and the death of his friend Aitzol Aramaio in 2011.

In naming his friend, the narrator aligns himself with the real Kirmen Uribe, adding another impolitical level to the text. In including his comments about why he wrote the book in the first place, the narrator distances the novel from the political realm—since above all else it was written for a friend, which leaves the reader sufficient space to identify the limits of totalitarian thoughts and the democratic responses they generate. In other words, there are no good or bad people in *Lo que mueve el mundo*. Instead of seeing strict divisions, one sees characters who act as they do out of love (and not as a chore or as a moral obligation). Likewise, the fact that the reader knows that, ultimately, Robert never returned to Ghent also adds to its impolitical nature. After returning from Spain, Robert joined the Allied forces and, when France fell, he was sent to a concentration camp on the last train, where he suffered a great deal. Thereafter, he was liberated and put on a ship that was mistakenly bombed by the Allies. While other prisoners were rescued from the concentration camp, Robert suffered the ill fortune of dying beside another 4,249 prisoners on a ship that supposedly represented his salvation. Thus, in the end, everything was in vain for Robert. He left his home to fight for his ideals, only later to die at the hands of his own compatriots in a tragic accident. As the narrator points out: "To be a hero also has its hidden face, its flipside. Look at how Vic [his wife] ended up, how Carmen ended up, without a husband and without a father. The flipside of being a hero is precisely that, all the suffering you leave in your wake. That is its dark side, having had clear ideas . . ." Once more, one can see how the novel gives voice to these silenced stories without offering any anti-political or political agenda, a technique one sees in many of Uribe's works.

3 Conclusion: Toward another splendid time

Through universal themes like love, heroism, and virtue, alongside the (non-teleological) narrative techniques he employs, Uribe's life and works present his readers with an impolitically optimistic perspective which examines the category of the political without imposing any explicit (counter)political agenda. In other words, Uribe's works point out the limits of monolithic perspectives, but he does not prophesize. He shows to what extent politics can alter our lives, but it is not what moves the world. He urges us to consider our own affiliations and what is really at stake with each decision we make, and he reveals to us the limits of thinking about identity, whether personal or collective, in a closed way by painting the world as a convergence of cultures, languages, and dreams instead of a series of rigid ideas that are worth dying for. With this new generational perspective we can perhaps conclude that a new, splendid time is advancing rapidly.

Bibliography

Delgado, Luisa Elena. 2014. *La nación singular: Fantasías de normalidad democrática española (1996–2011)*. Madrid: Siglo XXI de España.

Esposito, Roberto. 2006. *Categorías de lo impolítico*. Roberto Raschella transl. Buenos Aires: Katz.

Garaño, Jon. 2011. *Urrezko eraztuna*. With Alaitz Eguren & Kepa Errasti. Online: http://kirmenuribe.eus/es/multimedia/bideoteka/multimedia/bideoteka/urrezko-eraztuna/ 02/11/2019.

Kortazar, Jon. 2013. *Contemporary Basque Literature: Kirmen Uribe's Proposal*. Cameron J. Watson transl. Madrid: Iberoamericana.

Kortazar Billelabeitia, Paulo. 2012. *Bilbao-New York-Bilbao* de Kirmen Uribe: postmodernidad, nuevas tecnologías de la comunicación y modernismo tras la postmodernidad. *Oihenart: Cuadernos de Lengua y Literatura* 27: 67–80.

Redondo, Maite. 2018. Kirmen Uribe: "Como a mis personajes me gusta viajar, salir para luego volver." *Deia: Noticias de Bizkaia*. 14/09/2018. Online: https://www.deia.eus/2018/09/14/ocio-y-cultura/cultura/como-a-mis-personajes-me-gusta-viajar-salir-para-luego-volver 02/11/2019.

Sakai, Naoki. 2010. Translation and the Figure of Border: Toward the Apprehension of Translation as a Social Act. *Profession*: 25–34.

Sainz, Jorge. 2014. Cadena humana multitudinaria por el derecho a decidir. *El Diario Vasco*. 08/06/2014. Online: https://www.diariovasco.com/politica/201406/08/cien-personas-reclaman-cadena-20140608115654.html [2019/11/02].

Seisdedos, Iker. 2018. Con la A de Arte y la B de Bilbao. *El País*. 03/10/2018. Online: https://elpais.com/cultura/2018/10/03/actualidad/1538580054_889158.html [02/11/2019].

Uribe, Kirmen. 2001. *Bitartean heldu eskutik*. Zarautz: Susa.

Uribe, Kirmen. 2007. *Mientras tanto dame la mano*. trad. G. Markuleta y A. Arregui.

Madrid: Visor.

Uribe, Kirmen. 2008. *Bilbao-New York-Bilbao*. Donostia: Elkar.

Uribe, Kirmen. 2009. El idioma de la Virgen María de la playa. *El País*. 02/11/2009. Online: https://elpais.com/diario/2009/11/09/opinion/1257721212_850215.html [02/11/2019].

Uribe, Kirmen. 2010a. Berlin 2006. In *Culo subido. Y otros relatos de humor*, Juan Bas (ed.). Iruñea: Alberdania.

Uribe, Kirmen. 2010b. Hierba alta. *El País*. 01/12/2010.

Uribe, Kirmen. 2010c. *Bar Puerto*. Donostia: Elkar.

Uribe, Kirmen. 2011. Sobre el derecho a la individualidad. *El Correo*. February 27, 2011. Online: https://www.elcorreo.com/vizcaya/v/20110227/cultura/sobre-derecho-individualidad-20110227.html [02/11/2019].

Uribe, Kirmen. 2012. *Mussche*. Zarautz: Susa.

Uribe, Kirmen. 2013a. El salón de la señora Crowe. In *Un cuarto propio*. Virginia Woolf. Barcelona: Lumen.

Uribe, Kirmen. 2013b. *Jainko txiki eta jostalari hura*. Donostia: Elkar.

Uribe, Kirmen. 2013c. *Lo que mueve el mundo*. trad. G. Markuleta. Barcelona: Seix Barral.

Uribe, Kirmen. 2018. *La hora de despertarnos juntos*. trad. J. M. Isasi. Barcelona: Seix Barral.

Venuti, Lawrence. 2002 [1995]. *The Translator's Invisibility: A History of Translation*. London: Routledge.

Zulaika, Joseba. 2004. Nourishment by the Negative: National Subalternity, Antagonism, and Radical Democracy. In *Empire & Terror: Nationalism/Postnationalism in the New Millennium*, Begoña Aretxaga *et al.* (ed.), 115–136. Reno: Center for Basque Studies, University of Nevada.

NARRATIVE

3

Kirmen Uribe's literature: A way of looking at Basque society

Hasier Arraiz

1 An introduction to late postmodernism and Kirmen Uribe's narrative style

Two pervasive features stand out in Kirmen Uribe's narrative: first, the importance of the *self* and, second, the use of *fragmentary* writing. In regards to the second, Uribe plays constantly with the use of ellipses, thus assembling his narrative by means of fragments that readers must connect. These two persistent features in Uribe's narrative have experienced an intrinsic evolution.

The clearest expression of the importance Uribe gives to the self in his creative process is in his first novel, *Bilbao-New York-Bilbao* (Elkar, 2008; English-language version: Seren, 2014), which is based entirely on *autofiction*. Bearing in mind that only autobiography can give more importance to the self than autofiction—and that is sometimes open to debate—we could argue that, in his first novel, Uribe arrived at the pinnacle of what could be considered giving importance to the self. Although in his second and third novels, *Mussche* (Susa, 2012) and *Elkarrekin esnatzeko ordua* (The Hour of Waking Together, Susa, 2016), the writer from Ondarroa did not rely as much on autofiction, he followed the same procedure in constructing the two novels: at the beginning of each, the author himself explains why he decided to write it and, above all, what his own relationship is with what he is going to say. Likewise, at the end of each novel, the author appears again in order to explain how writing the novel—understood as a process—has changed him.

Both in *Mussche* and, especially, in *Elkarrekin esnatzeko ordua*, the writer describes the writing process for the reader as if he were doing it at that very moment. Through that technique, Uribe manages to create an illusion in which the writing and reading processes seem to take place simultaneously, as if the reader were receiving certain information at the same time as the writer. Through such writing, which today we consider totally contemporary (we could, for example, include in this tendency the significant works of renowned writers like Emmanuel Carrère or Laurent Binet), the author seeks a more horizontal relationship with the reader. Therefore, while in the novel *Bilbao-New York-Bilbao* (2014 [2008], 132–33) Uribe turned the canonical nineteenth-century novel upside down, in the two that followed he also abandoned the prevalent twentieth-century notion of the mysterious artefact novel in which *playful* structuring was often preferred to the story itself. In the three works, the Ondarroa writer explains to the reader that what he or she is reading is a novel, and also shows, one by one, the steps he has taken to write it, placing before the reader's eyes, in order to do so, what we term an *artefact*. In that process—in Uribe's view, a single procedure made up of writing and reading a novel—the reflections and feelings stemming from events (and stories) are more important than those same events and stories themselves, and he acknowledges from the outset that they may be different and even contradictory according to each reader.

For Uribe it is not complicated to perceive the importance of subjectivism behind the use of the self, nor to know that very different perspectives—even opposing ones—may emerge in the face of the same event, and yet all perspectives are true because each shows the truth of a person (of a self). Subjectivism, as a philosophical attitude, calls into question the idea of absolute truth from the perspective of the internal factors of each subject. However, relativism, which reaches the same conclusion and in the same way, calls into question the existence of absolute truth by focusing on external factors. This is because the basis of relativism is the complexity of reality. Reality is always too complex to guarantee that it is one thing or another; it is also probably always one thing, and another, and even contradictory too. There are not one but many realities and, although they may appear contradictory, some are not more real than others. This mentality, influenced by Gianni Vattimo's notion of *weak thought*[13], was not just widespread in late twentieth-century narrative, but also took the form of a particular way of writing in literature: specifically, *fragmentary writing*. Writing based on fragmentation seeks to convey the idea that reality is unattainable, because we can only detect pieces of reality and because those pieces, by nature, are always incomplete and sometimes contradictory among themselves.

In that sense, fragmentary writing seeks to abolish widespread early twentieth-century *metanarratives* that took on the appearance of ideologies or creeds, because there is no story that can embrace and express *totality*, whether of the universe, the world, history, human beings themselves, or human relationships. In literature itself, especially in the late twentieth century, the desire to relate a totality was not just perceived as arrogant, but refuted even as an option. The relativism which corresponds to fragmentary writing would like to be the vaccine against all totalitarianism and to demonstrate that reality is never totally black or completely white, but often that same relativism, as a thematic tendency to relativize absolutely everything, also developed into a foundation of negligence or indifference in the face of injustice. Of course, the cultural tendency to relativize every event, and neoliberalism as an ideological doctrine, did not predominate at the same time, because one was the cultural thread that the other needed, as demonstrated by the American cultural critic Fredric Jameson.

Likewise, the fact of having established certain limits on relativism in contemporary literature has contributed to creating a fitting context in which to express heterodox thoughts, with the specific consequence of skillfully calling into question most monolithic philosophical attitudes. In doing so, the narrative

13 In Vattimo's view, language can at best convey an interpretation of reality, but never the thing itself. (https://www.oxfordreference.com/view/10.1093/oi/authority.20110803121433242)

tendency to play with the blurred boundaries between fiction and reality proves to be very useful.

One could say that the importance of *self* and *fragmentary writing*, respectively, link Kirmen Uribe's narrative to postmodern literature. Or at least they reveal a postmodern source of his narrative. In the United States (and we should not look too far from the center of gravity of contemporary literature), Thomas Pynchon, John Barth, Don DeLillo, William Gaddis, Vladimir Nabokov, and William Gass, among others, formed the strong nucleus of *classic postmodernism*. Their heirs—David Foster Wallace, Jonathan Franzen, William T. Vollmann, Jeffrey Eugenides, A. M. Homes, Richard Powers, Joanna Scott, and Mark Leyner, among others—also acknowledged the influence of European literary theory and considered themselves the offspring of *late postmodernism*. With the publication of *Bitartean heldu eskutik* (Susa, 2001; *Meanwhile Take My Hand*, Graywolf Press, 2007), Kirmen Uribe emerged not just as a writer but also a reader due to the *intertextuality* of the book, among other reasons. In addition, we know that he has also studied literary theory. One of the main features of his literature is its very contemporary nature. His works have demonstrated time and time again that the writer from Ondarroa knows full well what he is writing about in the world and the type of literature he is creating. Therefore, the hypothesis that the roots of Uribe's narrative lie in late postmodernism is not, in my opinion, inappropriate, especially taking into account that most of the American writers we can situate in that current are only between seven and ten years older than Uribe.

David Foster Wallace, arguably at the head of the aforementioned generation, declared his wish to break with the literature of the previous generation, even though he confessed to having been influenced by its powerful writing. In my opinion, Kirmen Uribe and certain other writers have done or are doing something similar, too—on the one hand, also breaking with late postmodernism (although not in a traumatic way), and on the other, trying to create a new literary paradigm. While the novel

Bilbao-New York-Bilbao evinced clear traces of postmodern narrative (such as autofiction itself), in its desire to call into question the very nature of the novel, its fragmentary writing, the predominance of ellipses, its longing to play with readers, the lack of apparent structure, the constant leaps forward and backward through time, frustrating every linear story, and the importance of the Internet and other contemporary technological references, its form of writing has nothing to do with the *complexity* that predominated among the authors of classical postmodernism. The main feature of those writers' works, and arguably the only one that connected all of them, was the demanding of a great cognitive effort on the part of the reader, whom they expected to possess a high cultural level. In all likelihood, just as Pynchon's *Gravity's Rainbow* (1973) represented the summit of this literary tendency, so Wallace's *Infinite Jest* (1996) marked its last significant work. The writers that emerged thereafter tried to distance themselves from that literature whose main ideal was *complexity* (of course, literary complexity and literary quality not being considered the same thing), although one continues to find several features befitting of postmodern literature in their works. That is where the term *late* came from, specifically because while they retained its essence, their narratives were also under other influences and ready to move in other directions.

Chronologically, it is difficult to link Uribe to pure postmodernism and even more difficult to be sure what is meant by such an assertion, especially seeing how the very concept of postmodernism has been so disfigured through the meddling of so many hands over the years. Nevertheless, turning to the features of his narrative and especially the novel *Bilbao-New York-Bilbao*, we can note traces of the aforementioned late postmodernism. It is true that such traces are less common in the following novels, but the basic difference is not in this area so much as in the way his novels view society. Or in the relationship that Uribe's novels seek with contemporary society. Previously, I alluded to neoliberalism's *cultural hegemony*[14] which, although it began during the era of Reagan and Thatcher, was developed fully after the fall of the Berlin Wall. The global expansion of the belief that there was no alternative is the clearest indicator of cultural hegemony. Culture had a lot to do with that, which is why Jameson[15] and other thinkers considered postmodernism a cultural heir of neoliberalism. Yet in the face of the conformity resulting from the lack of alternatives in the field of culture, as well as in literature, some *celebrated* ("*postmodernism of reaction*") and others *lamented* the situation. Progressive writers that deplored the lack of an alternative in the face of neoliberal hegemony expressed their inability to accept injustices from a "*postmodernism of resistance.*"[16] From the same perspective, when Uribe looks at Basque society, we perceive a spectator that does not like the spectacle he is witnessing. To tell the truth, Uribe makes it clear that it is not to his liking, but he prefers to remain a spectator. In the novel *Bilbao-New York-Bilbao*, when discussing political violence, he expresses deftly the complexity of reality and his own impotence: on the one hand, the fear felt in his own home when ETA bombed the police station in Ondarroa and, on the other, as a consequence of that very explosion, when he describes *from his balcony* how the wife of a man murdered by the paramilitary Triple A group is picking up bits of glass. Uribe expresses the despair of many Basques of that era thus: "This fall I'll turn thirty-eight. I've lived the whole of my life with this. Thirty-six years with a conflict and only two or three with some peace. How little."

Kirmen Uribe's position as a writer began to change with his second novel. By that time, the political situation in the Basque Country had changed completely, or was on the way to

14 We are referring to the parameters of the concept of cultural hegemony theorized by the Italian thinker Antonio Gramsci.

15 In 1984, the American literary critic Fredric Jameson published "Postmodernism, or, the Cultural Logic of Late Capitalism" in the *New Left Review*. Six years later he developed his thesis in a book of the same name.

16 Perhaps it was not his original idea, but I am indebted to the American historian and art critic Hal Foster for the *postmodernism of reaction / postmodernism of resistance* dichotomy.

a decisive change, because ETA chose to call a definitive end to its use of violence on October 20, 2011. Amid great skepticism, hope for a new and long-unknown era began flourishing in Basque society. Peace processes anywhere always go through rough patches in which they frequently face many hurdles, but this step in the Basque Country peace process was definitive. The novel *Mussche* (2012) did not focus on concurrent Basque society but, rather, on the personal situation of a writer who at the time experienced both joy and grief, because within the space of a few months, the writer's daughter was born and his great friend, the filmmaker Aitzol Aramaio, died. Uribe thought that his situation at that time resembled that of the Flemish writer Robert Mussche, who also had a newborn daughter and lost a close friend (2012, 184). However, it is difficult to overlook the fact that, in his second novel, Uribe sought to tell the story of a *hero*. Specifically, a story in which a repressive situation forces a writer to act like a hero of resistance. The situation in the novel is not as nuanced as the Basque conflict because the Nazis are occupying Mussche's homeland and the threat of all of Europe falling into their hands is crystal clear.

When Kirmen Uribe wrote the novel *Mussche*, our world was also changing and, while hope reigned in the Basque Country for very specific reasons, at the global level, the massive economic downturn provoked by the financial crisis of 2008 brought with it lasting political and social consequences. The dominant tendency in postmodern literature, that *impotence*—and also the inability to even imagine another world—in its narrative, was on the way to disappearing. Perhaps it is not up to small heroes to change the world. Indeed, Mussche died a prisoner on a warship that was bombed by his British allies. That is why Uribe wrote the novel in his honor and, even though it is just paper, it is the only grave the family possesses. It is the story of a painful defeat, and yet the author is in no doubt, when he imagines a conversation between Mussche and his close friend, that what moves the world is love (Uribe 2012, 36). It does not appear that the title chosen for the translation of the book into

Spanish[17] was a coincidence. In some way, by means of this novel with its bitter end, Uribe contends that sometimes human beings must keep moving ahead, faced with no other option as a result of injustice and repressive situations, *for love*.

By means of his novel *Mussche*, Kirmen Uribe—observing a world that in many cases is changing for the worse—suggests that sometimes normal people are forced to carry out major deeds in the face of injustice, obliged by love, and, moreover, that the world can only be transformed that way. When great threats become attacks, even though there is no absolute truth, the time of all excessive relativism has finished. The development of Uribe's narrative is characterized by his longing to portray this changed perspective, and the desire to tell stories and go back into history—to go to the roots of a story—to do so. The writer seeks out, thus, more traditional narratives, but maintains the fragmentary writing—with its clever use of ellipses—and a *living* as well as changing (dialectical in nature) relationship between the text and the author.

2 *Elkarrekin esnatzeko ordua*, another way of examining Basque society

Uribe's change of perspective—this new way of examining society—is also present in his third novel, *Elkarrekin esnatzeko ordua* (The Hour of Waking Together, Susa, 2016), in which the writer focuses on Basque society. The concerns (and fears) one notes in the novel *Mussche* are more evident, because after the terrible tragedies suffered by twentieth-century Europe, the new century brought with it *old new* threats. In his third novel, nevertheless, Uribe extends and explores more deeply the direction he had taken in *Mussche* by not just including reality but also totality; in a novel of some 300 pages, Uribe narrates half a century of history from a Basque perspective.

Elkarrekin esnatzeko ordua abandons the relativism characteristic of late postmodernism—above all reflected in Uribe's poems and *Bilbao-New York-Bilbao*—in order to relate,

17 *Lo que mueve el mundo* (What Moves the World).

by means of investigating memory, a key part of contemporary Basque history. Any kind of playfulness with the reader disappears, because the narration is linked to reality. In *Postmodernism, or, The Cultural Logic of Late Capitalism* (1991), Fredric Jameson critiques the lack, among other things, of historicity in postmodernism, that is, an awareness of and specific tendency toward overlooking the relationship between cause and effect that we find throughout history. In *Elkarrekin esnatzeko ordua*, Uribe does not in any way connect the events he narrates in a chain by means of a cause-and-effect relationship. Indeed, in this novel the author does not show any justification for any event. Yet he does in some way try to explore the reasons behind each event. There is no attempt to gloss over any injustice that occurs in the book, and truths hitherto buried away are revealed. And with them, so are questions that appear to be sharp reflections, or questions that demand profound reflections on the part of every reader so that they may respond individually.

Uribe's literature always makes readers think that there are other questions and that, in all likelihood, nobody can answer all of them. It is difficult to find agreement on one single truth and we take refuge in that if we know that there are more questions without answers. Sometimes all our efforts are not enough to understand what has happened, and perhaps others—those who were here before us—possess a truth that we are completely unaware of. Kirmen Uribe observes Basque society and, far from clinging onto an absolute truth, prefers not only doubt but also empathy for others.

The totality in the novel *Elkarrekin esnatzeko ordua* presents a Basque society which, during the twentieth century, came out of rough and twisting paths. Even more importantly, I believe, this legacy implies our greatest challenges at the social level. It is essential to know what happened previously in order to understand our present social situation, or at least to get closer to understanding.

In the novel itself, as Uribe notes in the words of the Bilbao painter Antonio de Gezala (Uribe 2016, 70), the most important thing for him is not to relate what happened but what he thought or felt as a result of what happened. More than the experiences of his characters, he recounts the reflections of the author himself. That way, Uribe develops a full reflection of Basque society by means of a story.

3 In search of a Basque perspective on the world

Lehendakari (President) Agirre and his assistant Manu de la Sota appear in Uribe's novel, mainly because de la Sota is a friend of the main character. Through him, Uribe idealizes a generation of Basque politicians or imagines portraying their idealism, specifically, in an idealist way of understanding politics. In all likelihood, both possibilities are present, a touch of idealism and a literary feat in order to portray his idealism.

Uribe presents Jose Antonio Agirre, Manu de la Sota, and other politicians of that time as qualified and ready and, what is more, full of determination and ambition to make a place in the world for "Euzkadi" or the Basque Country. In other words, these men did not just have the skills, they also believed that the Basque nation had a place in the global concert of nations. Therefore, they decided to intervene in the difficult historical moment that they were faced with, with the aim of achieving, for once, representation for Basques everywhere. As well as creating its own currency and passport, through the force of its own actions, the Basque Government assumed jurisdictions that were not in the statute of autonomy passed by the Spanish Republic, as if it were a federal territory that, of course in special wartime circumstances, had almost full decision-making authority.

Agirre and his fellow cabinet members decided to get involved, and they lost. They lost against the fascists led by Franco in the War of 1936 but, later, as a result of the Cold War and the Allies abandoning the chance to help the Basque cause, they also lost their own war. Jose Antonio Agirre and his fellow cabinet members embodied in many ways the myth of God's chosen people dreamed up by Sabino Arana in the late nineteenth century, their mission being, despite all suffering, to guide the People home. Or put more accurately, they updated the myth that Sabino Arana created and, from a liberal Christian perspective, they took as a model the United States—the first nation to be created in the world as a result of the French Revolution—and its foundational process.

The main character in the novel, Txomin Letamendi, is also a child of that era. A friend of musicians and artists and quite bohemian, and likewise Catholic but liberal, he too links Basque nationalism naturally to the struggle for freedom. And he begins to take part in politics, until his life is put in danger, first because of his loyalty to the leaders of the Basque Nationalist Party (EAJ-PNV, founded July 31, 1895), and second because of recognizing the sharp teeth of fascism, the enemy of freedom.

His sad and lonely death, far from all heroics, is also a political defeat for Agirre's government. It is in some way the mournful end of the Basque national story. Years will pass, some in resistance, most in resilience, while the Letamendi Urresti family remain almost always in exile, long years in which one of the main characters in the book, Karmele Urresti, has to bear all the burdens, until a new Basque national story is created.

Karmele's son, Txomin, gives Uribe another direction in which to tell the story. During the Cold War years, in the harsh repressive atmosphere of the Franco dictatorship, a group of young Basques makes a connection between the national liberation processes taking place in the world and the situation in and needs of the Basque Country. Those young people feel disillusioned with the previous generation—with Agirre, de la Sota, and the rest—because it had trusted the United States and the other sponsors of capitalism that eventually decided, in the face of the Communist threat, to make an alliance with Franco. Thus, from another ideological perspective, those young people linked the freedom of "Euskadi" or the Basque Country to social freedom, to the need for revolution. These young people of the 1960s converted what their parents viewed as the chosen people into a revolutionary subject, symbolizing them as working-class people.

Obviously, that national story is also out of date today, because it was a specific way of explaining the world and the Basque Country at that time. The world, and Basque society too, is not like it was then. Basque society has completely changed in the last forty years. To some extent, if one were to highlight the most significant contemporary feature, it would be the lack of any heroic story. The long cycle of violence recently came to an end, and the harsh situations resulting from that long period of violence and its consequences distorted our image, so that now when we look at our true image in the mirror—so normal, so ordinary—we often do not know ourselves.

Clearly, national stories that have prevailed in the Basque Country are out of date in the contemporary era. There is no national story that explains Basque society today, or any story that explains the world from the perspective of Basque society. Indeed, those who choose, because of inertia or intellectual lethargy, to keep holding onto an already outdated national story deny themselves the possibility of creating a new national story.

Lately, it seems that we are adrift as a society, sometimes with the overwhelming illusion of being stagnant—perhaps because we keep looking toward the past or maybe because we are a society that is looking for direction one step at a time. New questions, such as those one finds in Kirmen Uribe's work, require new answers. Uribe's narrative project transcends individual will, highlighting instead the national story in order to connect Basque identity—specifically, as a set of particular features which distinguish it from all the rest—to certain dominant tendencies at the global level. It is well known that any people—or group of people therein who are conscious of the fact—searches for its place in the world by means of a national story, necessarily also seeking out connections with global tendencies.

Connecting with some tendencies allows a nation to confront others. Creating a new national story is a way of finding our place in the world. It allows us to adopt a position before the world as a community, to choose to build bridges, to open doors despite those who seek to build new walls in the world. A concern about fascism was one of the driving forces behind writing the novel *Elkarrekin esnatzeko ordua*. Uribe looks back toward the past with the aim of explaining threats to the contemporary world, believing that some of the lessons which history has left could be useful in order to understand some of the faults in our world today. The dominance of authoritarianism in political power, the closing of doors to immigrants within the European and American fortresses, and the restriction of civil and political liberties are in themselves alarming, since they indicate that the evolution of our societies is truly worrying, seeing that these processes occur thanks to the votes of citizens in *democratic* elections.

In a 1995 lecture at Columbia University in the United States, the Italian writer and thinker Umberto Eco (1995, 12–15) used fourteen features by which to unmask new versions of fascism. These are, respectively, *the cult of tradition* (preferably a millenarian tradition, because if not, *new* traditions have to be invented); *the rejection of modernism* (the values associated with the Enlightenment); *the cult of action for action's sake* (without any need for reflection); *disagreement is treason*; *fear of difference*; *an appeal to social frustration* (on the part of the middle classes); *the obsession with a plot*; *the enemy is both strong and weak*; *pacifism is trafficking with the enemy*; *contempt for the weak*; *everybody is educated to become a hero*; *machismo and weaponry*; *selective populism* (constantly calling into question the bases of democracy); and *Ur-Fascism speaks Newspeak* (with an impoverished vocabulary made up of specific and direct language in order to represent a binary reality through an elementary syntax).

The problem is not, therefore, that certain grotesque characters offer a pseudo-political discourse that would seem to us ridiculous, but that those symptoms which Eco details are increasingly obvious among ample sections of the population in our societies. This is ultimately because the Far Right searches for votes in those sections of society among whom the system has caused deception. And because numerous social sectors that have abandoned the permanent acceleration of neoliberalism find in the populist Far Right a political alternative.

In that sense, coinciding with its era, the novel *Elkarrekin esnatzeko ordua* is a call to be attentive. Attentive because, at the heart of Basque society, certain tendencies are beginning to be noted. Attentive because fascism does not come from elsewhere (not from Germany, not from Italy); rather, fascism is a beast that is at our core. There is no escape from the revived beast through the chronic increase of social inequalities as a result of neoliberal policies. And if there is one escape, we must intervene (as does culture, and with it, literature too). As the Nigerian writer Chimamanda Ngozi Adichie recently explained, the gravity of the situation demands that we intervene. She was asked which political position she would adopt, and she replied that telling stories is her natural way of taking a political stance. In my opinion, Kirmen Uribe conveys a similar message with his third novel: It is an opportunity to create a narrative that intervenes against inequality, against xenophobia, against sexism, against false heroes, and against ultra-right populism.

Without forfeiting any of the style characterized by his passion for expressing the doubts and heterodox thoughts befitting of his narrative, in the novel *Elkarrekin esnatzeko ordua*, Uribe undertakes a work that had already abandoned postmodernism as a literary model. According to Uribe, so that Basque society might take its place in a new world that has not yet emerged, it should choose its place in this strange world as soon as possible and act with ambition and determination.

3 Another way for Basque society to look at itself

When we look in the mirror after the cycle of violence has come to an end, it seems that we do not recognize that ordinary reflection. When all heroes have disappeared, we are all transformed into normal everyday people, unfortunately . . . Or fortunately. And in that new logic, we also have to change the way we look at one another in order to be able to transform the way Basque society views itself.

Our concept of identity has on most occasions been linked to how we were in the past. Identity was apparently a way of holding on to how we were. In my opinion, however, there is nothing to hold on to when there are steps forward to be taken. Nowadays, we do not need to go back into the past to look for identity, but instead look to the present and future. Basque identity is not what we were, but rather what we are today and, above all, what we want to be in the future.

If there is any Basque identity (and there is), if it comes from some place (and it does), it comes from the Basque language. But it will not come from a Basque language that has been well preserved in an archaeological museum, even though there may be agreement that it is a treasure. A national community that wants to create its own narrative looking to the future must conceive of and use its language as a means of communication, and to do so it must make it simpler, easier, more flexible, and less pure, so that it is an effective means of communication in our cities. In his novels as well as his poems, Kirmen Uribe's literary use of language goes in that direction. In referring to the literary importance of the Basque oral tradition, and without any insecurities about the surrounding Romance languages, Uribe is not usually a big fan of creating syntactic knots in order to write what he needs to express, because it is enough for him to respect the simple meter of Basque expressions and the musicality of their melody. Likewise, one of the chief strong points of his writing is his talent for giving poetic use to the words in simple speech.

We note in Kirmen Uribe's novel a Basque society which would like progress based on wisdom and preparation. An open society, a society which should know how to welcome those who are coming and will come from elsewhere, and one which should learn how to care for one another, so that it is a true *community*. In that sense, Kirmen Uribe also examines our contemporary tragedy honestly in his novel *Elkarrekin esnatzeko ordua*. For some, that began in 1978; for others, ten years previously. For still others, however, our contemporary tragedy began on July 18, 1936.

Kirmen Uribe begins the story slightly later and, describing what happened through to 1978, seeks to reflect on why we are in this situation today. Of course, one cannot overlook ETA in that story. Uribe, boldly, does not ignore anything in the novel. He explains how ETA emerged through the words of the son, Txomin. Writing Karmele's experiences and despair, he conveys how very ample sections of Basque society felt deceived by the transition after Franco's death. The book explains clearly the traumatic choice between reforming the previous regime or a sudden democratic transformation, as well as the manner in which the culture in favor of democratic transformation was not just rooted in Basque society but also persisted through time.

In my opinion, it is impossible to understand all of that without ETA. The violent action-repression-action chain provoked by ETA as a response to Franco's repression meant that the reform associated with the regime was not allowed to become established calmly, because those sections of society in favor of democratic transformation joined in the cultural resistance. Yet, trapped in a spiral of violence, as time progressed ETA became one of the main reasons to extend the need for reform at the social level. Thus, because of ETA's violence, widespread social sectors abandoned the culture of resistance to a position in favor of reform or toward increasingly more numerous political spaces situated between extremes.

In his critique of the novel *Elkarrekin esnatzeko ordua*, the Spanish literary critic José Carlos Mainer (*El País*) mentioned the word "indulgence" as regards Basque nationalism. There is nothing of the sort in the novel. In fact, when Uribe narrates the story of how the pro-Franco librarian of Ondarroa was assassinated, the very armed struggle which at one time was legitimized widely by society is called into question. Kirmen Uribe and all the writers of his generation are very clear in that everyone's human rights are above all other goals and that one injustice does not justify another.

However, Uribe also conveys in this novel the idea that violence in the Basque Country did not begin with ETA, because Basques knew suffering and pain before the emergence of ETA. Obviously, ETA brought great suffering and pain and that is undeniable. And all the victims of the suffering and pain of ETA deserve our recognition and respect. Likewise, it is important to know their story, all of their stories, because, unfortunately, they are part of our very history. Nevertheless, ETA was not the only one to bring suffering and pain. Regrettably, the suffering and pain did not end even when ETA disappeared definitively. And all the suffering must end, once and for all. That is why those stories must also be told. Those who favor a disputed narrative seek to condemn Basque society to continue its quarrels. It is time for new narratives, ones that narrate new times. Basque society wants to build peace, moreover, through cooperation.

Those of us who have been on one side or the other have committed or tolerated injustices, since often our silence has been understood as acceptance. As Uribe writes in his novel, all of us have at one time or another remained as stony-faced before someone else's suffering as the statues in the Ondarroa church (2016, 318). We must never forget that, because it will always be a heavy burden on our consciences. And, while all of our mistaken steps have led us to where we are today in what one might consider a "late" or "clumsy" way, we also have a new opportunity to repair the broken bridges among all of us, building new, more beautiful bridges with the rubble saved from the all-too-long cycle of violence.

Kirmen Uribe and some other writers of his generation have already begun to build such bridges. Abandoning the dualism and Manicheanism that have predominated in politically disputed narratives, they are working on new narratives so that we may renew the humanity lost on the path of generations; they are searching for stories in our recent past with the aim of giving new answers to new questions. Without forgetting the importance of each individual, taking into consideration the reality which embraces all realities (like putting the pieces of an always unfinished jigsaw puzzle together), and undertaking each step more with empathy and doubt than with absolute certainty, new narratives in favor of peace in the Basque Country are emerging.

Bibliography

Aldekoa, Iñaki. 2008. Euskal literaturaren historia. Donostia: Erein.

Alberca, Manuel. 2007. *El pacto ambiguo. De la novela autobiográfica a la autoficción*. Madrid: Biblioteca Nueva.

Casas, Ana. 2012. *La autoficción. Reflexiones teóricas*. Madrid: Arco/Libros.

Colonna, Vincent. 2004. *Autofiction & autres mythomanies littéraires*. Auch: Tristram.

Eco, Umberto. 1995. Ur-Fascism. *The New York Review*, vol. XLII, nº 11.

Foster, Hal (ed.).1985. *La posmodernidad*. Barcelona: Kairós.

Gasparini, Philippe. 2004. *Est-il je? Roman autobiographique et autofiction*. Paris: Seuil.

Gruppi, Luciano. 1978. *El concepto de hegemonía en Gramsci*. Mexico: Ediciones de Cultura Popular.

Jameson, Fredric. 1991. *Postmodernism, or, The Cultural Logic of Late Capitalism*. Durham: Duke University Press.

Kortazar, Jon. 2007. *Postmodernitatea euskal kontagintzan*. Donostia: Utriusque Vasconiae.

Kortazar, Jon. 2011. *Bitartean New York: Kirmen Uriberen literaturgintza*. Donostia: Utriusque Vasconiae.

Uribe, Kirmen. 2008. *Bilbao-New York-Bilbao*. Donostia: Elkar.

Uribe, Kirmen. 2012. *Mussche*. Zarautz: Susa.

Uribe, Kirmen. 2016. *Elkarrekin esnatzeko ordua*. Zarautz: Susa.

Vattimo, Gianni & Rovatti, Pier Aldo (ed.). 2006. *El pensamiento débil*. Madrid: Cátedra.

Wallace, David Foster. 2001. *Algo supuestamente divertido que nunca volveré a hacer*. Barcelona: Mondadori.

Žižek, Slavoj. 2008. *En defensa de la intolerancia*. Madrid: Sequitur.

4

Lehendakari Agirre and the Basque Government's cultural strategy (1936–1939) in *Elkarrekin esnatzeko ordua*[18]

Leyre Arrieta

Most of my historical research work has to do with the time of Basque exile; specifically, I have worked on subject matter concerning Basque nationalism and the Basque Government. Therefore, the historical era I am most familiar with, as regards Kirmen Uribe's literature, is the background to the development of Karmele and Txomin's story. As well as these "professional" and "academic" reasons, my motivation to contribute to this collection is, above all, personal and emotional. *Elkarrekin esnatzeko ordua* (The Hour of Waking Together, 2016) was a present from Kirmen himself, with a lovely dedication and another small gift. Kirmen and I are children of the same place, children of the same era. We both attended Ondarroa High School in the 1980s, a time in which classes were interspersed with demonstrations, strikes, and bomb warnings—one of those times which marks one's personality. However difficult it was, it was also one of the best times of my life.

Something else also connects me to this work of Kirmen's: his world is my world. When they read any work, any novel, readers picture the landscape created by the author, they imagine

18 This chapter forms part of a research project subsidised by the Secretariat of State for Research, Development and Innovation (reference HAR2015-64920-P, MINECO/FEDER) as well as the research carried out by the Communication Research Group at the University of Deusto, recognized officially and subsidized by the Basque Government.

it. For me, however, it is a case of seeing the world reflected by Kirmen—because it is my world. Places mentioned in *Elkarrekin esnatzeko ordua*, like Arrigorri, Francisco's shipyard, the images in the medieval church ("Kortxel's ghosts" for us), Saturraran, the walking paths of Lekeitio and Mutriku (my town), etc., are the landscapes of my youth, my adolescence, my life. For all those reasons, I said yes to the invitation to write about the cultural strategy of the Agirre Government. And that is what I will do in the pages that follow.

1 The initial months: Leizaola's department's initiatives

Agirre was appointed lehendakari (president) on October 7, 1936, in Gernika, in a ceremony replete with symbolism. The Basque Government was created immediately thereafter, a coalition government formed by the EAJ-PNV (Eusko Alderdi Jeltzalea-Partido Nacionalista Vasco, Basque Nationalist Party) and the parties of the Popular Front.[19] The government agenda clearly demonstrated its moderate Basque nationalist nature and intention to apply a progressive social program.[20]

The activity carried out by the government in Bilbao during those nine months was remarkable, bearing in mind that this was during a war. How was such work possible? On the one hand, because the government, due to the fact that the Basque

19 At that time, even at the international level, the composition of this government was striking, because it was the first time in history that a government presided over by a practicing Catholic included a communist within its cabinet. See Santiago de Pablo, *La patria soñada. Historia del nacionalismo vasco desde sus orígenes hasta la actualidad* (Madrid: Biblioteca Nueva, 2015), 228.

20 During the years of the Second Republic, Basque nationalists developed a Christian social dimension. Thus, the more moderate leaders gradually embraced an ideology that would later be termed Christian Democracy. Among them were José Antonio Agirre and, from Vitoria-Gasteiz, Francisco Javier Landaburu. Both were members of the Madrid Congress during the Republic and presented several proposals with a social dimension. The most thorough biography of Lehendakari Agirre is Ludger Mees et al., *La política como pasión. El Lehendakari José Antonio Aguirre (1904-1960)* (Madrid: Tecnos, 2014). On Agirre, see, moreover, Ludger Mees, *El profeta pragmático. Aguirre, el primer lehendakari (1939-1960)* (Irun: Alberdania, 2006). I explain the manner in which Basque nationalists understood and embraced Christian Democratic approaches in Leyre Arrieta, "Estudio introductorio," in *La causa del pueblo de F. J. Landaburu* (Leioa: EHU/UPV), especially 55–72.

territory was half isolated, took on jurisdictions that would have been impossible in another situation. For example, coins were minted, passports issued, the Ertzaintza (Basque police force) was created, along with a university, and so on. On the other hand, at the beginning, the government members did not think that the war would last so long and they wanted to give a sense of "normality" to their activity. Thus, in a very short space of time the Basque Government established its departmental groups and agendas.[21]

One of the most efficient departments was the Culture and Justice Department, headed by Jesús María Leizaola. The Autonomy Statute granted the Basque Government jurisdiction in the fields of education and culture, and it established a co-official status for Spanish and Basque. Leizaola made the most of the opportunities offered by the law and carried out important measures and initiatives in the fields of education, the Basque language, and culture. In education, priority was given to Primary Education. EAJ members wanted to create a network of confessional state schools rooted in the territory, and they established the so-called Euskadiko Eskolak (Basque Country Schools). The goal of those schools was to cultivate Basque language and identity. As well as the use of Basque, another pedagogical novelty was also introduced into those schools: physical education. Why? Because physical education was understood as something in favor of Basque culture, linked to traditional dance, Basque music, and the Basque language. I mention this because it is related directly to the nature of *Eresoinka*, as we will see later.

---

21 On the work undertaken by each Basque Government department during those nine months, see Leyre Arrieta, Eider Landaberea et al., *El primer Gobierno Vasco en Bilbao (1936-1937). En pie sobre la tierra vasca* (Bilbao: Bilbao 700, 2016). To describe that state of exception, some historians have used the expression "Basque oasis." However, that unusual situation was relative, because there was repression in the Basque Country, even though it went against the wishes of the EAJ and the Basque Government. Nevertheless, although there were excesses, the Government's aim was to avoid reprisals and offer humane treatment of prisoners. See Santiago de Pablo, *La patria soñada* (op. cit.), 226–245. See also José Luis de la Granja, *El oasis vasco. El nacimiento de Euskadi en la República y la Guerra Civil* (Madrid: Tecnos, 2007).

Without any doubt, one of the greatest achievements of the Department of Culture was the university. In the space of two months, during the initial months of 1937, the first faculty, the Faculty of Medicine, was up and running. Yet by the end of March, the Bizkaia offensive had begun and most students and some teachers had been forced to flee to the border. The war made all university activity impossible.[22]

Another preoccupation for the department was protecting the Basque historical, artistic, and cultural heritage—which was at risk because of the war. Responsibility for this cultural heritage was in the hands of the Office for Fine Arts, Archives and Libraries. The painter José María Uzelai—who would later be on the executive board of Eresoinka[23]—was its director. This office organized Basque participation at the Paris International Exposition from May to November 1937. The Basque presence at this exposition was most likely the Basque Government's most prominent external cultural act, at least during those months in 1937.

2 The delegation network

By the time the exposition finished, in November 1937, the Basque Government had already been in exile for some months. Following the fall of the whole Basque Country to the forces of Franco, a new era began with the initial period of Basque Government exile, first in Santander and later, from October onward, in Barcelona. Government members, political leaders, and refugees were increasingly dispersed and it was essential to create a relationship network among Basques spread all over the world. Likewise, it was vital to appeal to political and social sectors in Europe and the Americas in search of their involvement and help and, in general, to create currents in favor of the Republic and the Basque "cause."

22 In order to better comprehend the aims and work of the department headed by Leizaola, see Miren Barandiaran, "Jesús María Leizola Sánchez. Universidad en tiempo de guerra," in Leyre Arrieta, Eider Landaberea et al., *El primer Gobierno Vasco*, 167–213.

23 Dancing group.

In order to achieve those goals, and making the most of the state of exception, the Basque Government used jurisdictions that were not recognized by the Statute of Autonomy, specifically those pertaining to foreign relations. And, using those, delegations were established in several cities throughout Europe and the Americas. The delegations did not represent political parties but were the first delegations of an institutional nature. Obviously, as those delegations were not embassies of an independent state, they did not receive the typical diplomatic treatment, but they did achieve political recognition, without a doubt.

Among the most important delegations were those of Paris and New York, both of which have something to do with *Elkarrekin esnatzeko ordua*. The Paris delegation was opened in November 1936. Rafael Pikabea, who had been a member of Congress in Madrid, was appointed chief delegate. This delegation worked very closely to establish close relations with the French Government and French politicians and intellectuals, in search of help in favor of Basques and the Republic. This delegation also coordinated aid given to refugees and exiles. In the summer of 1937, when Lehendakari Agirre went into exile in France, the seat of the Basque Government was established in Paris, in a beautiful building on the city's Avenue Marceau. Following the Second World War, too, when the lehendakari returned to Europe, the government seat was in Paris.[24]

During the war years, however, Agirre and his colleagues were in New York, as explained in the novel. The delegation in that city was created in August 1938. Its goal was to carry out propaganda work and forge relationships with American leaders, European intellectuals exiled in the United States, and Basques who lived there. What was at the beginning a provisional delegation became permanent because of the risk of the Second World War breaking out. Anton Irala, Ramón de la Sota, Juan

24 The story itself of this mini palace is befitting of the history of Basque exile as a metaphor. Elsewhere, I have examined the symbolic value and history of the building. Leyre Arrieta, "El simbolismo poliédrico del nº 11 de la Avenue Marceau de París" in *La celebración de la nación* (Granada: Comares, 2012), 117–134.

Aranburu, Eustasio Arritola, José Urreti, and the novel's third main character, Manu de la Sota, made up the working group of the delegation.

All the delegations had two main goals: one, to help the exiles; and two, to carry out political and cultural propaganda. The main topic of this chapter, as I will now explain, is the latter.

3 The cultural strategy (1937–1939)

In effect, when we speak about the Basque Government's cultural strategy at that time, we cannot think of it as a strategy to promote culture. We must bear very much in mind the context. At that precise moment, the Basque Government's main goal was not to promote Basque music, dance, or art—not, at least, as it had been before or would be in the future. No. At that time, culture was a means that the Basque Government wanted to use to make propaganda. The chief aim was achieving help to win the war. The propaganda war was a very important struggle because, to a great extent, the future of the Republic was subject to foreign aid. And the lehendakari knew that the Basque Government could reach moderate foreign democracies more easily than the Republican Government.[25] Agirre was clear about that, because he had very close contacts in Europe. For the Republic, it was essential to gain international help; and then, when it was obvious that this was impossible, they sought to at least achieve mediation between the two sides.

Meanwhile, we should bear in mind that, although it was a diverse government, the main departments in the Basque Government were controlled by the EAJ. This party was Catholic and wanted to explain to the world the reasons for giving aid to the Republican side in the Civil War. The Basque Government wanted to show France, the United Kingdom, and the United States that the EAJ was still a Catholic party, and that the Spanish

25 As a note from the lehendakari's office stated in late 1937, "the Basque Government could reach much further than that of the Republic, to 'temperate democracy and the field inspired by Christian principles' " (Ludger Mees et al., *La política como pasión*, 2014), 377.

Republic was not a revolutionary regime. For that reason, a Catholic party like the EAJ had a place there.

Moreover, the Basque Government sought to demonstrate before international public opinion that the Basque Country was different, that its culture was distinct and nice, that it was a peaceful nation, that it was a nation that loved culture. Thus, through that cultural propaganda, it sought to dispute the negative image of Basques portrayed by Franco's propaganda. The chief means used in the Basque Government strategy were: the press (especially the journal *Euzko-Deya*); publishing books and short stories; film; sporting teams; the International League of Friends of the Basques (Ligue Internationale des Amis des Basques, LIAB); and tours by artistic groups. Agirre was involved personally in all of these.

Agirre's team was very clear that film was valid as great propaganda, especially to explain the history of Basque nationalism and the social perspective.[26] While the Basque Government was based in Bilbao, it produced two documentaries of a religious nature: *Entierro del benemérito sacerdote vasco José María de Korta y Uríbarren, muerto en el frente de Asturias* (Burial of the honorable Basque priest José María de Korta y Uríbarren, who died on the Asturias front; 1937) and *Semana Santa en Bilbao* (Holy Week in Bilbao; 1937). In both films the compatibility of the Catholic faith with the defense of the Republic is emphasized.

Following the fall of Bilbao, the Basque Government continued to use film with propaganda aims in mind. Film propaganda was produced from the Paris headquarters. Nemesio Sobrevilla directed three films: *Guernika* (1937), *Elai-Alai* (1938) and *Euzko-Deya* (1938). All three have a similar structure. All of them offer an idealized picture of the Basque Country: A rural, peaceful, Catholic, and democratic image. An image of a people that have seen their way of life interrupted all of a sudden by war. They were films aimed at audiences in the

26 The information in this section is taken from Santiago de Pablo, *The Basque Nation On-Screen: Cinema, Nationalism, and Political Violence* (Reno: Center for Basque Studies, University of Nevada, Reno, 2012), especially 51–58.

Western democracies, always with the same demand: do not abandon the Republic at that moment when Nazi Germany and Fascist Italy are aiding Franco.

The title of one of those three films was *Elai-Alai*. Elai-Alai was a children's artistic group, founded in Gernika, without any name, in 1927. Its director was the musician and choreographer Segundo Olaeta. It took its name in 1931. Following the bombing of Gernika in April 1937, the group broke up, but in June 1937, following a request by Olaeta on Radio Bilbao, most members met up at the La Citadelle children's camp in Donibane Garazi (Saint-Jean-Pied-de-Port).

Olaeta added dances from Zuberoa (Soule) to their repertoire. In the spring of 1937, the Elai-Alai members settled in Donibane Garazi. They gave their first performance on the Feast Day of Saint Ignatius in 1937. In the spring of 1938, they danced and sang in Paris in front of the Archbishop of Paris. That image (that of Archbishop Verdier with the children of Elai-Alai) was worth more than a million words from a propaganda perspective.

The pinnacle of Elai-Alai's activity came in May 1938 when they appeared at the Trocadéro Concert Hall. However, they performed mostly outside in the streets. In August 1939, as war was fast approaching, their worried parents began asking for their children to return, and Elai-Alai broke up at that time. There remains one record from that era released by Lumen in 1940.[27]

Within the cultural strategy, another initiative also had a major impact: the Basque national soccer team. From the early twentieth century onward, Basque nationalism encouraged sports as a means of developing national identity, especially among young people. In October 1936, because of the war, the Spanish Football Federation decided to suspend the league. Basque leaders then thought that they could use the pool of Basque soccer players for political purposes. It was Manu de la Sota's

27 For more on Elai-Alai, see José Antonio Arana Martija, *Elai-Alai, Euskal Herriko lehenengoko koreografi taldea* (Bilbao: Elexpuru, D.L., 1977).

idea. At the time, another charity campaign was underway by the name of Pro Avión Euzkadi. Pilota (Basque handball) games were organized in the Euskalduna fronton (handball court) and Manu de la Sota thought that something similar could be done with soccer.

During the initial months of 1937, some Basque soccer players got together to play three games. The goal was to raise money to buy a plane. They played the first game in the San Mamés stadium. It was attended by Lehendakari Agirre as well as the department heads Aldasoro, Aznar, Gracia, Leizaola, and Monzon.[28] After two more games were played, Manu de la Sota came up with the idea of creating a national team. Lehendakari Agirre was enthusiastic about the idea, all the more for being an ex-player for Athletic Bilbao.[29]

The goal was to carry out propaganda at the international level: to introduce the Basque Country, to spread information about the situation Basques were experiencing, and, at the same time, to raise funds for the refugees. When FIFA (the Federation Internationale de Football Association) recognized the new Spanish Football Federation which had been reorganized by the Francoists, the Euzkadi (Basque Country) team was in exile in Mexico, and was invited to take part in the league there during the 1938–1939 season.[30]

The team took as its badge the coat of arms of the autonomous region and as its symbol the "E" that was used in the journal *Euzkadi*. The design for its uniform was based

28 As Fernando Estomba states, 19,000 spectators attended and 8,000 *duros* (five-peseta coins) were collected. Fernando Estomba, *Competir en años convulsos. Deporte, política y sociedad en Bizkaia durante la II República y la guerra civil* (Bilbao: Artgerust, 2016), 207.

29 In truth, a Basque national team played its first games during the 1915–1916 season, but without any kind of political aim, because these were encounters between regional federations. Later, as Basque nationalism grew, a closer relationship between the new ideology and soccer developed. Thus, in 1922, a Basque team played in South America. And in 1930 and 1931, teams that were de at the time called "Vasconia" played against a Catalan national team. In the 1934–1935 season the Basque Soccer Cup was established, in which the four best teams in the territory competed. Fernando Estomba, *Competir en años convulsos*, 193.

30 For more information on the Basque soccer team, see the aforementioned Estomba, *Competir en años convulsos*.

on the colors of the *ikurrina* (Basque flag), newly designated the official Basque standard: green shirts, white shorts, and red socks, a uniform full of symbolism. The team name was Euzkadi, the neologism created by Sabino Arana.[31]

Agirre appointed Manu de la Sota as the government representative on the soccer team. Jean-Raymond Larrouyet helped the team in Paris. This lawyer and former soccer player from Zuberoa organized matches in Paris. From May 1937 onward, the team played in several European countries: Czechoslovakia, Poland, Russia, Finland, Norway, and Denmark. On its return from the tour, it paid tribute to Manu de la Sota in Paris. This is mentioned on page 41 (page 52 in the Spanish edition) of Uribe's novel: de la Sota and Txomin meet at the Chistera restaurant and speak about a book on caviar brought from Russia. Later, the soccer team went to the Americas, but now without de la Sota because he was involved in other matters, namely in Eresoinka—that so-called "Basque embassy," that initiative in which the lives of Karmele Urresti and Txomin Letamendi crossed paths.

4 Eresoinka[32]

Gabriel Olaizola, the former conductor of the Eusko Abesbatza,[33] suggested to Lehendakari Agirre the idea of creating a choir, formed by Basque exiles in France. Agirre happily accepted the proposal. Following the success of the Basque soccer team's tour of Europe, the lehendakari thought that the cultural propaganda could be completed with a choir, making use of the strong singing tradition in the Basque Country. One should not forget

31 For more information on the history and symbolism of the *ikurrina* and the word "Euzkadi," see Jesús Casquete and Ludger Mees, "Ikurriña" and Ludger Mees, "Euskadi/Euskal Herria," in Santiago de Pablo et al., *Diccionario ilustrado de símbolos del nacionalismo vasco* (Madrid: Tecnos), 508–531 and 294–319.

32 Information on Eresoinka in this section is taken from the following books: José Antonio Arana Martija, *Eresoinka: embajada cultural vasca 1937-1939* (Vitoria-Gasteiz: Gobierno Vasco, 1986) and Xabier Sáenz de Gorbea, *Aranoa eta Guezalaren Gernikak: Eresoinka Kasua* (Gernika: Euskal Herria Museoa, 2014).

33 Basque choir.

that he was also a musician and had played the flügelhorn in the Urduña (Orduña) Jesuit school band. And moreover, the project was viable because the necessary infrastructure already existed in Paris: on the one hand, the aforementioned important artistic infrastructure sent there for the Paris Exposition and, on the other hand, the Basque artists who lived in Paris too.

A few years later, Lehendakari Agirre recalled the task he had delegated to Olaizola in the book *De Guernika a Nueva York pasando por Berlin* (*Escape via Berlin* 1945 103):

> It is possible that we will remain here," I told him, "without being able to leave. But that is no reason to end the fight. I order you to leave immediately for France and to form among our refugees the best choir possible, which will carry to all the world, through our melodies, the memory of a people who die for liberty, because there are many who do not know yet that we are fighting for them. If we fall, you will remember us and continue singing.

That was the message sent to Olaizola, an order to create an exceptional choir. Among the documents the Basque Government sent to Olaizola, there was a letter signed and dated August 22, 1937 in Santander, from the lehendakari to Rafael Pikabea and Felix Urkiola, the Basque Government delegate in Paris and the editor of *Euzko-Deya*, respectively. Therein, he told them to help Olaizola: "[Olaizola] is officially heading the important artistic mission to create a Basque National Choir, based on select voices and a group so perfect that it is first-class material for theatres, the main ones in Europe and the Americas (. . .) in theatres of the highest order or renowned concert halls anywhere" (Arana Martija, 60). Agirre told them to spare no expense and to help Olaizola through their contacts in Paris.

In order to get the project up and running, the lehendakari called on a friend, an educated man, with excellent cultural training and who loved culture: Who was it? Specifically, Manu de la Sota (1897–1979). The son of an important ship-owning family, he studied law at university in both Salamanca and Cambridge. A fervent Basque nationalist, he was an avid reader of literature, wrote poetry, staged plays, wrote for the journal *Hermes*, was a member of Euskaltzaindia (the Basque Language Academy), the president of Athletic Bilbao, the first editor of the mountaineering journal *Pyrenaica*, and the representative of the Basque national soccer team. Consequently, it is understandable that the lehendakari chose him to set up the project. The goal was to project the Basque Country in the world by means of culture, establishing a "cultural embassy," and who better to do that task than de la Sota?

In fact, the idea for the Eresoinka project came from de la Sota, that is, the concept of opening it up to other fields as well (in addition to the choir)—specifically dance and the scenic arts. In August 1937, de la Sota finished his tasks as the sports representative and he traveled to Sara (Sare) from Paris in order to fulfill the mission on the orders of the lehendakari. In order to achieve his objective, de la Sota chose the most talented artists: musicians, experts in dance and choreography, painters, and playwrights. The executive committee members were: the president Manu de la Sota and the committee members Gabriel Olaizola, representing the choir; Jesús Luisa, representing the dance group; Enrique Jordá, in charge of putting the music together; Antonio Gezala, in charge of the scenography and decoration; and José María Uzelai, as a Fine Arts curator. The historian Xabier Sáenz de Gorbea, however, does not mention Uzelai, although he does note José Etxabe, the choir instructor, and Aurora Abasolo, the singing teacher (Arana 65, Sáenz de Gorbea, 14–15).

It remains unclear who thought up the name "Eresoinka." Some group members said that José Etxabe invented it. Others, however, said it was Manu de la Sota's idea. Whoever came up with the idea, it seems that its meaning is "sung dance" or "group that sings and dances."

If not the name, we do know who created the symbol: the painter Antonio Gezala. Gezala designed an oak leaf with two acorns as the mark of Eresoinka, with everything located in a concave-sided hexagon-like shape. Kirmen Uribe presents this artist in his novel. Gezala was de la Sota's friend. He was one of the most innovative and singular painters of the early twentieth century. He painted *Noche de artistas en Ibaigane (Night of Artists in Ibaigane)*, which Uribe uses to begin his story. Therefore, it is not surprising that he was chosen to make up the main group in Eresoinka. He also created Eresoinka's promotional poster and scenography. Some of his works reflect the everyday nature of Eresoinka (recall that *Elkarrekin esnatzeko ordua* cites the paintings *Eresoinka 8.45* and *Eresoinka 20.45*, which reflect two everyday moments of the group).

Another important figure in that early era of Eresoinka was the Filipino-American Manuel Inchausti. Inchausti was very wealthy, and he placed his money at the service of the Basque Government. Thanks to his financial support, the government managed, for example, to acquire a Paris headquarters on one of the main avenues. Likewise, thanks to Inchausti, Agirre went to New York. And it was the former who secured a teaching position for the latter at Columbia University. Furthermore, the children's camp at Jatsu (Jaxu) was established with his money.

Now that we have introduced some group members, let us return once more to Sara. As soon as he arrived there, Olaizola began bringing together people from different artistic and folkloric groups in Donostia-San Sebastián. One of them was part of the initial group: that is, our main character, Karmele Urresti from Ondarroa. José Etxabe, one of the technical directors of the choir, recruited Karmele while she was working as a nurse at the La Rosarie hospital. Karmele began as a dancer and later joined the choir as a contralto.

Among the women in the choir were, among others, Julene Urzelai and Haydée Agirre, who had both been members of Emakume Abertzale Batza (Basque Nationalist Women's Council) and public speakers during the Second Republic. Among those members who arrived later to the choir were José Luis Arriola and Paulin Urresti; the latter was Karmele's cousin.

They arrived in November 1937. A few days before Ondarroa fell to Franco's troops, on October 4, Arriola, Paulin Urresti, and Antonio Ortiz fled the town for Donibane Lohizune (Saint-Jean-de-Luz) on the steamboat *Jontxu*, which was owned by Francisco Urresti, or "Malaletxe," Karmele's father. Uribe also mentions that steamboat in his novel. The choir members were lodged in the Eskualduna and La Poste hotels in Sara as well as in private homes, but they met at the Eskualduna to eat and rehearse. The dancers and txistulariak (Basque pipe and tabor players) lived separately and rehearsed in the fronton, under Jesús Luisa's direction.

While they prepared everything in Sara, in Paris some executive committee members (de la Sota himself, Uzelai, Jordá, and Gezala) prepared the stage decorations, costumes, choreography, and music. At the same time, with the help of the delegation, there was a major effort to book shows. They did not forget the lehendakari's wish: Eresoinka had to become a "cultural embassy" in Paris; shows had to take place in major concert halls; and the Basque cultural message had to be clear, forceful, and impressive, the goal of propaganda within a wider ultimate strategy. *Euzko-Deya* was used to promote the shows, and small advertisements appeared in some French newspapers: *Paris Soir*, *Paris Midi*, *Le Matin*, *Le Journal*, *La Lumiere*, *Ce Soir*, *L'Art Musical*, *Le Petite Gironde* and *L'Ouvre*. Karmele and Txomin appear in some publicity photos.

The group members left Sara for Paris on November 19. In the capital they lodged in hotels in Montmartre and rehearsed in a parish church in the days prior to the show. The show took place in the Pleyel, the biggest concert hall in Paris, on December 19, 1937. The lehendakari of the Basque Government and its department heads were there, as well as the Republican government minister Manuel Irujo. Karmele danced and sang. Txomin played the trumpet in the orchestra. There were 63 singers in the first official photo of Eresoinka taken at that Paris show. Later, according to the sources, they ended up having 110 members. Around 30 had also been members of the Eusko Abesbatza and the Donostiako Orfeoia choirs.

It was a great success and one that attracted impresarios from the world of entertainment. One of those, the Parisian Arnold Meckel, became Eresoinka's agent. He organized a tour of Belgium and the Netherlands which lasted nearly two months. In Belgium, they performed in Brussels, Ghent, and Antwerp; and in the Netherlands, in Amsterdam, The Hague, Utrecht, and Haarlem. In the latter two venues the audience was fewer in number. Apparently, not enough publicity was carried out and the resident orchestras were not very good (as the Eresoinka members explained).

The choir's repertoire was a blend of religious music and Basque songs, as Uribe states in his novel: "tradition and modernity together" (page 21 in the Basque edition). As well as singing, following de la Sota's idea, in each show they danced and performed short theatrical pieces in the form of song and dance. By means of those short theatrical pieces or stage productions, they depicted extracts of Basque life for a foreign audience. In the written statements of de la Sota, they gave a mythologized view of the Basque Country.

On April 17, 1938, the first Aberri Eguna (Basque national day) in exile was celebrated. That day, Eresoinka put on two shows at the Théâtre de Paris. In the evening show, Txomin Letamendi conducted the orchestra. By that time, as we know thanks to *Elkarrekin esnatzeko ordua*, Letamendi was already performing in Francisco Canaro's orchestra. And as a matter of fact, Txomin introduced a young Eresoinka singer into the world of Paris musical shows. The name of the singer was Mariano Eusebio González García. Later he became very famous under the artistic name Luis Mariano. Another choir member who became well known later was Pepita Enbil, the mother of the famous tenor Plácido Domingo. From that Aberri Eguna day onward, Txomin performed with Eresoinka not just as a trumpeter but also as an *irrintzilari* (a performer of the Basque deep-throated yell, originally a war cry).

From June 1938 onward, Eresoinka performed in London. But once that tour finished, the manager Meckel left the group, in all likelihood because by that time there was little future in it as a business. Indeed, as Agirre acknowledged in a letter, there were financial issues making it difficult for the group to continue.

Nevertheless, Eresoinka lasted one more year. There still remained its last phase: that of the Château de Belloy. While Eresoinka was in London, the group's administrator, Karla Billalabeitia, remained in Paris in order to look for a residence for the group. On its return from London, a beautiful house surrounded by gardens was ready for Eresoinka, a mansion bequeathed by a wealthy Basque—a mansion that was the privileged witness to the love between Karmele and Txomin, the Château de Belloy.

That was surely one of the best times in the lives of Karmele and Txomin. Yet the problems were beginning for Eresoinka. The economic state of the Basque Government was increasingly precarious. It was impossible to organize another Eresoinka tour and it wanted to assure the continuation of the group, but without financing its publicity. From that time on, stage design would be sacrificed because it was too expensive. The txistulariak, singers, and dancers continued rehearsing at the Belloy, but without performing for people, they were downcast.

One event freed them from that tedium. In October 1938, Agirre wanted to show Eresoinka to Lluís Companys, the president of the Catalan Generalitat (government). They sang "Els Segadors" (the Catalan national anthem) for Companys. That moving event is also recorded in *Elkarrekin esnatzeko ordua*. However, with the exception of that visit, that autumn was boring and tedious. The executive committee was weakened: Uzelai left; by that time, de la Sota was involved in diplomatic matters that would take him to New York; Jordá continued in the group but also worked for the Paris Symphony Orchestra; Gezala was working on his bookplates and seals; and Jesús Luisa also had other responsibilities. Olaizola continued to be very involved, but he was not very skilled at promotion.

At that moment, however, at the close of 1938, the International League of Friends of the Basques (LIAB) was created. It was founded with a humanitarian goal in mind, to make known the situation of the Basques. It was made up of very well-known figures, including the philosopher Jacques Maritain and the novelist François Mauriac as well as the aforementioned Archbishop Verdier. This association had direct influence in the French administration for a few years.[34] The LIAB promoted Eresoinka. Its members used their influence and Eresoinka once more performed in the Pleyel concert hall, with great success as before.

One of Eresoinka's last appearances was at the 1939 Aberri Eguna. That was also celebrated at the Château de Belloy. The notes of "Agur Jaunak,"[35] performed by Txomin Letamendi on the trumpet, welcomed Lehendakari Agirre. As Uribe says in the novel, after lunch Txomin's solo was preserved for posterity by Josean Elosegi in a photo.

That spring, Eresoinka took part in some propaganda activities organized by the LIAB. The last of these took place at the Palais de Chaillot Theatre on May 26. That performance was its swan song. At the time they did not know it, but it was the last time the whole group would perform together. Thereafter, they met up again at Belloy.

That July, Txomin and Karmele were in Larresoro (Larressore), Lapurdi (Labourd). Ikerne was born there, on July 13. By the end of the month, they returned to Belloy and, as we know, that is where Joseba, Karmele's brother, married them, on the Feast Day of Saint Ignatius, Karmele's birthday.

Then, at the end of July or the beginning of August—according to different accounts—Perico Garate, the Basque Government representative in Eresoinka, went to Belloy with bad news: the group would be disbanded officially. The situation was by then unsustainable. Once more, we find an explanation for

34 Jean-Claude Larronde, *Exilio y solidaridad. La Liga Internacional de Amigos de los Vascos* (Bidasoa: Bilbao, 1998).
35 Basque traditional song.

this in the historical context. On the one hand, by order of the new president of the French Republic, Albert Lebrun, all exiles in France had to sign up for conscription into the French army. War was approaching and the army needed to be reinforced. On the other hand, the European powers had recognized Franco's government, and the dictator decreed that all exiles with no political responsibilities should be returned to Spain. He gave a deadline: between August 15 and September 15. It was a very difficult decision for the men of Eresoinka to make. The only way out was to flee to the Americas. And that is what many did.

By the beginning of September 1939, when the Second World War had already broken out, there was almost nobody left at the Château de Belloy. On September 10, *Euzko-Deya* offered an emotional farewell to that beautiful mansion that had been home to Eresoinka for a year, to what had been a nest in which Karmele and Txomin had spent their most lovely and hopeful months. For the moment at least, they returned to Larresoro on September 15. A few months later, though, they did decide to cross the Atlantic. On May 12, 1940, Karmele, Txomin, and Ikerne arrived in Caracas.

We will end the story of Eresoinka as we started it, with Gabriel Olaizola. Olaizola stayed in Baiona (Bayonne). While he was there, he received a letter from Lehendakari Agirre dated December 4, 1939. In that letter full of emotion, Agirre congratulated him on the work he had done and, in the name of the Basque Country, gave him thanks. He asked him to extend the thanks to all of the Eresoinka members.

As always, so now, too, Agirre sought to bring Eresoinka's journey to an end with a positive message. This is what the letter said:

> 'Eresoinka' has fulfilled its mission to awaken among different people, and above all specific figures, a noble affective emotion toward the Cause of our people, an emotion which would have been difficult to achieve by

> other propaganda procedures. The exquisite art of our music and the perfection achieved by the choir as a whole, above all, alongside the magnificent dances of 'Eresoinka', have been an instrument of peaceful diffusion into the souls of those who did not know us, or those others who were unaware of us and they were many (. . .) Eresoinka has existed, has sung in the main squares of Europe and has carried out work that our patriotic dreams had entrusted to it. (Arana 1986, 251)

And that is how it was. Eresoinka was a key piece of a strategy prepared by the Basque Government to make the Basque Country known throughout the world. Making use of culture, forming a "cultural embassy," the goal was to project the Basque Country abroad. Agirre and his groups sought to present a whole people to the world; they wanted to show that they were different, and they used culture to do so. And they managed to do so. Even though, looking at the historical perspective, we know full well that the main objective was not achieved because the Western democracies soon recognized the Franco regime, which lasted forty long years, in my opinion Eresoinka's journey was successful, looked at from many angles. First, because it was useful as a means of sparking hope among Basques in difficult times; second, because it was valid to spread the word about the Basque Country and Basque culture and because the contacts made at that time were truly valuable later; and third—if you will allow me to abandon the role of historian and once more, as at the beginning, turn to sentiment—because the lives of Karmele and Txomin crossed paths and, on account of that, because Kirmen Uribe wrote this beautiful novel.

Bibliography

Aguirre y Lecube, José Antonio. 1945. *Escape via Berlin*. New York: The Macmillan Company. (Original publication in 1943).

Arana Martija, José Antonio. 1977. *Elai-Alai, Euskal Herriko lehenengoko koreografi taldea*. Bilbao: Elexpuru, D.L.

Arana Martija, José Antonio. 1986. *Eresoinka: embajada cultural vasca 1937-1939*.Vitoria-Gasteiz: Main Publication Service. Basque Government.

Arrieta, Leyre. 2011. *Fondo Gobierno de Euzkadi (1936-1979). Historia y Contenido*. Vitoria-Gasteiz: Basque Government.

Arrieta, Leyre. 2012. El simbolismo poliédrico del nº 11 de la Avenue Marceau de Paris. In *La celebración de la Nación*, Ludger Mees (ed.), 117–134. Granada: Comares.

Arrieta, Leyre, Landaberea, Eider et al. 2016. *El primer Gobierno Vasco en Bilbao (1936-1937). En pie sobre la tierra vasca*. Bilbao: Bilbao 700.

Arrieta, Leyre. 2017. Estudio introductorio. In *La causa del pueblo de F. J. Landaburu*, Leyre Arrieta (ed.). *Colección Textos Clásicos del Pensamiento Político y Social en el País Vasco*, 9–112. Leioa: University of the Basque Country.

Barandiaran, Miren. 2016. Jesús María Leizola Sánchez. Universidad en tiempo de guerra. In *El primer Gobierno Vasco en Bilbao (1936-1937). En pie sobre la tierra vasca*, Leyre Arrieta, Eider Landaberea et al., 167–213. Bilbao: Bilbao 700.

Estomba, Fernando. 2016. *Competir en años convulsos. Deporte, política y sociedad en Bizkaia durante la II República y la guerra civil*. Bilbao: Artgerust.

Larronde, Jean Claude. 1998. *Exilio y solidaridad. La Liga Internacional de Amigos de los Vascos*. Bilbao: Bidasoa.

Granja, José Luis de la. 2007. *El oasis vasco. El nacimiento de Euskadi en la República y la Guerra Civil*. Madrid: Tecnos.

Mees, Ludger. 2006. *El profeta pragmático. Aguirre, el primer lehendakari (1939-1960).* Irun: Alberdania.

Mees, Ludger, José Luis de la Granja, Santiago de Pablo & José Antonio Rodríguez Ranz. 2014. *La política como pasión. El lehendakari José Antonio Aguirre (1904–1960).* Madrid: Tecnos.

Pablo, Santiago de. 2012. *The Basque Nation On-Screen. Cinema, Nationalism, and Political Violence.* Reno: University of Nevada.

Pablo, Santiago de, José Luis de la Granja, Ludger Mees & Jesús Casquete, (coord.). 2012. *Diccionario ilustrado de símbolos del nacionalismo* vasco. Madrid: Tecnos.

Sáenz de Gorbea, Xabier. 2014. *Aranoa eta Guezalaren Gernikak: Eresoinka Kasua.* Gernika: Euskal Herria Museoa.

Uribe, Kirmen. 2016. *Elkarrekin esnatzeko ordua.* Zarautz: Susa.

5

Kirmen Uribe and translation: An endless journey[36]

Miren Ibarluzea Santisteban

1 Introductory words: Kirmen Uribe, travel and translation

In order to begin this study, we would like to emphasize the existent nexus between Uribe and translation. We would like to recall that, making metaphorical use of language or using parallelisms, the translator's task has been equated on repeated occasions with travel or with the transportation of texts. The word itself that means the act of translation in Basque, *itzultzea*, is the image of return on a round trip: it is, specifically, a question of a succession of steps which have to be taken in order to return after having left.

Returning to the mention of borderland spaces, we would like to recall, likewise, that translators have often been termed mediators between frontiers; as such, we would like to underscore the fact that such mediation is, as well as linguistic, also cultural and political (and, as we will see in the following analysis, the writer that is the object of our study is acutely aware of that). Moreover, one should remember that fictional translators have also been represented as travelers (Delabastita & Grutman 2005, 11–34) and that, among other things, it is typical to hear or read that a translator is a guide, a travel guide, a carrier that takes travelers, healthy and safe, from one riverbank to the other or that guides authors in their journeys

36 Paper prepared within the projects IT 1047-16 (Basque government) and FFI2017-84342-P (MINECO) developed by the level A consolidated research group MHLI (Memoria Historikoa Literatura Iberiarretan / Memoria Histórica en las Literaturas Ibéricas / Historical Memory in Iberian Literatures).

abroad. Uribe also articulates these latter ideas, expressed in phrases like: "The translators themselves encourage translation" or "The translator acts as a bridge or as a driving force" (Uribe 2013).

Therefore, what does Uribe say about translation? What is translation for him? What is it that is transported, from where and where to, by Uribe as a translator or by means of his translations? In what follows, we will attempt to reveal the characteristics of Uribe's endless translation journey,[37] as we did in the case of other authors (see Ibarluzea 2016 and Gandara & Ibarluzea 2018). In effect, Uribe has taken a route made up of many paths in the terrain of translation: he reads translations, he makes use of them as a tool for his writing process, he has translated on various occasions both his own texts as well as those of other writers, he has been in contact with the translators of his texts, and he has fictionalized translators. We will explain all that here and, in order to do so, we will take as our starting point Uribe's responses to a questionnaire on the topic (Uribe 2013).[38] In addition to those responses, we will include other kinds of notes, interpretations, and what critics and translators have said and written about him. In the same vein, we will also analyze several passages in the novel *Mussche* (2012) in which he places a translator in the story, in order to link him to the writer's own thought process. In other words, we will try to reveal Uribe's translation habitus.

2 Kirmen Uribe's translation habitus: discourses, positions, and experiences

Uribe and his translators form part of a structure that makes up the transnational, multi-directional, and relatively autonomous sub-field of Basque literature in translation (Ibarluzea 2017, chapter 3). They are agents in a specific social environment and they adopt specific positions and attitudes, in other words, a

37 This study is useful in order to understand the sub-field of Basque literature in translation and the dynamics that occur therein.

38 Unless otherwise stated, references to Uribe's comments here are taken from that interview.

specific habitus:[39] they are conditioned by the features of Basque literature and translation models, subject to the authority of the forces therein, but, at the same time, they too build and nourish that model, as well as its development and representation.

In general, we can say that, like other writers who live in plurilingual spaces, translation is very close to Uribe's experience and he coincides with the approach of writers who increasingly divide their time between creative and translation work (Ibarluzea 2015). Uribe is from a generation of writers who completed their basic education in Basque, and like the other writers of that generation, Basque has been his creative language from the very beginning (ibid.). Uribe is also comfortable in Spanish, and he also feels it as his own language, but when it comes to writing he chooses Basque, his literary language: "I have not had to choose my literary language, the language already chose me when I was born" (in Perret 2014, 22). This is a common issue in the field of Basque literature, since, as some observers have explained previously, such as Manterola (2011), literary bilingualism is not typical among Basque writers. As well as Basque and Spanish, Uribe also has some knowledge of English, and in different interviews he has said that he reads Italian, Catalan, Galician, and French.

In Uribe's own words, he has had "a very long relationship" with translation "of all kinds": on the one hand, he has done translations (of his texts and those of others) and, on the other hand, other translators have translated his texts, and he has

39 For more information on habitus in Basque, see Ibarluzea 2017, chap. 2. In any event, habitus may be defined briefly in the following terms: it is a virtual situation that is felt profoundly in a specific body which, in one way or another, makes it react (Bourdieu & Wacquant 1992, 28). In other words, it is a kind of universal grammar, a system of internalized attitudes which have to do with someone's perceptions, thoughts, discourses, actions, and practices. In the same way, it is also a creative schema which makes one respond or act in one way or another in the face of different situations, since subjects usually act according to an interiorized schema. Whatever the case, the habitus is not fixed, it varies according to a specific situation and according to the directions taken by subjects; thus, the habitus is connected to both habits and improvised responses. The habitus is dual in several senses: it interiorizes and exteriorizes; it is collective and personal; and it articulates individuality and sociability (ibid.).

followed those projects closely. As a matter of fact, through translations of his works, Uribe has entered into both national and international spaces. As Professor Sally Perret (2017, 26) explains, Uribe has also managed to enter into the Chinese- and English-language markets, both difficult to gain a foothold in. It is even more difficult for a writer in a small language to go down that route, as Perret makes clear (2017, 24), as Casanova and Olaziregi state, gaining an international projection is more difficult for writers from the periphery. It is worth noting, however, that Uribe won the Spanish National Literature Prize for Narrative by means of a translated version of his work. In that case, contends Perret (2017, 28), instead of seeing translation as an exercise in domestication, it should be understood also as a political act and one should also bear in mind the liberating effects of translation.

As well as being a translator and a writer of texts that are translated, Uribe is also a reader of translations. He says: "I read more works translated into Basque than written originally in the language. I'd say that most of my reading is in translation. It's an important fact because it also has an effect on my writing." In effect, there is much to learn from translators: "Translators help to spruce up Basque and raise the level of Basque. Our style has also been influenced, [because] we would write a lot more coarsely [without it]. A translator offers you a lot of solutions so that you can then write." In that vein, translation is for Uribe "a learning method," and he uses the corpus of texts translated into Basque as a consultation tool in his writing process. That is what he said in an interview after completing the novel *Mussche*: "In order to write *Mussche*, I read a lot of novels translated into Basque, and that also had an influence. *Pereirak dioenez* [*Pereira Maintains*], *Elurra* [*Snow*], *Loti Ederra* [*Sleeping Beauty*] . . . Natalia Ginzburg . . . What's more, I kept some books by my side, on the table, and consulted them frequently." He confesses to being self-taught in the field of translation, and that he also started on his own account when he was young, yet he would not define himself as a translator.

While he is a member of the Basque writers' association, he is not in the translators' association. In any event, he knows many Basque translators, some of whom are friends. He says, "I also admire some of them. I'm also a fan of some of them." In effect, some translators "get a following. You see who has translated a text and you say: 'this is well translated.' " Asked about his general opinion on translation into Basque, Uribe is "very positive," and he believes it has had a major influence on writers of his generation, above all because texts that translators have rendered in Basque offer a great number of solutions to the choice of language when it comes to writing.

As stated above, Uribe has translated his own and others' texts; he has been a self-translator as well as a translator.[40] As regards his texts, he worked with Gerardo Markuleta and Ana Arregi on the Spanish translation of the book of poems *Bitartean heldu eskutik* (*Mientras tanto dame la mano*). It was first published in 2004, and then again in 2008,[41] 2010, and 2013, all four editions being bilingual (in Basque and Spanish). The texts in that collection were also used in other projects.[42] In 2004, Uribe himself translated his children's and young adult literature work *Ez naiz ilehoria, eta zer?* (I'm Not Blonde, So What?, 2004) into Spanish: *No soy rubia* (La Galera, Barcelona). Moreover, his poems, alongside those of other authors, were translated into Spanish for the 2006 anthology *Montañas en la niebla: Poesía vasca de los años 90* (Mountains in the Fog:

40 The information on translations cited here comes mainly from the EIZIE (Euskal Itzultzaile, Zuzentzaile eta Interpreteen Elkartea, Association of Translators, Correctors and Interpreters of Basque Language) database *Nor da Nor* (Who is Who). On occasion, though, in order to clarify something, other sources have been consulted.

41 In editions thereafter it was titled *Mientras tanto cógeme la mano*, because it was felt that the verb '*coger*' (take) was a more precise rendering of '*heldu*' than '*dar*' (give).

42 Preparatory works carried out for the first edition appeared on the basqueliterature.com website in 2002. Most of the poems included by Perret in the 2014 anthology *Kirmen Uribe Vidas y Ficciones* are in that collection. Likewise, the Spanish version of the 2016 text *Ezin esan* (One Cannot Say), titled *No se puede decir*, was included in an itinerary designed by Esther Ferrer as part of the Donostia/San Sebastián, European Capital of Culture 2016 project.

Basque Poetry of the 90s), with the translation coordinated by Ana Arregi.

As noted, Uribe has also been a translator for other authors. He translated three of Raymond Carver's poems in the book *Ulamarine*—"Balsa Wood" ("Baltsa-ohola"), "Jean's TV" ("Jeanen telebista"), and "Bonnard's Nudes" ("Bonnarden biluziak")—from English into Basque, which were published in numbers 15/16 of the journal *Hegats* (1997). Prior to the poems, which appear in both the original English and in Basque translation, Uribe also pens a short introduction for each. After the poems there is a list of Carver's poetry books (as well as his work published in French and Spanish), which also includes the book *Katedrala* (*Cathedral*, 1983), translated into Basque by J.M. Mendizabal. That same year, Uribe published another translation in numbers 17/18 of the same journal, *Hegats*, an edition that included nine poems by the Nobel-Prize-winning Polish poet, Wisława Szymborska, translated into Basque by Kirmen Uribe, Rikardo Arregi Diaz de Heredia, and Magdalena Węgrzyn ("Ahizparen laudorioa eta beste zenbait poema"). Here, some introductory words were also included, and the translators remark that, in addition to the original texts, they also utilized their translations into Spanish, French, and English.[43] As in the previous example, the poems are published in two languages (Polish and Basque) followed by bibliographical data. In 2004 Uribe also took part in group work at a translation workshop in Estonia:[44] "Each of us translated the others' poems into our native tongue."[45] Lastly, one can cite Uribe's translated work

43 "Rikardo Arregi and I really loved Szymborska, and that's why we translated her. I used Spanish and English, Rikardo French, and Magdalena translated them directly from Polish. In the translation we did, we took into account the original and the three translations" (Kirmen Uribe, personal communication).

44 With Benno Barnard (Flanders), Sigurdur Pálsson (Iceland), Cathal Ó Searcaigh (Ireland), Jan Erik Vold (Norway), Robert Alan Jamieson (Scotland / Shetland Islands), Mererid Puw Davies (Wales), and Doris Kareva, Kalju Kruusa, and Hasso Krull (all from Estonia).

45 One of the poets who took part in the workshop, Robert Alan Jamieson, discusses the experience here: http://www.estlit.ee/centre/index.php?mact=News,cntnt01,detail,0&cntnt01articleid=20&cntnt01origid=27&cntnt01returnid=27 [December 28, 2020].

at the armiarma.eus website: in 2011 (the same year Tomas Tranströmer won the Nobel Prize), in the "Euskarari ekarriak" (Translated into Basque) section at this site, Uribe published a collection of his poems titled "Zeru amaitu gabea eta beste poema batzuk" ("The Half-Finished Heaven and Some Other Poems," Swedish to Basque),[46] comprised of "Zeru amaitu gabea" ("The Half-Finished Heaven"), "Bekoz beko" ("Face to Face"), "Goizeko txoriak" ("Morning Birds"), "Izena" ("The Name"), "79ko martxoan" ("March '79"), "Oroimenaren ikuspegia" ("Memories Look at Me"), "Apirila eta isiltasuna" ("April and Silence"), and "Haikuak" ("Haiku Poems").[47] Then, in 2014 and at the same website, Uribe also translated Mark Strand's poem "Elegy for My Father" as "Aitaren eresia."[48] In addition to all this, Uribe has also used his translations of other people's poems in recitals and his other texts.

Not all of Uribe's translations have been published, and he himself has said that he did them as a kind of exercise in order to learn how to do so, as mentioned above: "Above all in poetry, I noted how the problems that emerged in other authors' poems were resolved in Basque." Put another way, for Uribe translation is an exercise in training to write:

> I asked myself: How would Plath write in Basque? Or how would Carver write in Basque? That's how I have translated several authors, from several languages. And it has been a very intimate, private, activity. I've published them, but they have been above all tests and trials, exercises

46 In order to translate Tranströmer, Uribe used the Spanish versions of his poems. "I knew of Tranströmer before he won the Nobel Prize, and when they gave him the award, I wrote about him in *Berria*" (Kirmen Uribe, personal communication).

47 The following year, the translator Juan Mari Agirreurreta published a collection of Tranströmer's poems, *Bizientzat eta hilentzat. Poema guztiak, 1954-2004* (Elkar, 2012), which were translated prior to those that Uribe translated. Agirreurreta's translations are, therefore, other versions.

48 Uribe used the original English-language version to translate Strand (Kirmen Uribe, personal communication).

> to learn how to write. Translation has served me as a means to write, as an exercise or as training.

Asked about translation strategies, Uribe observes that he does not like to take too many liberties. Here he is above all alluding to poems: "A poem has its moment, and I do not like a version that is very different from the original. The translator must respect the moment at which the poem was born, whether the poem is that of the translator or someone else." Moreover, as regards the language register, one tries to maintain the poetic spirit, to reconstruct the rhythm and musicality. Likewise, one tries to "purify" texts: "In other words, instead of the poem becoming very cryptic in relation to the original, I try to use a well-lubricated Basque. In the end, the writer writes clearly in their language and in ours, too, it must appear clear. The poems must appear as if they had been written in Basque." In Uribe's view, "translation is a creative exercise," and it is not the same to translate your own text and someone else's. "When one does it oneself, they rewrite it. Translation is a lot like creative work, and in the end, literature comes from deep inside, also a lot through intuition, and not everything is rational. Thus, the translator must go deep into those abysses again and look for a new, although similar, rhythm."

When his texts have been translated into other languages, Uribe notes that he has had two options: in poetry translations, when he has had some knowledge of the language in question, he has taken part in the translation: "I have also taken part in poetry translations. The language of the poems is very important for me, and I took part in the Spanish translation of the poetry book *Bitartean heldu eskutik* (*Meanwhile Hold my Hand*). Of course, when it came to French I did not participate, but I did in the English-language version, I flicked through it. I did not take part in the Russian and other versions." The French version of this book, translated by Kattalin Totorika, was published in Bordeaux in 2006 by the Le Castor Astral publishing house. The English-language version of the text, published in the United

States in 2007 by Graywolf Press, was translated by Elizabeth Macklin.[49] The Russian version, translated by Roman Ignatiev, was published in Moscow by the Gernika Press in 2010.[50] That same year, in 2010, the Proa publishing house in Barcelona published an anthology in Catalan, edited by Jon Elordi and Laia Nogera, which included Uribe's poems in *Bitartean heldu eskutik* as well as several unpublished poems from his recitals. As on other occasions (and we will return to the issue later) Uribe praises the mediatory role of translators when he mentions this work:

> The translation team did a great job, not in publishing it because I found the publishing house, but in the talks and readings they gave. That makes me realize that literature, especially narrative, is a business. One can get out there with grants, but the relationship with a publishing house is very commercial. That said, thanks to translators one can establish another kind of relationship, another kind of publication, other kinds of circles, more human, and still maybe reach a bigger audience, one thing doesn't rule out the other.

That human circle or relationship, and the writer-translator connection, is a very typical one which happens in both directions between Uribe and his translators. In the words of the translator Nami Kaneko, "The chance to meet the author himself in person has also had a big influence on me: I think that the experience I've had with him, in conversations both in the Basque Country and in Japan, have helped me a lot in developing a more intimate relationship with both Basque and Basque literature" (Kaneko 2018). In effect, Kaneko agrees with Uribe in believing that personal relationships help to create other kinds of circles. "I totally agree with Kirmen on that subject. To put it one way, in

49 This was a finalist for the 2007 PEN American Center award for the best work translated into English in the United States.
50 This translation was done via the bridge language of Spanish.

the world of literature those that create and organize translations are not the invisible hands of the market, but the hands of people who are involved in the translation and publishing process (agents, people who work in publishing and in bookshops, readers, critics . . .) (Kaneko 2018). An example of these circles and collectives is the fact that translations into certain languages are always carried out by the same translators.

Uribe believes that not having to use a bridge language and being able to translate directly from Basque into other languages represents progress. As regards this, it seems worth highlighting that in the case of the book of poems, *Bitartean heldu eskutik*, almost all the translations were done from Basque.

> I'm also very happy about something else: when it came to translating *Bitartean heldu eskutik*, I tried to find translators who would do so directly from Basque. For example, Elizabeth Macklin translated it into English, and always from Basque, without the bridge language of Spanish. We've come a long way in that too. With *Bilbao-New York-Bilbao*, it was a case of many translations being done from Spanish. But with publishers I have always stood up for, if possible, looking for a translator who knows Basque. That happened to me with Japanese. *Bilbao-New York-Bilbao* is in thirteen languages, and when it came to translating it into Japanese, for example, it was done so from Basque.[51]

Nevertheless, as regards subordination to linguistic dominance (in this case, that of Spanish), the words of translator and researcher Nami Kaneko are worth noting. "I think that there is a lesson to learn here: indirect translation should not be completely ruled out, because sometimes it acts like a bridge" (Kaneko and Manterola 2016, 10). Moreover, Kaneko thinks

51 On the question of bridge languages, translation strategies, and the document called "vulgata" that writers passed on to translators, see Kaneko and Manterola (2016).

that "those in contact with a major language have an advantage in being able to achieve recognition in that language and, thanks to that, in being disseminated in many other languages too" and "one must make the most of that, even though it may create some other problems" (ibid., 26–27). Meanwhile, one should remember what kinds of strategies are used in order to highlight or suppress territoriality, because they can alter the function of translation (Ibarluzea and Olaziregi, 2016). Thus, we believe it necessary to underscore the fact that different editions of Uribe's poems are bilingual, or that editions of the same work by him in different languages have been published, as part of a strategy to demonstrate territoriality. As such, we agree with Kaneko when she states that "what most conditions the fact that Basque literature is spread through Spanish is, precisely, the view one has of that literature" (Kaneko and Manterola 2016, 15), and not so much the language in which we approach it. In Kaneko's opinion, if direct translation from Basque becomes merely a symbolic act, it loses value and she thinks it better to do "something that will be reflected in the result of and reception for the translation" (ibid., 25).

In the case of his narrative work, Uribe does not take part in the translation (except to answer translators' questions) and he explains that he has always opted for Basque translators:

> In all the other cases, with the novels, I opted in favor of the translator. I don't translate my own work, even though I know Spanish and English. It is an option, 1) in favor of Basque, because Basque is my only literary language and 2) in favor of the translator, because I believe there are good translators and that they do good work. That should be backed, I think.
>
> Markuleta did the last one, and he did a great job of translating *Mussche*, much better than me. So, why would I do it? I know Spanish, yes, but in my case, I don't self-translate in spite of being bilingual. The novelist David

> Crossman told me the same thing, that he just writes in Hebrew, even though he knows English well. I think that we need to normalize all that too, we write in Basque and then a translator transforms it into Spanish, English, French . . . into whatever language. (. . .) I tried with *Mussche*, and in the end I managed to make it a normal process: [the publishing house] Seix Barral made up a contract to publish *Mussche*, and they hired Markuleta. It wasn't a case of me doing it and telling them, all my doing. I was very firm on that point: "Deal with me as if I were German" I told them, "You hire a translator." I think it must have been one of the first times we achieved something like that: that a commercial publishing house hired a paid Basque-Spanish translator, with them paying, without any subsidy.

Today, one can read the novel *Bilbao-New York-Bilbao* in Basque (2008) and fourteen other languages.[52] We can read *Mussche*, meanwhile, in Basque (2012), Spanish (2013, trans. Gerardo Markuleta), Catalan (2013, trans. Pau Joan Hernández), Japanese (2015, trans. Nami Kaneko)[53] and Chinese (2015, trans. Huang Yehua). On the topic of translations of *Mussche*, Uribe commented, "In the case of *Mussche*, they all did so from Basque. In that regard, we're making progress." In the case of Chinese, we should be clear, the translation was done from Spanish. As the Japanese translator Nami Kaneko states, "From what I have heard in China, *Mussche* was translated from Spanish, the title

52 Specifically, in Galician (2010, trans. Isaac Xubín); Catalan (2010, trans. Pau Joan Hernàndez); Spanish (2010, trans. Ana Arregi Martínez); Portuguese (2011, trans. Pedro Vidal, revised by Clara Joana Vitorino); French (2012, trans. Gersende Camenen); Bulgarian (2012, via bridge language Spanish, trans. Boriana Dukova); Japanese (2012, trans. Nami Kaneko); Russian (2013, via bridge language Spanish, trans. Roman Ignatiev & Zoia Khibrikova); Georgian (2013, via bridge language Spanish, trans. Vladimir Luarsabishvili); Albanian (2013, trans. Bashkim Shenu); 2013, Serbian (via bridge language Spanish, trans. Zorica Novakov-Kovacevic); English (2014, trans. Elizabeth Macklin); Slovenian (2014, via bridge language Spanish, trans. Marjeta Drobnič); and Estonian (2017, trans. Merelin Kotta).

53 It received the award for the best translation into Japanese. For more information on this, see Kaneko and Manterola (2016).

appeared in Spanish, not Basque, on the front cover, and it was presented as a new publication in Spanish literature" (Kaneko and Manterola 2016, 15).

Kaneko herself has always made an effort to make sure Uribe appears as a Basque writer in contemporary literature collections and to underscore his distinctiveness (ibid.).

As regards *Elkarrekin esnatzeko ordua* (The Hour of Waking Together, 2016), the following translations are available: in Spanish (2016, trans. José María Isasi), Catalan (2016, trans. Pau Joan Hernández), Portuguese (2017, trans. Artur Gerra & Cristina Rodríguez), Galician (2017, trans. Isaac Xubin) and French (2018, trans. Edurne Alegria).[54]

In the field of children's and young adult literature, besides Spanish (2004), Uribe's aforementioned *Ez naiz ilehoria, eta zer?* (2004) has been translated into Galician (2004, trans. Hadrián Laureira), Catalan (2004),[55] and Asturian (2004, trans. Carlos González Espina). Moreover, Nere Lete translated *Garmendia eta zaldun beltza* (2003) into English (as *Garmendia and the Black Rider*, 2015).

The audio-visual project *Bar Puerto* is trilingual: it was translated into Spanish by José María Isasi and into English by Elizabeth Macklin (2010).

Lastly, translations of Uribe's poetry have been published in English and German in several anthologies and on various websites: In 2006, ten of Uribe's poems (four of them translated by Petra Newiger and the remaining six by Ludger Damm)[56] appeared on the Berlin website Lyrikline. In 2007, his work appeared in the book *Six Basque Poets*, translated by Amaia Gabantxo.[57] And in 2008, the US critics Kevin Prufer and Wayne

54 As we write this chapter, there are plans to translate the work into Serbian, Greek, Japanese, and English. Likewsie, Asier Altuna will make a film based on the book and titled *Karmele* (Kirmen Uribe, personal communication).

55 We do not have any information about the translator.

56 The texts, translations and audios can be accessed here: https://www.lyrikline.org/es/poemas/kukua-3072?showmodal=de

57 All the poetry translations by Gabantxo are new in this anthology, and therefore different from those of Macklin (Kirmen Uribe, personal communication).

Millar included three of Uribe's poems in their anthology *New European Poetry*.

It is worth pointing out that many of these translations have been undertaken thanks to the promotional efforts of local agents in the field of Basque literature and thanks to public subsidies, and that is another of the distinctive features of the sub-field of Basque literature in translation (Ibarluzea 2017). In any event, Uribe has not just moved around in those local circles and, as we saw in the previous quote, he has made an effort to function as if writing in the major languages and also to be present in commercial publishing houses and circles. In that vein, Nami Kaneko's position coincides with that of Uribe:

> In the same sense, the kind of publishing house and collection in which the translation is published is, I think, really important. To tell the truth, I don't think it's such a good idea to publish translations in the academic world or in specialized Basque literature collections; here, in Japan, although I've received offers like that, I haven't been keen to do it. It's a personal opinion, and I won't deny the importance, for example, of publishing with the University of Nevada or a German publishing house, but I have my doubts, because they are aimed at a very limited kind of reader (. . .) It's important to publish books, but I'd give (and I do give) priority to aiming for the greatest number of readers possible. That's why I've always tried to carve out a path in the commercial world (even though it's in the extremely small market of literature in translation), so that works by Basque writers may be published by important publishing houses, in one of those collections that readers of literature in translation are interested in. (Kaneko and Manterola 2016, 22)

As regards the motivations to translate Uribe, clearly the Spanish National Prize has helped to raise his profile and awareness of his work (Kaneko herself found out about the novel *Bilbao-New*

York-Bilbao as a result of the prize), yet translators also point out other features. For example, Uribe's Georgian translator, Vladimir Luarsabishvili, highlights the exchange between minority literatures and the universality of a writer's work (2016, 136–139): "Uribe avoids addressing the typical Basque subject matter; on the contrary, he uses that to develop certain values, and those are equally attractive to Basque, German, English and readers of any nationality."

Kaneko also felt the same kind of connection: she felt a link between the effects of recent events (the earthquake and tsunamis) on Japanese coastal towns and the stories in the novel *Bilbao-New York-Bilbao* (Kaneko and Manterola 2016, 27). Similarly, like the Georgian translator, in Kaneko's opinion too, promoting Basque-language translations "could create their own relationships and new dialogues" (ibid., 7).

The translator Edurne Alegria also felt a bond with Uribe's latest novel, because she knew the events and characters portrayed: Alegria was born in exile, and knew the Urresti Letamendia family personally (Alegria 2018).

It appears, then, that the local and global nature of the themes Uribe explores (or a combination of both) is one of the bases in strengthening the connection between him and his translators. Additionally, it is worth noting too that there is a direct relationship between the writer and the translators. In effect, as noted above, Uribe gives a lot of importance to the relationships he shares with translators because they help him develop other more human ways to reach readers:

> What I have learned from my relationships with translators is that there are many directions, not just the commercial route, but also the route of those who love literature, and that is how translators fall in love with a book and promote it. (. . .) And they do so because of literature (. . .) Loyalties also emerge and groups of translators are created around one writer. That is lovely (. . .) Think about it, for example, *Bitartean heldu eskutik* would

> not have been published in English if there had been no translator (. . .) Translators have been very important when it comes to helping me, in encouraging and persuading publishers (. . .) That's why relationships with translators are wonderful. They often do more work than an agent, and in the end, publishers know a translator, like they were family, and they trust them. There is trust in an agent but one knows that it's a commercial relationship, and so on. If a translator promotes the book, there is a greater chance it will get published. That has been very nice for me.

Specifically, the nature of the leading character in Uribe's novel *Mussche* (a translator himself) is an attempt to show the human side of a translator and, to put it one way, Uribe reconstructs in his fiction opinions about translators.

3 Kirmen Uribe's habitus reflected in the role of the translator

Perret contends that one of the key features of Uribe's literature is its human side (2014, 7): "What most stands out in Uribe's work, as well as its originality and innovative spirit, is his peaceful worldview and his positive position in defending the human in all its complexity." Moreover, the topic of translators in fiction is not new, although we appear to have experienced a boom in Basque literature in recent years (Ibarluzea 2017, chap. 5),[58] and, at the same time, the so-called fictional turn has enriched research in translation studies. This last reflection must, therefore, be situated in that line of research, on the understanding that what is fictionalized is a representation of writers' habitus, and that it is valid when it comes to both describing the subfield of Basque literature in translation and expressing perceptions about it (ibid.).

---

58 Therein, several fictional translators that have appeared in contemporary Basque literature are studied, following the notion of the fictional turn and comparing the image of the role of Basque translators with those of other literatures.

Mussche begins in Belgium in 1937 with the story of the child war refugee Karmentxu Cundin, and then Uribe leads us from the Spanish Civil War to the context of the Second World War, specifically to that of the Flemish writer and translator Robert Mussche (who took Karmentxu Cundin into his home at a young age). Uribe says the following about the character of Robert Mussche:

> Each of us chooses our characters, whatever they are like, and each chooses what they offer you in the novel. Then they are adapted. Although Mussche was a real person with certain real biographical data, most of it is made up. As regards being a translator . . . To tell the truth, that is what sparked my interest in starting the novel. Who was Mussche? Well, he was a Flemish translator that took in a Basque child. The fact he was a translator, that he spoke different languages, attracted me a lot.
> The translator is a very attractive character, humble, in the shadows, they recover the universal literary tradition. The writer is more egotistical . . . You won't believe it, but I like translators more, it's lovely sharing the voices of others.

Specifically, in the last chapter of the novel, the author himself makes an appearance in the story, and he offers a synthesis of the leading character's nature, as well as justifying his reasons for writing the novel[59]:

> Our daughter Arane was born on 28 November 2010. My friend Aitzol died on 24 April 2011. One of the last times we were together this is what Aitzol said to me:
>
> "You should tell the story of a hero."

59 All the English quotes of *Mussche* are our translations, as the novel has not been translated into English.

> "But there are no heroes for me. I like the fragile side of people, not their feats. I'm scared of heroes."
>
> "I'm not speaking about those kinds of heroes. I'm speaking about normal people. Heroes are all around us, before and now, here and all over the world; small heroes, those that devote themselves to helping others."
>
> Then I fell silent. Now I agree with him. There are heroes all around who, once they've been developed, pass away.
>
> So, there's the story of a hero, my beloved friend. (Uribe 2012, 194)

The translator is an everyday hero and, therefore, for Uribe, suitable for demonstrating the fragile side of his characters. Here, too, as Thiem (1995) observed, the translator is far from being on par with the "Conan the Translator" hero. Yet, as Uribe explains, contemporary society acknowledges all kinds of heroes, and translators can also become heroes. The changing defintion of the "hero" concept leads in some way to a change in the image of translators themselves. Furthermore, rejecting Thiem's contention that, "when not wholly invisible, we appear as marginal figures" (1995, 207), the translator has gone from being a marginal figure to being the central character in novels. In Uribe's novel, Robert Mussche is presented as a person of firm ideas (Uribe 2012, 19) who is a charming speaker (ibid.) with a talent for making people feel at ease (35) and knows how to use the appropriate words for anyone he speaks to (ibid.). He is a character that is desperately in search of freedom, whose dream was "to roam the world free, without any kind of tie" (41). As for the nature of this character, he is a bank employee but then gets fired having been accused of stealing (86). From that moment on, he will earn a living as a journalist (73) and translator. It is mentioned in the narration that, among other occupations, he has taught Spanish classes in schools organized for the children of war, and, with the words of his preferred writers, he had made a notebook of dictations for the classes, because he was in the habit of copying extracts from his favorite authors (63). As regards personal relationships, one should highlight the fact that his basic relations are established through "conversation." The dialogues and reflections of Robert Mussche and his friend Herman Thierry (who is also a writer) are one of the main pillars of the novel. Mussche also acts in the same way as regards sentimental relationships. Yvonne (Robert's partner) explains their relationship to Herman in the following way:

> "I don't know if Robert loves me," says Yvonne, changing the subject. (. . .) "He doesn't want a relationship with me. For him, I'm a beautiful woman, bright, well-read. Just a conversation partner. A piece of shit. So he's not even capable of kissing me, caressing me, he doesn't . . ." (Uribe 2012, 75)

In fictional works, the labor of the translator is often linked to isolation (Ibarluzea 2017, chap. 5.2), yet in this novel one notes signs of change as regards that tendency: Robert Mussch has no problems whatsoever when it comes to social relations. Although how we interpret his affective relations is another question altogether.

As the story progresses, Robert Mussche abandons his normal life and, embracing his commitment like a traveling companion, joins the Resistance (Uribe 2012, 117). Here is the image of the committed active agent and activist, as described by Ilse Logie: "The translator is recognized today as a figure that takes an active form or that, due to political motives, takes sides" (2005, 43). It is at that moment, when the character goes underground, that translation is mentioned for the first time:

> The days are endless, I've finished my translation work, but the book is so ridiculous that I'm completely exasperated with the blatantly non-natural sentiments in it. And

> meanwhile we're experiencing a real tragedy here, a tragedy taken from real life. So, that's why I'm so angry with the style of these shallow exercises by this bourgeois author. I don't see any advantage in this translation, but I'll carry on doing it for two reasons: first, because it helps me to pass the time; second, because it will help us make a bit of money, with such an uncertain future. (Uribe 2012, 105–6)

Robert complains about his lack of identification with the author and inability to feel committed to the translation. As he makes clear in one section of the text, translation has a dual value at this moment: on the one hand, it is a pastime; on the other, it is a source of income. Robert's translation languages are also mentioned in the novel, as is a positive side of his work: being able to work from home.

> The best thing was working in the apartment, without having to go to a workplace everyday. Herman got a suitable job for him: he would do translations. Robert could translate from German, French and Spanish into Dutch and he was a writer, he would be well suited to that job. He met up with Herman once a week in the Café de Paris in Brussels and he gave him the things to translate. (Uribe 2012, 113)

Robert also reflects on writing (and translating?) in Dutch on one occasion:

> "My language is not very rich," Robert remarked. "Why write in Dutch, in a language between the two great traditions of France and Germany?" he asked himself. "Because it situates me in the world as a person," he said in a hushed voice, clenching his fists as he gazed at the raindrops soaking the ground. "I wouldn't be me

> without the language of the workers on Ferrerlaan Street in Ghent." (Uribe 2012, 119)

Returning now to the images of translation, since Robert does not just consider translation a pastime and source of income; he also learns a lot from translation and praises the stylistic and literary value of translation:

> He reflects on translation at the café table. For many long days those writers have been his only company. And those voices help him to keep going more than those of real flesh-and-blood people. The solitude forces him to take as company those people who are not there, those who you have not seen for a long time, the dead, they are right there, in the same way as someone you'd run into every day when crossing the street, as real as they are. As the years go by something similar happens, the living and the dead, one recalls all their voices. "It's strange," he often thinks, "but it is clandestinity that has most drawn me to literature." Since he left the bank, he's never spent more time reading and writing. Robert learns a lot from translating all those foreign writers into Dutch. He likes repeating what is said in those foreign languages in his own language, it's like entering into unexplored territory for him. The work of translation opens up windows onto unknown landscapes or, what amounts to the same thing, sentences that have never been written. (Uribe 2012, 118–9)

4 Some final words: The brief chronicle of a journey

The affective link between literature and translation is to some extent a reflection of the author's own habitus: for Uribe, the work of translation is, on the one hand, an act of learning when it comes to writing in Basque, and we have seen that, as a published translator, he emphasizes the stylistic and literary value of translation. On the other hand, the translator is a traveling companion to traverse the world, a traveling companion to free up the world, one who is committed and skilled in the art of conversation. Those features, which Uribe has found in translators, have helped him to find his place as a Basque writer (indeed, Uribe is a firm proponent of normalizing language practices in small languages) in the national and international space (making use of occasional strategies such as, for example, drawing attention to not using bilingual versions or bridge languages) as well as both in commercial circles and those of the Basque-speaking community, but always emphasizing the human side of the exchange.

Bibliography

Alegria, Edurne. 2018. Unpublished questionnaire responses for the summer course roundtable "Kirmen Uribe: Life, Fiction."

Bourdieu, Pierre & Wacquant, Loïc J.D. 1992. *Reponses: pour une sociologie reflexive.* Paris: Editions du Seuil.

Delabastita, Dirk & Grutman, Rainier. (ed.). 2005. *Fictionalising translation and multilingualism (Special Issue of Linguistica Antverpiensia New Series 4/2005.* Antwerpen: Hogeschool Anterpen, Hoger Instituut voor Vertalers en Tolken.

Gandara, Ana & Ibarluzea, Miren. 2018. Representaciones transtextuales y heterolingües (para la memoria) en la novela Manu Militari. *Fontes Linguae Vasconum,* 125 (January–June): 191–220. Online: http://www.culturanavarra.es/uploads/files/06-FLV125.pdf [August 1, 2018].

Ibarluzea, Miren. 2015. The Translation Habitus of Contemporary Basque Writers. *Estudios de traducción,* 5: 59–75.

Ibarluzea, Miren. 2016. Urretabizkaiaren eta Sarrionandiaren itzulpen-habitusak. *Fontes Linguae Vasconum,* 122:

153–67. Online: http://www.culturanavarra.es/uploads/files/04-Miren%20Ibarluzea%20issn.pdf [August 1, 2018].

Ibarluzea, Miren. 2017. Itzulpengintzaren errepresentazioak euskal literatura garaikidean: eremuaren autonomizazioa, literatur historiografiak eta itzultzaileak fikzioan. PhD thesis. UPV/EHU.

Ibarluzea, Miren & Olaziregi, Mari Jose. 2016. Autonomización y funciones del subcampo de la traducción literaria vasca contemporánea: una aproximación sociológica. *Pasavento*, IV-2: 293–313. Online: http://www.pasavento.com/pdf/02Ibarluzea_Olaziregi.pdf [August 1, 2018].

Kaneko, Nami & Manterola, Elizabete. 2016. Interview with Nami Kaneko (full version). *Senez* 47: 1–30. Online: http://www.eizie.eus/Argitalpenak/Senez/20161103/03manterola [August 1, 2018].

Kaneko, Nami. 2018. Unpublished questionnaire responses for the summer course roundtable "Kirmen Uribe: Life, Fiction."

Logie, Ilse. 2005. Una escena de traducción en América Latina: `Las dos orillas' de Carlos Fuentes. In *Fictionalising translation and multilingualism*, Delabastita, Dirk & Grutman, Rainier (ed.), 35–46. Antwerpen: Hogeschool Anterpen, Hoger Instituut voor Vertalers en Tolken.

Luarsabishvili, Vladimir. 2016. Itzulpena, kulturen elkargune (Kirmen Uribere's and Harkaitz Cano's poetry in Georgian. *Senez*, 47: 133–43. Online: http://www.eizie.eus/Argitalpenak/Senez/20161103/09luarsabishvili [August 1, 2018].

Manterola, Elizabete. 2011. La autotraducción en la literatura vasca. In *Aproximaciones a la autotraducción*. Dasilba, Xosé Manuel & Tanqueiro, Helena (ed.), 11–40. Vigo: Academia del Hispanismo.

Perret, Sally. "Un tiempo espléndido," in *Vidas y Ficciones* (Iruñea: Pamiela, 2014), 7–13.

Perret, Sally. 2017. "Fish and Trees Are Alike": The Movement of Identity in Kirmen Uribe's *Bilbao-New York-Bilbao*. *Hispanic Review*, Winter 2017: 23–45.

Thiem, Jon. 1995. The Translator in Postmodern Fiction. *Translation and Literature*, 4, 2: 207–18.

Uribe, Kirmen. 2012. *Mussche*. Zarautz: Susa.

Uribe, Kirmen. 2013. Unpublished email questionnaire about translation habits submitted by Ibarluzea.

Uribe, Kirmen. 2014. *Vidas y Ficciones*. Iruñea: Pamiela.

6

Writing and the Internet in Kirmen Uribe's novel *Bilbao-New York-Bilbao*[60]

Jon Kortazar

1 Writing

In 2007, Irene Zoe Alameda published a brilliant article in *Cuadernos Hispanoamericanos* titled "La era Gates y la reinvención del lenguaje," in which she explored the relationship between the Internet and literary writing, and the influence of the former on the latter. It was not about direct literary practice on the Internet (the use of blogs and things like that), but rather the form in which the new Internet era conditioned the way of writing in conventionally written texts.

That same year, in *La luz nueva*, and the year before, in *Pangea. Internet, blogs y comunicación en un mundo nuevo*, Vicente Luis Mora simultaneously examined the same topic: the way in which new technology was influencing new writing.

Behind all of this there was an old axiom of Walter Ong, who had already explained that a change in the paradigm of writing (that of oral to written technology) implied a change in the development of cognition and the ways in which literary creation was carried out (1987). It is certainly true that Walter Ong's thesis has been critiqued, given that the paradigm may be constructed for Western society, but not so much for other cultures, so that it has also been classified as ethnocentrist.

60 This work falls within Research Project IT 1012-16, by the Established Group LAIDA (Literature and Identity), which is part of the Basque Government Group Network.

Yet it is still a compelling premise. That same year, 2007, Professor José María Pozuelo Yvancos referred to the novel *Nocilla Dream* by Agustín Fernández Mallo in the following terms:

> Each radical change in the communication system has brought with it a significant modification in literary genres. The transition from orality to writing modified lyrical and epic series; the coming of the printing press once more redrew the panorama, with the emergence of the novel, its great ally. Later, journalism and photography implied the downfall of that nineteenth-century realist illusion and led to the unphotographable interiority of Joyce's and Virginia Woolf's subjectivity. It will not be long before the Internet once more disrupts the physiognomy of genres. On such occasions, it makes no sense to adopt apocalyptic or integrated alternatives. Literature, which is a need that does not depend on the medium, has survived each profound change in channeling its diffusion. And it will likewise do so in the twenty-first century. But it will not be the same. Nor is it desirable that this should be the case.[61]

As one can infer, technological change is not tied to a transformation in perceptive cognition and in the form of creation, which is what Walter Ong was contending, but, rather, one discerns that technological alteration will have as a consequence a change in literary genre, which is not the same. Yet the basic idea that one affects the other, remains.

Following these methodological bases, this work attempts to explore in what way the influence of the Internet is present in the writing in Kirmen Uribe's *Bilbao-New York-Bilbao* and in what form those characteristics of new writing, defined by both Irene Zoe Alameda and Vicente Luis Mora, are reflected in this novel.

---

61 Translated by Cameron Watson.

2 The inclusion of graphic information

Irene Zoé Alameda (2007, 23–24) notes that novels have moved away from a formerly normal tendency: the inclusion of images which may accompany the text and may enrich the meaning through iconic representations. However, according to this author, through the influence of film, different levels of illustrations are increasingly present in texts.

One of the singularities in the novel *Bilbao-New York-Bilbao* consists of inserting into the work a color reproduction of Aurelio Arteta's mural *En la romería 1*, which is kept in the Fine Arts Museum in Bilbao, a painting that decorated the house of the architect Bastida in Ondarroa, which, as we know, is the writer's hometown.

The reproduction of this image was not accidental. It offers several keys to interpreting the novel. In the first place, it is the starting mechanism in the novel, in a highly emotive scene, for the recollection that *Bilbao-New York-Bilbao* becomes.

The grandfather, one of the key protagonists in the novel, walks over to take a closer look at the painting in the company of his young daughter-in-law, after he has just been diagnosed with a terminal illness. So, at the moment death is announced, the old fisherman arrives at the museum to see a renewed past, the memory of his young wife represented forever in Arteta's painting. Past and present, memory and nowadays are joined in the grandfather's nostalgic vision, accompanied by his son's young wife in a *ritornello* of time.

> [Mum] would never forget that day, how on the very day they told him he was going to die Granddad took her to a museum. (*Bilbao-New York-Bilbao*, 8)

In the second place, the protagonist of the painting, the writer's grandmother, wanted to appear in the painting and pose as a model.

> The thing is, Granddad told our mother that [the farm girl in the mural] was Grandmother Ana, not to tell anyone, but he wanted to share the secret with her. (*Bilbao-New York-Bilbao*, 175)

In order to understand what this means and symbolizes, we must examine what is said in the novel about another woman who wanted Arteta to paint her, to understand the attitude of Benigna Burgoa, who accepted an offer to pose for the painter against the will of her parents and did so furtively when she went to the drinking fountain to get water. Both Benigna and Ana represent a female independence which rebels against a family veto on posing for the painter. She wants to be painted and appear in Arteta's painting, and hence her decision prevails over the convention of the epoch:

> One of Arteta's models was Benigna Burgoa. Benigna was a lithe eighteen-year-old. Arteta saw her on the street and asked if she'd pose for him. She went home all happy . . . but [her parents] gave her a scolding.
>
> Modelling was something fallen women did, they told her, and don't even think of it. Since they knew Benigna had been happy around the painter, they forbade her to leave the house. She could only go as far as the old bridge . . . for water [. . .] She arranged to leave her water jug with an acquaintance and, with that pretext, go on to Arteta's studio to do some modeling. (*Bilbao-New York-Bilbao*, 25)

In the third place, the painting itself, with its blend of women from a rural background and stylized young women dressed in modern fashions, represents one of the great symbolic questions in the Basque Country and its entry into modernity. Being modern and how to be so has been one of the recurring questions in the cultural history of the Basque Country. What is more, the arguments linking tradition and modernity—or, if one prefers as regards this novel, the local and the global—were fundamental in establishing Basque literary modernity and have been an essential source of many artistic and cultural movements in the Basque Country (recall Txillida and Oteiza, not to mention Arteta), aspiring to create an art that can be universal without losing its roots. The two cities in the novel's title are merely an expression of that need for universality based on personality.

> In the mural two worlds appear, together at one and the same time. On one side are the *baserritarrak*, the people of the farmsteads, and on the other the townsfolk. The farm girls are in traditional dress. Their skirts come down to their ankles, scarves on heads and their necklines modest. The city girls, though, don't look like that at all. Their dresses are lightweight, the wind moves them. Their hemlines are shorter, their knees allowed to show, and their necklines are wide open. (*Bilbao-New York-Bilbao*, 9–10)

They are distinct but united worlds.

As a side note, Kirmen Uribe also used this technique of referring to a painting as a starting mechanism in the novelistic situation in *Elkarrekin esnatzeko ordua* (The Hour of Waking Together, 2016), this time resorting to a painting by Antonio Gezala, *Noche de artistas en Ibaigane*.

3 Typographic games and the awareness of the scope of the printed page as an image

There is a considerably rich use of different typography in *Bilbao-New York-Bilbao*. I will attempt to be exhaustive since the reader, thanks to the fact that the narrator has created a distinct network of texts, can register those key fragments without much effort. There are plenty in the text and they are markedly varied. There is a reference from Wikipedia (17); the narrator reproduces a letter from Bastida to Arteta (46) and one from

Arteta to Bastida (47–48), using different fonts for both; Jabier Kalzakorta's email explaining a popular legend (53–55) and that of Nerea Arrieta on a comment during a writers' meeting (90–91); a transcription of the young Bastida's diary (60, 60–61, 61, 63, 68, 71–72, 72–73, 74–75); the reproduction of an entry in Eneko Barrutia's *Biscayan Fishermen's Lexicon* (64); the citation of a popular song (77–78, 138); a poem (87); the lyrics of a Nora Jones song (118); a fragment from his personal diary (96–97); a message on Facebook (129–130); a fragment from the personal diary of Uribe's mother Antigua (146); and a poem by the author (179–180). And lastly, there is the almost photographic transcription of the *Boletín Oficial del Estado* (BOE, Official State Bulletin), which registers the deep-sea vessels in Ondarroa in 1982 (182) and, as an extra-textual note, closes the book.

As one can observe, there are clear references to the Internet: emails, Wikipedia entries, and Facebook messages. The Internet is present in the life of the author-character, but he does not overlook communication written in the form of diaries (three different ones in the book), literary creativity, and the memory of traditional oral poetry, in the form of song or sung prayer.

On the presence of the Internet in contemporary novels, Vicente Luis Mora comments (2007, 34):

> The *constitution* of our world (*and* the world, therefore, of writers and about which people of letters write) has been defined gnosiologically by the intervention of the media.

He also cites José Antonio Pérez Tapias, from his work *Internautas y náufragos*, who reinforces this idea and states:

> The technological revolution underway reinforces even more the role of technology in our culture to the point of being able to consider it one of the principal, if not the principal, determinant in our pragmatic and cognitive relationship with the world. (Mora 2007, 34)

Following Walter Ong's trail, Vicente Luis Mora explains that technological change evolves into cognitive change:

> That diffuse concept on which so much has been said from every perspective in the study of the literary, *the gaze*, can, as of 2007, only be *the gaze of the writer born after 1960 and, therefore, fascinated and burdened mentally by the way in which the ubiquitous audio-visual culture has carved out its method of communication in the world.* (Mora 2007, 36)

He concludes with the expert in digital communication, Marc Prensky:

> Presky deduces, rightly, that a type of digital learning and an immediate contact with television and computers indicates a mental behaviour which does not have much in common, of course, with the old learning through books and paternal oral stories. (Mora 2007, 37)

So, we return again to the influence of the Internet and its importance in configuring the fluid narration offered in *Bilbao-New York-Bilbao*, not without first underscoring the fact that the three forms and styles of transferring information—oral transmission, written communication, and digital writing—are present and amalgamated in Uribe's novel. And the author takes from each of these three communications that which best matches his aesthetic interests.

4 Polyglossy

There is no need to insist on the fact that the use of distinct typography offers the printed page the configuration of an image. Irene Zoé Alameda links the concept of polyglossy to the use of neologisms, then extends it to the management of different means of expressive and discursive communication.

> Polyglossy does not just allude to the blending of languages; in general it refers to the blending of different kinds of discursive molds. The introduction of song lyrics into literary texts. (Alameda 2007, 21)

The classification also contains other dialogical forms such as "the use of phrases or words in the field of advertising" and makes a note of the use of "scientific language," or contends that in past decades "languages originating in other areas of knowledge, such as journalistic, notarial, and administrative language were used" (2007, 22–23). (The words in bold are in Alameda's original.)

Let us look now, specifically, at those messages which, in *Bilbao-New York-Bilbao*, represent communication that has been transcribed in a literal manner and that represents a certain image. I am referring to short texts which are singular on account of their typography and brevity, and which may respond to that concept of polyglossy. They are short messages which belong to much lesser genres (if one can use the word). They are the following: the Bastida Films flyer (34), Bastida's printed letterhead (Ricardo de Bastida /Architect) (45), the small screen in the plane that the writer is traveling in (62, 76, 109, 148, 157, 167, 168, 169), the names on the gravestone in Käsmu (85), the obituary page for Fabián Larrauri (112–113), the film information on the plane screen for *Entre les murs* (121), an ad for a watch (148–149), the code used to know how much fish had been caught (153), and a short citation from Mozart's *Figaro* (161).

The deliberate "advertising" dimension of some of these messages, insofar as they seek to make potential readers take part in the news that has been announced (the obituary page), or want to communicate the authorship of a letter (the letterhead), or simply offer information on the plane screen about the distance traveled and the distance still left to complete to the destination, can resemble these demonstrations of advertising language, which is indeed reproduced in the ad for the watch in the airline magazine.

"Administrative language" is also addressed when the author inserts into the novel a page from the BOE which lists the vessels in Ondarroa. Moreover, the author searches for a "scientific language" in the abstract of an academic article published in a specialist journal. Thus, when speaking about the size of waves, the narrator says:

> In the results section of a 2006 scientific paper in volume 33, L056, of *Geophysical Research Letters*, 'Were extreme waves in the Rockall Trough the largest ever recorded?' Naomi Holliday said this. (*Bilbao-New York-Bilbao*, 28)

But this is not the only example; all of the information Uribe includes about the name of the cormorant in Basque is no different from the scientific use of language—in this case dialectological—in the narrative work (*Bilbao-New York-Bilbao*, 63–67), or in recounting the story of the island of St. Kilda (116–118).

The purpose of using such messages is to reinforce the idea of the image within the monotonous typographical sequence of the narration and dialogue. But what is more, Irene Zoé Alameda concludes that:

> The adoption of such narrative formats seems to many people 'anti-literary,' and requires of readers an interpretative competence and certain knowledge of things they often do not possess. Nevertheless, the authors' intention is to seek out channels which might regain emotion, whether by means of peculiarity, subconscious evocation or attentive participation in the mental processes into which it invites one. (Alameda 2007, 23)

There are two elements in this quote that are worth extra consideration. The first resides in the allusion to a reader attentive to the constant changes offered by the tide of narrations, which come and go in *Bilbao-New York-Bilbao*. In a recent interview with Caroline Conejero, the writer declared that he writes "leaving the reader to reconstruct part of the narrative plot" (2018, 84). The second is found in the appeal to emotion. Indeed, on many occasions *Bilbao-New York-Bilbao* has been described as a novel that appeals principally to the emotions. And that is what one passage in the book does indeed suggest: "[Foster] Wallace was an innovator, he loved to experiment, but in one of his last interviews he said this: 'Emotion is fundamental' " (*Bilbao-New York-Bilbao*, 128). This is a quote that suggests the essence of Kirmen Uribe's aesthetic intention: innovation in order to create emotion.

5 Mixing of creative process with text

Literary criticism has abounded in pointing out the metaliterary agency present in the novel *Bilbao-New York-Bilbao*. In other words, the reflection on and recounting of the process of writing this novel. Irene Zoé Alameda terms this narrative agency the "confusion of process and product," and defines thus the relevance of using this narrative technique:

> This procedure contributes to the mimesis of the author's intellective process, from which not only is there the hope of saving the conclusions but, moreover, a desire to rescue the intermediate states of reasoning. (Alameda 2007, 24)

And she offers as an example the work ¡Otra maldita novela sobre la Guerra Civil! by Isaac Rosa, a novel well known for its use of that technique, in which he creates a first novel to which he returns reflexively and, alongside the action, offers a reflection on the writing process in which he "comments on the successes and naïveties of the novel of his youth, and recalls how and why he wrote it" (Alameda 2007, 24).

In the case of Kirmen Uribe's work, passages are recalled in which the author comments on the story line of his work and his purpose behind writing it. There are three different passages. Already in the first chapter there is a statement about the direction that the author wants to give the novel:

> . . . Several years ago, I started tracking down the clues. I felt that *Dos Amigos* had a novel somewhere inside it, a novel about the fishing world that's in the process of disappearing. But this was the plan only at the outset. And the search for facts for the novel has taken me down several roads I hadn't expected. (*Bilbao-New York-Bilbao*, 15)

Later, he says something similar to Renata, who is sitting next to him in the plane taking them to New York, as regards the initial idea of a literary work:

> "My first idea was to write about my grandfather's boat. And simultaneously, about a way of life that's in the process of getting lost. The way of life that's bound up with the sea. The name of the boat is suggestive too. *Dos Amigos*. Two Friends."
>
> "Really nice."
> "I've always wanted to know why our granddad named his boat that. I've been looking into who that alleged friend of his was, but nothing's come clear." (*Bilbao-New York-Bilbao*, 91)

Yet in chapter 15, in response to a publisher's question, the author offers a more complete version of the central argument. Now he still speaks about a narration that follows the story of a family, but a new element is introduced: fragmentation as a form of writing a work that distances itself from the nineteenth-century novel and in which the writing project takes on a specific importance that it did not have in the two previous descriptions:

> The idea had gone on evolving, I said, and finally I'd be setting everything on a flight between Bilbao and New

> York. How else would I talk about three generations of a family without going back to some nineteenth-century novel? I told her about the process of writing the novel and in bits, in very small bits, stories of the three generations. (*Bilbao-New York-Bilbao*, 119)

Here there are two important changes with respect to the two notes with which the author summed up the story line (mentioned above). First, he attends to the "writing process" as an important part of the narration, and which probably is associated with having to use autofiction in the novel. And second, it is no longer a question of recounting a "story" or a "way of life," but short "stories"—now without any teleological aim—about the generations that make up the family, which, incidentally, are the generations of the grandfather, the father, Kirmen Uribe himself, and that of his son Unai, which makes four generations rather than three.

Yet as well as recounting the main story line, the autofictional author-narrator (a technique that we will not discuss, due to it being beyond the scope of this work) talks, above all at the beginning of the work, about the vicissitudes he experienced in order to write the novel. For example, he recalls the first interviews he carried out in order to get information:

> [Maritxu is] the youngest of our grandmother Ana's sisters. When I took up the project of the novel for the umpteenth time, in the spring of 2005, Maritxu was the first person I interviewed [. . .] When I paid her a visit, I heard stories I'd never, ever heard before, ones Dad never told us. (*Bilbao-New York-Bilbao*, 17–18)

The reference to Carmen Bastida, Ricardo's daughter who would offer the author key information about the history of his family, is similar: "Nerea and I had gone to visit Carmen at the house in Bilbao" (*Bilbao-New York-Bilbao*, 32).

Something resemblant happens when the author contacts José Julián Bakedano, a curator at the Bilbao Fine Arts Museum, and, to a lesser extent (given that in this case the communication takes place via email), with Professor Javier Kalzakorta, and with Eneko Barrutia. In other words, the author-narrator explains the process of gathering material.

Yet the reflection on the process does not end there. The character-author asks questions about the opportunity to make a choice, or not, at a crossroads, as happened to Arteta when he was offered the chance to paint something on the topic of the bombing of Gernika, and he reflects on the need a budding writer has for support:

> A writer needs protection. Especially at the beginning. He wants to gain confidence, to hear from outside that he's on the right track, hasn't made the wrong decision at that last crossroads. (*Bilbao-New York-Bilbao*, 37)

In contrast to more intimate notes, the author-narrator also seeks meaning in his writing through the stories that other writers tell him, such as in chapter 11, "The Gravestones in Käsmu," in which the writers' retreat serves Uribe to reflect on modernity and the capacity of new technologies to create distinct aesthetics:

> Our small cultures had to get renewed. The ways of doing things renewed. To adapt to the times. The medium has changed. Nowadays it's not just books. Right there, you've got your new technologies. And who's on the receiving end has changed too. No one was writing solely for the fellow members of their own community now. (*Bilbao-New York-Bilbao*, 88)

It could be that the passage contains a declaration in favor of the Internet, which the author undertakes enthusiastically, and an affirmation of seeking a readership outside the Basque community. If anything defines Kirmen Uribe's aesthetics, it is his resolve to depart the Basque Country and explore important questions for all peoples, and that is evinced in his second novel, *Mussche* (*Lo que mueve el mundo*), which takes place in Europe, addresses the topic of anti-Nazi resistance in Belgium, and explores the symbol of international solidarity, all as a form of creating a literature which is not just centered on the Basque Country and its circumstances.

There is a technique in the novel *Bilbao-New York-Bilbao* that I will term indirect, which is linked to all those mentioned thus far in highlighting the creative process. It is a question of seeking the assistance of other artists to describe the aesthetic foundations of the work itself. Thus, for example, the film *Entre les murs* is mentioned because it is a likeness, a parallel the author wants to draw: blending and linking, by means of autofiction, truth and fiction, and moving nimbly between two spheres. He says: "The movie's a fiction, a film that looks like a documentary" (*Bilbao-New York-Bilbao*, 121), in which the actors represent their real lives.

But the novel itself explores the play between reality and fiction, the evident creation of the text which the writing process describes, in a more symbolic passage, as I understand it, than that which mentions the French film. It is the allusion to the painting "St. Francis in the Desert" by Giovanni Bellini, signed by the author on a fictitious bit of paper painted into a corner of the painting itself. The reflection the writer makes recalls that which he made at the beginning of the novel regarding Arteta's mural, but in this case it is more eloquent. Bellini's real name written into the painting on a represented, fictitious piece of paper leads Kirmen Uribe to ask himself about the importance of autofiction:

> That detail gave me something to think about. How I had to deal with the narration of the novel. How to speak about those closest to me without appearing myself. I had to talk about my grandfather, my father, my mother. Put my world on the page. But how to do that? Was I

> supposed to invent a set of mendacious names or was I myself going to appear in the novel as storyteller? (*Bilbao-New York-Bilbao*, 126)

The quote is loaded with all the meaning that Kirmen Uribe promotes in his aesthetics, and once the novel was published one could see how he resolved this issue which is at the root of his narration: How to shape the figure of the narrator and his voice? The answer is obvious: the author opted for autofiction in a novel which, at the same time, tells stories, explains how these stories and not others were chosen, and the way he did so.

6 Fragmentation and speed

Let us now leave Irene Zoé Alameda's theoretical work and focus on what the author says. In a recent interview with Caroline Conejero, Kirmen Uribe insists on fragmentation as one of the most important characteristics of his aesthetics.

> Kirmen Uribe is especially interested in literary experimentation, as if the novel were a canvas on which to set about placing objects, a space in which to blend fiction and reality, different points of view with diverse narrative techniques. And leaving to the reader the role of finishing off the jigsaw means not leaving everything done and finished.
>
> According to Uribe, this narrative matches the present moment, in which communications are in part shaped by the Internet and social media. A channel through which stories pass fragmented into installments of times and styles. (Conejero 2018, 84)

The declaration returns to the conviction that the use of the Internet has changed the way of telling and conceiving narration. But in addition to that faith in new technologies as producers of new forms of writing, the writer puts forward some of the key aspects of his narrative: fragmentation and mobility, two intimately linked elements.

Resorting to fragments brings with it mobility in the focus of narrative threads; that is, fragmentation implies a constant change in the matters to be considered, the stories to be told, within leaps in space and time. The definition Vicente Luis Mora makes of the postmodern novel is an apt reflection of the aesthetic characteristics influencing Uribe's novel:

> A. Time: fragmented, discontinuous.
> B. Subject: mosaic or multiple.
> C. Notes: pop, non-sublime, decanonization, blend of high and low culture [. . .].
> D. *Topoi*: nodes of communication between cities, spaces or fictitious or symbolic cities and global and local sites at the same time.
> E. Concept of truth: questioned. Falsifiability is transferred to the narrator and the poetic I is fictionalized. Semiology emerges and it stops concerning itself with the concept of truth, although the latter does still exist [. . .].
> F. The postmodern type novel would have this general shape: it would be a spatially and temporarily disintegrated novel; it would tend to disjointedness [. . .] It would have a notable thematic presence of audio-visual references [. . .] Finally, the postmodern novel would possibly have a very open ending and avoid moralizing at all costs; it would be a work tending more toward playfulness than to ethical reflection. (Mora 2007, 29–30)

Nevertheless, *Bilbao-New York-Bilbao* shares with the pangeic novel a key element:

> The pangeic *type* novel is not yet definable, but it should have at least some of these textual features: the structural presence of expressive visual resources from the electronic mass communication media, the adoption of the image

> (positive—a drawing or photograph—or negative—a correction) as one *more* element of discourse. (Mora 2007, 73)

The first few chapters in *Bilbao-New York-Bilbao* clearly demonstrate that wandering through memory, through consciousness, and through writing, which recalls that "subconscious evocation" to which Irene Zoé Alameda refers. The unmotivated union of the surrealists is echoed in the mobility of topic, space, and time.

Let us see some examples. In chapter 5, discontinuous stories are threaded together. The narrator refers to the importance of protection at the start of a writer's career, which leads him to consult his father, who uses the parable of the two priests that offer different kinds of sermons in order to reflect on two forms of writing: one which describes, and one which suggests. Here the narrator introduces the subject of memory and how it works, and places the focus on a family story that alludes to a disaster at sea in 1908. This event constructs a link to the story told by Aunt Maritxu, whose memory had altered locations, moving the drowning of her grandfather and uncle to Ondarroa, although it had actually happened in Santander, and the thread of memory in the hand of history jumps from family to towns and relates the story of an emigrant to Latin America and his Peruvian wife in Elorrio, and the changes that memory (and the interpretation of events) cause in real history (*Bilbao-New York-Bilbao*, 37–42).

In another example, the narrator-author goes out fishing with his uncles. While they are fishing, he remembers that they were fishermen in Venezuela and the narrator-author asks them how they got there, and the uncles answer him. They talk about an incident with the Venezuelan military which commandeered the boat, and they continue telling stories such as that about Franco's arrival in Bilbao and the manipulation of a propaganda film. They continue to fish, while the author-narrator refers to the story that opens the chapter. Gestures are noted and recalled which do not exist today. And when they arrive back to port, one of the uncles hands the author-narrator a document that tells the story of the name *Dos Amigos* and "there was no mystery at all." Grandfather Liborio had nothing to do with the name. It already had it when he bought it (*Bilbao-New York-Bilbao*, 162–166).

This switching between fiction and reality, this play between past and present, the narrative techniques which introduce stories within stories, and the changes in space recall the game that someone plays when they surf the Internet, going from page to page, jumping from one to another, without spending too much time on any one site.

Surfing the Internet. Surfing *Bilbao-New York-Bilbao*.

Bibliography

Alameda, Irene Zoé. 2007. La era Gates y la reinvención del lenguaje. *Cuadernos Hispanoamericanos* 668, X: 11–28.

Conejero, Caroline. 2018. La novela de Uribe en Nueva York. *El Correo*. September 25, 2018.

Kortazar, Jon. 2013. *Contemporary Basque Literature: Kirmen Uribe's Proposal*. Madrid-Frankfurt: Iberoamericana/ Vervuert.

Mora, Vicente Luis. 2006. *Pangea. Internet, blogs y comunicación en un mundo nuevo*. Sevilla: Fundación José Manuel de Lara.

Mora, Vicente Luis. 2007. *La luz nueva*. Córdoba: Berenice.

Pozuelo Yvancos, José María. 2007. Llega la estética del blog. *ABCD de las Artes y de las Letras*. January 6, 2007.

Ong, Walter. 1987. *Oralidad y escritura*. México: Fondo de Cultura Económica.

Uribe, Kirmen. 2008. *Bilbao-New York-Bilbao*. Donostia: Elkar.

7

The origins of what I am: Family, collective, and historical memory in the narrative of Kirmen Uribe

José Martínez Rubio

1 A recognizable formula

After many texts and many interpretations in the new millennium (or not so new now) there is a recognized *incipit* by readers which has a double virtue: on the one hand, it refers to a novelistic (by now) tradition of investigation, in the same way that the formula of the discovered manuscript struck gold through the centuries; and on the other, it shapes a text strategically and narratively which is assembled on the basis of the tension among different pairings, since it will contain at the same time reality and fiction, it will appeal to the present through the past, or it will combine fictitious and non-fictitious categories, in such a way that the characters in the action blend together with the author and even, occasionally, with readers themselves.

This formula could be demonstrated in the following way:

> I found the first mention of Filek in *Franco: A Biography*, the monumental biography of the dictator written by Paul Preston. There were barely ten sentences, and therein it was noted how the Austrian had gained Franco's trust and convinced him of the qualities of his invention: a fuel superior in quality to petrol, created on the basis of a mixture of water and plant extracts and other secret

> ingredients. [. . .] The first thing I thought was that there was a good story there. (Martínez de Pisón 2018, 7)

That is how Ignacio Martínez de Pisón begins to tell the story of the life of Filek, in *Filek. El estafador que engañó a Franco* (2018). Almost as a preliminary note, almost as paratext (paratext?), the narrator (perhaps author?) reveals how he discovered by chance Filek's name and, above all, how he reworked his story on the basis of the 1920s and 1930s, and the fraud that he perpetrated in order to trick the intellectual leadership of the Franco regime. That narrator's voice, the voice of whom discovers the case, appears in a timely manner throughout the novel (novel?) in which the life of this Austrian chemist is detailed. And at the same time as that narrator voice allows the biographical story to be transmitted, it introduces conjectures about Filek's travels in Spain, it details the clues that he follows about Filek's activity, it presents documents which corroborate all of the above, and it sanctions the most probable hypotheses. The final result is a biography discussed by the biographer, a life which unfolds in parallel to the voice that discovers it; in sum, it is a novel in which the reader is conscious both of the outcome of the story and of the work undertaken in elaborating the discourse.

To put it another way, in *Filek* (and in this type of investigation novel), the literature does not contain only one story about reality at the ontological level, but, moreover, it undertakes an epistemological reflection on the capacity to recognize and, ultimately, project a deontological position on how to manage in the present that traumatic or recoverable inheritance which history has bequeathed us. From that same deontology, many writers, and especially those who are part of the current memory novel, have presented their works either as a means of raising awareness (even on the basis of work-in-progress narrative) or as a tool for knowledge.

It is not by chance or whim that I have added question marks to some key aspects of such narrations. Is the narrator-investigator a category of fiction? Has the author as a truthful category or the autofictional game been so in vogue in recent decades? Are the initial pages of the novel the prior note to the narration, the paratext, or, given that there is no signal, are they assimilated as a motor of the story within the novelistic plot? Is the end result a biography—that is, a non-fiction text in which the author may be accused of lying in the event of introducing false data or poetic license? Or a novel—a fictional text in which the author is qualified to write about or even invent something? It is, then, a kind of text about the past, about the capacity of the past to intervene in the present, and how ambiguous novels, in the words of Manuel Alberca (2007), call into question the categories of author, narrator and fiction itself, in such a way that readers never know for sure if it is the author's story or not, or if what they are reading was true or the result of an invention on the part of the person who wrote it.

Ignacio Martínez de Pisón's work, published in April 2018, is the perfect example of what in another work I termed the "writer's investigation novel" (Martínez Rubio 2015). From then until the moment I write this, only three years have passed, and the formula, far from waning, has continued to produce numerous variants. While in 2015 there were around thirty novels in the Hispanic, transatlantic, and Iberian context[62]

62 In order of publication: Juan Manuel de Prada, *Las esquinas del aire* (2000); Javier Cercas, *Soldados de Salamina* (2001); Carme Riera, *La meitat de l'ànima* (2004); Isaac Rosa, *El vano ayer* (2004); Juan Gabriel Vásquez, *Los informantes* (2004); Ignacio Martínez de Pisón, *Enterrar a los muertos* (2005); Javier Cercas, *La velocidad de la luz* (2005); Benjamín Prado, *Mala gente que camina* (2006); Francesc Bayarri, *Cita a Sarajevo* (2006); Isaac Rosa, ¡Otra maldita novela sobre la *Guerra Civil!* (2007); Jordi Soler, *La fiesta del oso* (2009); Jordi Soler, *Anatomía de un instante* (2009); Rodrigo Rey Rosa, *El material humano* (2009); Leonardo Padura, *El hombre que amaba a los perros* (2009); Elvira Cambrils, *El bes de l'aigua* (2010); Kirmen Uribe, *Bilbao-New York-Bilbao* (2010); Clara Sánchez, *Lo que esconde tu nombre* (2010); Juan Gabriel Vásquez, *El ruido de las cosas al caer* (2011); Justo Navarro, *El espía* (2011); Alberto Fuguet, *Missing* (2011); Patricio Pron, *El espíritu de mis padres sigue subiendo en la lluvia* (2011); Leopoldo Brizuela, *Una misma noche* (2012); Kirmen Uribe, *Mussche,* (2012); Pablo Martín Sánchez, *El anarquista que se llamaba como yo* (2013); Paco Roca, *Los surcos del azar* (2013); Jaime Martín, *Las guerras silenciosas* (2014); Javier Cercas, *El impostor* (2014); and Rafael Reig, *Un árbol caído* (2015).

which displayed this kind of investigation, in 2018, one would have to revise this and include a dozen more novels[63] such as:[64]

La abuela civil española, Andrea Stefanoni, 2015
Chicas muertas, Selva Almada, 2015
Les darreres paraules, Carme Riera, 2016
La hora de despertarnos juntos, Kirmen Uribe, 2016
El monarca de las sombras, Javier Cercas, 2017
Carmen de Mairena. Una biografía, Carlota Juncosa, 2017
El salto de papá, Martín Sivak, 2017
Filek. El estafador que engañó a Franco, I. Martínez de Pisón, 2018
El asesino tímido, Clara Usón, 2018
Doble fondo, Elsa Osorio, 2018
Honrarás a tu padre y a tu madre, Cristina Fallarás, 2018
El dolor de los demás, Miguel Ángel Hernández, 2018

Were we to open up our perspective to other formulas of inquiry, could we incorporate as remembrances (Martínez Rubio 2013) *El comensal* by Gabriela Ybarra (2015) and *Mejor la ausencia* by Edurne Portela (2017), in order to recover—via memory and tracking of the past itself—family and childhood stories of the narrators and authors?

Such a profusion of variants in this type of narration demonstrates some things: first, the indefatigable fascination with a past in which stories abound that demand being rescued from forgetting on the part of post-memory generations (Hirsch, 1997); second, the ethical use of those stories from the past to replenish that historical memory which may give us human and political instruments to define the collective story of our community in the present; and third, the narratological interest in blending elements, techniques, and strategies (Schilschke and

63 And incorporate into the period 2000–2015 novels such as: Ernesto Semán, *Soy un bravo piloto de la nueva China* (2011); Maria Teresa Andruetto, *Lengua madre* (2010); Elsa Osorio, *La Capitana* (2012); Leila Guerriero, *Una historia sencilla*, (2013).

64 And partially *Patria o muerte* by Alberto Barrera Tyszka (2015).

Schmelzer 2011) which belong to those fictional stories and non-fiction stories in search of discourse authenticity. Memory, reality, and narrative ambiguity continue to inundate the second decade of the twenty-first century.

2 Kirmen Uribe, investigator and writer

A quick and prototypical definition of the "writer's investigation novel" could be the following: A "casual element" sparks in someone sufficient curiosity to make them carry out a more or less methodical investigation in order to unearth a story that remained hidden or forgotten. That person who investigates—a journalist, writer, doctoral student, teacher, etc. (an etc. outside classic detective fiction)—culminates their investigation, satisfies (or not) their curiosity, and only after this process, begins the task of writing, so that the final novel, as I noted above, relates that case investigated as well as the investigation itself.

More than a decade ago, in 2007, Isaac Rosa already recognized and criticized the formula in *Otra maldita novela sobre la guerra civil*:

> Too exposed. Dozens of examples spring to mind only among novels in recent years. A writer at a low ebb comes across an old story by chance from whose narrative thread they will draw until they discover a terrible drama and some fascinating characters–one of whom, still alive, will give them a complete human and moral lesson in the final pages. Following her father's death, a woman, right in the middle of a personal crisis, devotes herself to reconstructing the dramatic family story from the papers and photographs she finds in a trunk in the attic. A journalist investigates a case of local corruption and ends up uncovering a civil-war-like drama. A disenchanted alcoholic policeman takes charge of a murder case in a small village in the heart of Spain whose plot leads to a

> long-deferred story of wartime revenge. And like these, many more similar plots that any reader may have in mind. (Rosa 2007, 24)[65]

Kirmen Uribe is part of this short "tradition" of writers-investigators. In *Bilbao-New York-Bilbao* (2014, English version), the autofictitious narrator decides to trace, during a transatlantic journey and following the death of his father, the story of his grandfather, Liborio Uribe, and that of a boat called *Dos Amigos*. That investigation, which includes documents, diaries, tapes, paintings, photographs, oral memory about fishermen in the area, email exchanges, Google searches, and Wikipedia information, ends by revealing the meaning of the "war between Basques" (Uribe 2014, 124) which the Spanish Civil War hid, the "wrong" choice of his grandfather, as well as the lives of the architect Ricardo Bastida and the painter Aurelio Arteta. The trigger for the story, again, is ignorance, mystery, and curiosity:

> About my grandfather I don't know too much. Liborio Uribe. By the time I was born he was dead and our father didn't talk to us a lot about his father. He wasn't big on the past, himself. A seaman by nature, he preferred to look to the future. About the people in our mother's family, on the contrary, yes: we knew a thousand tales from Mum's side, stories about one relation and another. But on our dad's side very few. Maybe because of this, that grandfather made me curious. (Uribe 2014, 14)

Chance and curiosity (that recognizable formula, that newly found manuscript) are the circumstances which will trigger the protagonist's investigation, the process of which is narrated in the first person. Besides that inquiry, the narrator asks himself what is the best way to narrate that flooding of memory which has been buried for so long by silence and which unnerves him because he does not share the same ideas as his grandfather.

65 Translated by Cameron Watson.

Yet, at the same time, he reflects on the value of memory and connects his generational experience to the symbolic-mythical stories of his place of origin, to the family landscape, to the history of his town, to Basque identity in the transnational global era (Kortazar Billelabeitia 2012), and, especially, to Euskara, the Basque language,[66] thereby tracing a physical and emotional journey into the past (Bilbao) and toward the future (New York). In other words, Uribe constructs "a story which demonstrates an autobiographical connection to a past linked to a memory measured and formed by multiple layers" (Norgaard 2014, 274) and, as a last resort, he seeks to track the past ontologically, to show epistemologically the mistakes and virtues of memory and of the data, and to define himself, deontologically, as a Basque linked to a family, a strong identity, and a postmodern time.

Kirmen Uribe carries out a similar exercise in *Mussche* (2012), or *Lo que mueve el mundo* (its title in Spanish, "What moves the world," 2013). On this occasion, family memory gives way to collective memory and historical memory, understood as that mosaic of individual and family fragments which make up and shape a specific time and community, coordinated in concrete historical events (Halbwachs 1968). The story recovered is that of Robert Mussche, the Belgian writer who in 1937 took in, in his house in Ghent, Karmentxu Cundin, a Basque girl among the 4,500 that set sail from Bilbao aboard the ship *Habana*, by order of the lehendakari (Basque president) José Antonio Agirre, in order to save them from fascist bombardments and the violence of the war. Belgium became one of the countries that took in refugees, especially children who were evacuated from the Basque Country, during the Spanish Civil War.

Another prototypical feature of investigation novels is to be found in the indistinct use of fictional and non-fiction materials, as if they were documents which accredited the truth under investigation (Martínez Rubio 2012). Thus, the narrator

66 The latter two aspects have been analyzed in detail in Nafría Fernández, María Jesús (2014): "*Bilbao-New York-Bilbao*: Un viaje por el universo literario de Kirmen Uribe." *Revista de lenguas y literaturas catalana, gallega y vasca*, vol. 19, 267–287.

begins to know and relate that story from the past by means of distinct resources: the somewhat doubtful stories of the Mirante sisters, and the letters and photographs kept by Carmen Mussche, the writer's daughter. Among the gaps left by the documents, imagination colonizes the true facts, introducing readers into an ambiguous world of docufiction (Martínez Rubio 2014).

Once again, besides the will to recover history, the narrator-investigator confronts the problem of how to communicate it:

> "I had not written anything for months," I told him, "and I did not even know what my next book was going to be like. The death of a great friend had left me completely devastated. That loss coincided with the arrival of our youngest daughter. I felt disoriented, on the one hand happy, on the other sad. Of course I knew some stories about the children of the war, their experiences had always attracted my attention, but it was very complicated to relate them as they should be." (Uribe 2013, 212)

Robert Mussche's story allows the narrator to get acquainted with one of the most painful and, at the same time, human episodes of the civil war: the evacuation and reception of the children by numerous families across Europe, Mexico, and the Soviet Union. Beyond historical interest, Uribe suggests fiction as a commitment to the memory (Nafría 2017) of those children and those families: a humanitarian legacy which projects the values of Human Rights in the present. Thinking about that act implies an "affiliative act" (Faber 2014), in whose values the narrator, and, by extension, the author—and, in the best-case scenario, the reader—recognize themselves. Thus, ontology, epistemology, and deontology combine once more in a text which jumps from the historical to the emotional and from the verified to the imagined, in a limitless ambiguity and in which the most important truth overcomes the limits of the verified and the contrasted.

La hora de despertarnos juntos (its title in Spanish, "The Hour of Waking Together," 2016) picks up once more some of the elements, techniques, and strategies, not just of the so-called writer's investigation novel, but also some characteristics with which Kirmen Uribe constructed his previous novels. This occurs at the start of the novel in a protocolic way:

> Some stories live in the writer's head for a long time, even years, before seeing the light of day. In that interval, most of them fade away, right there, lost in the depths of the mind, without coming to life, but a few, however, remain latent forever.
>
> This is one of those stories.
>
> The Urresti family had been spoken about a lot at home. [. . .] I remember the day well, during my time at university, on which Ikerne, accompanied by her mother, Karmele Urresti, visited us in our family home in Ondarroa. [. . .] The background to that conversation stuck in my mind and, over the years, far from forgetting, it sparked my interest in and concern about the subject, simply because I understood that Karmele's experiences, everything that happened to her, that era, that context, also formed part of my own history and lurked in the history of who I am, the seed of my identity. As is typically said, we are not isolated beings, but children of our time, of our education, of our culture, but also, in the same way, children of the past. [. . .] It was not until 2010 when I convinced myself that I had to write a book based on the life of Karmele Urresti. (Uribe 2016, 9–11)

Once again, we come across well-known elements: a story in the past which deserves to be told, a voice that takes on the ethical commitment to tell it, an identity that gets mixed up with identities from the past, and a key moment in which inquiry and writing are activated. It will be a painting (an element that also appears in *Bilbao-New York-Bilbao*) exhibited at the Bilbao Fine Arts Museum that contains the first clues: *Noche de artistas en Ibaigane* (Night of Artists in Ibaigane), by Antonio Gezala, recreates an entertaining evening gathering at a well-to-do home, at which the guests dance a cakewalk, a fashionable dance in the 1920s. The painting features Txomin Letamendi Murua, the future husband of Karmele Urresti, and the painting will be one of the multiple documents (together with letters, announcements, medical certificates, images, and diaries) used to detail the existence both of Karmele Urresti, a nurse, Basque nationalist, and exile in Venezuela, and Txomin Letamendi, a trumpeter and *gudari* (Basque soldier) captain, a political prisoner in Franco's Spain who dies in Carabanchel prison.

The unpleasant life experiences of Karmele and Txomin allow the narrator to inquire into interwar Ondarroa and the Basque Country, the cultural life of the capital Bilbao, as well as to go through the tragic history of the civil war and Francoism. That inquiry not only retells the biography of two real figures with novelesque avatars, but also the biographies of *lehendakari* Agirre (who also appears in *Lo que mueve el mundo*) and the shipowner Manu Sota, who owned the largest shipping firm at the beginning of the century and who organized the transport to evacuate the refugees during the war, such as those involved in tours by the Basque national football team and those performing folkloric shows put on by the Eresoinka group, as a kind of cultural embassy for the Basque Country. It was precisely at one of those shows that Karmele and Txomin met and their biographies would intermingle through the Spanish Civil War, exile, and the Second World War, until the latter's death in Carabanchel.

Clearly, *La hora de despertarnos juntos* persists in the will of the author to attach himself to "affiliative" pasts as a part of his identity. The recovery of characters, figures, and scenes from the past, which is very closely connected to his place of origin and intermingled in the conflicts that continue to assess the weight of memory in our country, attempts to help define a solution of continuity with the identity of the present. In that sense, the writing is triggered by both aesthetic and ethical reasons, renovating that commitment to the memory (family, collective, or historical) that we observed in Kirmen Uribe's previous novels. We read an exploration of the lives of Karmele and Txomin and we recreate, at the same time, a symbolic-mythical past about Basque tradition, which has been cut short by forty years of the Franco dictatorship, and that only now, through democracy and through the exercise of memory and literature, is open to being rescued and valued.

That narrative voice, which leads the investigation into Karmele and Txomin, will appear at the beginning of the novel and continue during its course, although it gradually gives way to the biographies of Urresti and Letamendi. It will also trace out clues, open up or close down possibilities, work out conjectures, and present possibilities for understanding a lost history: that of a family pierced by a civil war and a world war, which moves between Ondarroa, Paris, and Venezuela, which suffers exile, and which contributes to the struggle against Franco by carrying out espionage tasks.

As part of both the autofictitious and docu-fictitious tension, the final note will contribute to placing us once more in that ambiguity of representation, in which we do not know if the page that we are reading belongs to the world of history or the world of fiction:

> This is a novel and the logic it follows is that of fiction. Even so, as every single one of the characters that appears in this book is real and, equally, the story they are involved in is true, I have taken the license to imagine and fictionalize some of the landscapes and dialogues which appear in the novel. (Uribe 2016, 439)

Novel? Fictionalized biographies? How much truth does imagination contain? What degree of license is an artist allowed before they may be accused of manipulating the truth, the past, and history? What legitimacy does this kind of story accomplish? These are pertinent questions, and they deserve a complex response which attempts to determine what part of the fiction and what part of the non-fiction is necessary in order to configure a new category of "truth" on the literary level.

3 Conclusion

In Kirmen Uribe's literary investigations we find a representation that oscillates between veracity and imagination, a symbiosis that novels with ambiguous fictional norms have promoted in recent years. That ambiguity, moreover, is constructed simultaneously both with the representation of the past and with the explicit presentation of the process of understanding of and inquiry into the case. And of course, the ambiguity increases with the appearance of a narrative voice which is blended together in a premeditated way with the author and which talks about past and present, but which, moreover, conjectures on, comments on, and takes a position on the ethical questions raised in the novel. That narrative ploy, this writer's investigation novel, contains not just an investigation but a reflection on the best way to relate what is important for our individual, family, and collective identities. The fact that there is a writer both catalyzes the raising of awareness on the part of the author and the reader with respect to some events in the past, and mediates the ethical and political commitment of the writing. It is an ethical and political commitment for which it is necessary to trace and rebuild the roots of identity itself, inserting it within Basque collective identity. In order to do that, Uribe's inquiries enter into the meanders of family memory, collective memory, and historical memory, three variants of inquiry into the past that allow him to insert himself into an ancestry, a people, and a historical moment that is the heir to successive events which have shaped the lives of his forebears.

Kirmen Uribe connects to that rich literary tradition from the beginnings of the millennium. A tradition which is on the way to completing two decades, which goes beyond the Hispanic world to other traditions (Roberto Saviano, Emmanuel Carrère, Goran Vojnović) and other languages (documentary film, television, and comic books, to name a few, in which often the "truth" recounted is told by a presenter, journalist, or researcher, to themselves, in search of the truth).

I am not interested so much in detecting the extent to which there is a formula in these novels, nor how accurately the blueprint is used in the different variants. It seems to me much more intriguing to demonstrate that there is literature which is committed to understanding the past, that there is a new generation of narrators that is delving into the buried history of our communities in order to rescue histories and scenes which have a value that transcends the literary, and that recovery is helping to redefine our identities and calibrate the values of freedom, generosity, and humanity, on the one hand, and pain, suffering, and injustice on the other. We encounter these values in a literature that seeks to be a weapon of the future once more. And it does so, above all, through speaking about and raising awareness of our past.

Bibliography

Alberca, Manuel. 2007. *El pacto ambiguo: de la novela autobiográfica a la autoficción*. Madrid: Biblioteca Nueva.

Faber, Sebastiaan. 2014. Actos afiliativos y postmemoria: Asuntos pendientes. *Pasavento. Revista de Estudios Hispánicos* 2. lib, 1: 137–155.

Kortazar Billelabeitia, Paulo. 2012. *Bilbao-New York-Bilbao* de Kirmen Uribe: postmodernidad, nuevas tecnologías de la comunicación y modernismo tras la postmodernidad. *Oihenart: cuadernos de lengua y literatura* 27: 67–80.

Halbwachs, Maurice. 1968. *La mémoire collective*. Paris: PUF.

Hirsch, Marianne. 1997. Family Frames: Photography, Narrative and Postmemory. Cambridge, Massachusetts & London: Harvard University Press.

Martínez de Pisón, Ignacio. 2018. *Filek. El estafador que engañó a Franco*. Barcelona: Seix Barral.

Martínez Rubio, José. 2012. Del documento como verdad al documento como mentira: apropiaciones de la ficción en la novela española actual. In *La tinta en la clepsidra. Fuentes, historia y tradición en la literatura hispánica*, Sònia Boadas, Félix Ernesto Chávez & Daniel García Vicens (ed.), 413–422. Barcelona: PPU.

Martínez Rubio, José. 2014. Autoficción y docuficción como propuestas de sentido. Razones culturales para la representación ambigua. *Castilla. Estudios de literatura* 5: 26–38.

Martínez Rubio, José. 2015. *Las formas de la verdad. Investigación, docuficción y memoria en la novela hispánica*. Barcelona: Anthropos.

Nafría Fernández, María Jesús. 2014. *Bilbao-New York-Bilbao*: Un viaje por el universo literario de Kirmen Uribe. *Revista de lenguas y literaturas catalana, gallega y vasca* 19. lib.: 267–287.

Nafría Fernández, María Jesús. 2017. La responsabilidad del autor en un contexto de crisis: Kirmen Uribe y el compromiso con la memoria. *Revista de lenguas y literaturas catalana, gallega y vasca* 22. lib.: 155–168.

Norgaard, Palle. 2014. Autoficción y autoridad en la memoria: *Bilbao-New York-Bilbao* de Kirmen Uribe. In *El yo fabulado. Nuevas aproximaciones críticas a la autoficción*, Ana Casas (ed.), 268–269. Madrid: Iberoamericana-Vervuert.

Rosa, Isaac. 2007. *¡Otra maldita novela sobre la guerra civil!* Barcelona: Seix Barral.

Uribe, Kirmen. 2008. *Bilbao-New York-Bilbao*. Donostia: Elkar.
Uribe, Kirmen. 2012. *Mussche*. Zarautz: Susa.
Uribe, Kirmen. 2016. *Elkarrekin esnatzeko ordua*. Zarautz: Susa.

8

Kirmen Uribe's displacements

Luis Martín-Estudillo

Displacement is one of the central notions in Kirmen Uribe's narrative. This chapter addresses its dual meaning in the first three novels by the author from Ondarroa. On the one hand, in its ethical and historical dimension, which Uribe deals with by means of focusing on characters in movement owing to political and economic pressures. On the other, in its aesthetic dimension, in whose sphere displacement is understood as the realization of a series of formal features (fragmentariness, polyphony, etc.) which fit together with an anti-dogmatic idea of literature and have characterized an important portion of Western fiction during the last half century. Displacement has also been a particularly productive concept in poststructuralist thought. In prioritizing this dual displacement, Uribe's narrative is situated in a tradition that, in the European context, we associate with artistic options opposed to exclusivist or reactionary discourses in the face of mobility phenomena which are especially significant in the human geography of the continent.

Toward the end of Kirmen Uribe's work *Mussche*, the narrator visits the son of Flemish writer Herman Thiery, better known by his pseudonym, Johan Daisne. The conversation about Daisne's work and experiences within the tumultuous Europe of the 1940s leads the characters to consider the way in which some extreme circumstances, like war, provoke a forced fluidity, from which it seems like nothing or nobody can be extracted. "In a war everything that was previously solid—a home, family, work, absolutely everything—is turned upside down. Nothing is fixed, which obliges people to act in another way. They experience things more profoundly [. . .]" (216). Fluidity is associated, therefore, with a particularly intense form of experience which will be of literary interest for Uribe. Thereafter, on being asked about *Baratzeartea*, the title of one of Daisne's novels, Evert Thiery replies:

> —As far as I know, my father travelled to the French Basque Country, apparently to visit a writer friend. He heard it there, and they told him what "*baratzeartea*" meant: the narrow bit of ground between a house and vegetable patch.
> —A border between two worlds . . .
> —Yes, my father liked those divisions: everyday life and desire, life and death. He was always in that space. His literature is also like that. (217)

Out of a journey—perhaps the most obvious form of fluidity, of displacement—came an encounter. And in that encounter there appeared a word, *baratzeartea*, which once again accentuated a borderland, a transitional space, which ended up becoming the title of a novel published in 1962. Its full title, which the narrator omits, includes thereafter "*een baskisch avontuur of de roman van een schrijver*" (a Basque adventure, or a writer's novel). It is curious that Daisne and Uribe coincide in both terms: the latter has dedicated many pages to the experiences of Basques, who appear to leave clear traces in the writing process; that is how one would have to understand the apparent pleonasm implied by *a writer's novel.*

As well as an appreciation of the literature of the Flemish author, these sentences in *Lo que mueve el mundo* include an idea that serves, likewise, to characterize a significant part of Kirmen Uribe's own writing. The key word in the passage cited, I would surmise, is *between*. In the same way as in the case of the literature of his character Daisne (who, like several others in Uribe's pages, is researched, on the basis of his historical existence, in order to be later fictionalized), Uribe's work also demonstrates a strong interest in exploring those interstices: it aims its attention especially at the displacement between eras (such as "the leap from old world to new" in his first novel (*Bilbao-New York-Bilbao*, 10)), between geographical spaces, between stages of life . . . Even between life and death, as evinced by the passages which he dedicates to the interval between the physical disappearance of a person and their dissipation in the memory of those who knew them.

In an essay with an important component of self-reflection, Uribe defines himself (following Claudio Magris) as "a borderland writer" ("El idioma de la Virgen María de la playa" 21). This word, "border," also figures in the fragment cited above: that *baratzeartea* is thus defined as "A border between two worlds . . ." (217). He is a borderland author who explores the interstices of life, stressing the displacements that run through them. At the end of the day, an interstice is a place of transition, of passing through, which fosters displacement. In this chapter I focus on some variants of this rich notion, *displacement*, particularly on its meaning in Uribe's narrative work. The author himself has called attention to the relevance it has for him: "I write from the Basque Country, my homeland is the Basque language; but in my books, I always tend toward migration, toward the displacement of people. I am inclined to make my characters move around the world, something which is constant in these times" (n.p.: 2017). I understand that, for Uribe, displacement is a narrative and epistemic strategy which helps him to raise, first, a moral issue deeply anchored to history; and, then—in a less obvious although equally important way—in the construction of his own literary world, an aesthetic issue. In the face of both dimensions (the moral and the aesthetic) he chooses displacement as a response.

Uribe's first two novels, *Bilbao-New York-Bilbao* and *Lo que mueve el mundo* (its title in Spanish, "What Moves the World") make explicit already in their titles something that, in *La hora de despertarnos juntos* (its title in Spanish, "The

Hour of Waking Together"), despite not figuring on the cover of the work, is also essential. Perhaps that interest in movement, in displacement, is also in that syntagma of the latter title, if only through opposition: those who wake together know the value of this, precisely because they have experienced even the most extreme of separations. Within the pages of these three vibrant books we come across characters in almost constant movement. However, they only coincide tangentially with what is typically understood as travel literature. Even so, the sensation of displacement is continuous; and not just concerning their plot. As we shall see, it is something that goes beyond reiterating geographical movement in the story.

Uribe's is not, essentially, travel literature, because the central element in his novels is not made up of the unexpected events of characters which would be at the service of presenting a changing landscape, or encounters with so-called 'exotic' locals, or a consciousness which registers its observations as it explores new territories. It is possible that our author—who is an assiduous and alert traveller, as Sally Perret points out (2014: 8)—owes something to that type of travel literature. Yet, in spite of the visibility of journeys in his texts, I believe that in his work reflexive processes on identity are ultimately more important than those factors. Displacement allows Uribe to highlight identity issues poignantly.

These preoccupations are very clearly located in Kirmen Uribe's narrative in a context that is, in principle, patently Basque and—in a possibly less obvious but equally significant way—more broadly European. One could add a third, all-encompassing global dimension, but I think there are both sociohistorical and personal determinants which make Uribe a writer we can characterized as markedly European. Not just on account of his Basque origins or his education, which took place both in the Basque Country and abroad (with Comparative Literature studies in Italy), or because of his readings of the great works of European literature. Perhaps it is within the Europeanness I am referring to where one of the keys to his productive fixation on displacement resides; because displacement, or mobility, has been considered a fundamental factor in reflections on Europeanness, at least since Immanuel Kant associated the development of European cosmopolitanism with *wanderlust*, the travel restlessness of the ideal inhabitant of the continent that the enlightened philosopher envisioned.

Nowadays, fluid displacement (that which the intradiegetic narrator enjoys, unlike the characters he or she investigates) is one of the principal metaphors for the process of Europeanization and the search for a sense of pancontinental cosmopolitan identity. That is how it is articulated by authors who have dedicated significant works to the matter, such as Vittoria Borsò, Jacques Derrida, and Ulrich Beck. Others, like Claudio Guillén, while rejecting the call to a shared European identity, underscore the importance that movement and fluidity have in approaches to the complexity of Europe, which he finds—relapsing into that same semantic field—"movable" and of a "never fixed profile" (1998: 377). For her part, the philosopher Rosi Braidotti conceives the associations between displacement, mobility, and identity—as the heir to Gilles Deleuze that she is—through a "nomadic" identity, out of which a European subject emerges, "in transit with different identity-formations, but sufficiently anchored to a historical position to accept responsibility for it" (2006: 75). We should be thinking, then, about some displacements connected to certain civic obligations, marked by the development of history. In this sense, Braidotti foreshadows "the end of pure and steady identities, or in other words, creolization and hybridization producing a multicultural minoritarian Europe, within which 'new' Europeans can take their place alongside others" (79).

Braidotti's argument, and her aesthetic equivalent in a literature like that of Uribe, present an alternative to the static essentialist notion of "fortress Europe," whose defenders demand, more or less explicitly, the preservation of a set of exclusivist values which they link to a restrictive concept of the legacy that may be the foundation of a common Europeanness. This position, which thinkers like Giovanni Sartori and Samuel Huntington present with some subtlety, and politicians like Viktor Orbán, Marine Le Pen, and Matteo Salvini have exploited recently in a much cruder way, has been used as rhetorical ammunition in debates on migration, mobility, and the growing diversity of the current population in the European Union: they contend that the free movement of people (above all when it is a question of people of different ethnicities and not "originally" European) may undermine the security of the continent and, ultimately, fatally corrupt its identity. For them, displacement is a threat.

These divergent ideas around the effects that mobility may have on Europeanness have very real consequences for many people. We see it clearly each time we read a newspaper; or a novel by Uribe, in his case with greater care and imaginative density. From the moment European integration, which has shaped the horizon of the latest generations of Europeans, was conceived, the experience of displacement in its full complexity has been one of the key factors both in constructing and in questioning a unified Europe. While the European Union has been broadly acknowledged to have facilitated mobility in abolishing borders among its member states, national governments occasionally express their discomfort at such openness, especially when segments of their populations see the identity or origins of the possible beneficiaries as a concern. For example, migrants from countries in Eastern Europe that look for work in the West, as well as members of the Roma minority, have encountered strong opposition, both popular and official, to their intra-European migrations—in spite of the support that in principle the Union offers to such movements. And yet, at the same time that it defends free movement within its territory as one of the pillars of Europeanness (with its clearest manifestation in the application of the Schengen Treaty), the Union also creates increasingly greater obstacles for those trying to enter from outside, especially when they are marked by poverty and racial difference. This incongruence produces what Ginette Verstraete terms "a Europe distinguished by intense mobility through a landscape of cultural differences" (2010: 11) and that, simultaneously, "requires sophisticated strategies of identification that can fix the distinction between Europeans and non-Europeans or, in this case, that can legitimate certain mobilities and exclude others" (2010: 89).

The tension between defenders of open mobility and those who advocate notions of identity which serve to justify exclusion is one of the most significant manifestations of the conflicts at the root of the process of European integration. From the early 1950s on, the dominant official discourse in the European project has been based on an idea of unification guided by principles of fluidity and solidarity. But its critics have shown signs of alarm from two opposing positions. On the one hand, the European Union has been condemned for not having been sufficiently rigorous in defending equal mobility for all. On the other hand, the Union has been attacked by those who, from the opposite end of the spectrum, discriminate against people who are positioned within the framework of certain ethnic and religious ideals of Europe they consider problematic.

Within this context, stories such as those Kirmen Uribe creates on displacement themes open up cracks in the grand narratives used to establish certain identity parameters, Europeanness, and our understanding of them. One of the ways in which his literature questions this is on the basis of an estrangement from the familiar; there are some questions that displacements lend credence to. In this respect, we should recall briefly a reflection by Karmele in *La hora de despertarnos juntos*. Settled in Caracas, finally reunited with her children, Txomin's wife feels uncomfortable with the idea of focusing her life around the exiled Basque community: "She looked toward the future with an air of renewal and leaving the past behind, and in the Euskal Etxea [Basque club] she came across an atmosphere corrupted by closed places, endogamic relations which narrowed walls and transformed hope and the future into fossilised rocks" (343).

With their vindication of the uncomfortable, with their questioning of the typical, Uribe's fictions can have an impact in the conceptualization of the common European home in this decisive period in the history of the region. He writes at a moment which demands new metaphors for that common European family or home, and urges us to recall the stories of displacement which have marked our recent past. Kirmen Uribe's work is exemplary in both senses.

Of course, his narrative does not emerge in a vacuum, but instead updates previous debates and stories. Some of the most celebrated European fictions question, by means of displacement, the relevance of these origins in the construction of identity. Frequently, in an effort to produce a certain image of Europeanness as a set of values rooted in a common, pure, and fixed heritage, the category of icons of those same identitarian values is elevated to the main roles of those stories—even when, closely observed, we realize that, in fact, those characters question precisely an ideology that we could classify as *nativist*. This would be the case, for example, of Aeneas, a kind of inaugural hero for Italian fascists and neo-fascists . . . although, as Virgil presents him, he could be a war refugee.

Upon closer reading, it seems clear that these fundamental European fictions offer more complexity than solutions to the topics that emphasize the sense of belonging to a place and a lineage. In many of these stories the search for or invention of one's own genealogy takes place within the frame of a displacement. That is the case of the aforementioned *Aeneid*; or in the *Odyssey*, with Odysseus's long pilgrimage and the adventures of his son Telemachus while he searches for news of his father; or in *Don Quixote*, a novel in which Cervantes associates the journey of his characters with the problematization of notions of identity. These and many other stories in which legacy and displacement are articulated—such as the myth of the Phoenician princess Europa, or the picaresque tradition—have contributed to debates about European identity for centuries, and make up a potent corpus with which Uribe's literature is connected, in which questions of identity, memory, and displacement have a prominent role.

Yet the dynamism of his prose is not only due to the numerous journeys his characters undertake, whether by their own free will or forced by circumstances. This includes the narrator, who is flying in *Bilbao-New York-Bilbao*, to the fishermen so central in this novel, and Basques displaced in South America in *La hora de despertarnos juntos*, by way of the characters in *Lo que mueve el mundo*, with their lives shaken by war, such as the little girl Karmentxu Cundin, and Robert Mussche, whose dream was, very significantly, "to walk freely in the world, without any ties" (47). For most of them, there have been one or several important displacements which have radically determined the outcome of their existence. This is further emphasized by the difficulty implied by those movements, in contrast to the apparent fluidity of those of the narrator, whose journeys do not come across notable obstacles in any of the fictions.

Displacement is, then, a central motive in Uribe's narrative; however, not just as regards his thematic dimension. To put it one way, and in a somewhat antiquated manner, Uribe conceives this *content* or travel theme out of a *form* that is also appropriately changeable, agile, wandering. The characters are marked by their displacements, and the narrative structure does so too. How? Uribe makes use of several resources, picked up on already some time ago by Jon Kortazar (2013). To cite a few: short chapters; the attention he shows to spaces; the inclusion of different kinds of materials, from letters, songs, and poems to extracts from other people's diaries, files in archives, and texts taken from the Internet, as well as reproductions of paintings or photographs; linguistic flexibility, with which short passages in different languages are included; a chronological agility, with frequent changes in transitoriness, threading past and present together while barely noticing the transitions between them; the manner in which he inserts short samples of texts from popular tradition; and so on.

Likewise, Uribe's full texts, at another level, experience numerous other movements, those that go from Basque to other languages: those that are geographically close, such as

Catalan, French, Galician, and Spanish, and those that are further away in space such as Chinese and Japanese, with translations which allow those of us unfamiliar with the original version to participate in those movements. The importance of this kind of displacement for Uribe leaves a clear trace in his pages: various reflections on translation are included in an intradiegetic way. In the solitude of his hideout in Brussels during the German occupation, Robert Mussche, who barely earned enough money to survive in this activity, thinks about how much he has learned through translation: "For him it is like entering into a terrain which has never been stepped on" (139). The displacement metaphor is here used as the image of an explorer who is discovering new worlds, delving into those that are mapped in other languages. It is something Mussche does for his own benefit and, by extension, for that of the literature in his language. This exercise leads Mussche to reaffirm himself as a writer in Flemish, a language located "between the two great traditions of France and Germany." He does so, he contends, for himself, going as far as to enunciate words in a low voice, "because it places me in the world as a person" (139). Language is presented as a medium by which to move about, but also to understand, ultimately, where the individual is located. The analogy also appears in *Bilbao-New York-Bilbao*, when the writer Phillis Levin says to the narrator about Basque: " 'Your language looks like a treasure map' [. . .] 'if you just forget all the rest of the letters and focus in on the *x*, it looks as if you could find out where the treasure is' " (22).

Displacement, the notion under consideration here, is a term that had enjoyed critical success within literary studies for a while before Kirmen Uribe began to write professionally. It is a malleable concept which has proven very productive in quite different, although interlinked, theoretical areas such as psychoanalysis, deconstruction, and postcolonial criticism. As Mark Krupnick points out, it became ubiquitous in post-structural theory, which was almost hegemonic in the overhaul of the humanities during the last quarter of the twentieth century.

Let us mention two names associated with such approaches and ponder how Kirmen Uribe would establish a certain dialogue with them: Jacques Derrida and Edward Said.

Displacement serves Derrida (although he would never put it in those terms) to subvert some of the hierarchies on which much thinking in the Western tradition are based. A key concept for the French thinker of Algerian origin, *différance*, would refer, in the first instance and according to Derrida himself, to "the (active and passive) movement that consists in deferring by means of delay, delegation, reprieve, referral, detour, postponement, reserving" (*Positions*, 8). In other words, Derrridean displacement implies never arriving at a fixed place, at a definitive conclusion. Its spirit is that of permanent evasion, an exploration by means of writing that must not be completed, because the highest fulfilment of the intellect is to be found in its continuous search—and because meaning remains continuously postponed, as it cannot be totally established. One immediately notes the similarity with Uribe's writing; we should point out in this regard the deliberate absence of linearity, the exploration of different juxtaposed textual territories, and the outline of stories that one can only glimpse fleetingly. History is an element which determines that this literature should find no satisfaction or comfort in mere digression, which is another form of mental displacement. María Zambrano and Walter Benjamin, both of them displaced digressers, visited in their writing something of that history which is illuminated in a moment of danger, as the German thinker would suggest in his *Theses on the Philosophy of History*. It seems necessary, then, to root formal and thematic displacement with historical depth. That is how Uribe approaches it.

A clear historical sensibility, reflected in his interest in the personal drama implied by forced displacements in tandem with political and social upheavals, links Uribe's work with what has been a fundamental question for numerous artists in recent decades. The comparativist Edward Said, in the wake of Freud and of Derrida, called our attention to the intellectual and aesthetic consequences of rootedness and uprootedness. In one of clearest political aspects of his work—one marked by the Palestinian experience—Said studied the importance of exile. For him, the defining characteristic of our era is displacement and what surrounds it: ours, he argues, is "the age of migrants, curfews, identity cards, refugees, exiles, massacres, camps and fleeing civilians" ("The Art," 17). In the face of all this, the most alert intellectuals and most illuminating artists would, precisely, be those who find themselves displaced, cut off from comfort and harmony with their original emplacement. Yet this circumstance does not, in itself, bestow a critical perspective: the key is in situating oneself in the chiasmus between the known and the unknown, the familiar and the other; and in order to do so, living in exile is not an essential requisite. Out of an awareness of inhabiting that interstice one can manage to access the plurality of perspectives and be free of all ties, which then allows one to develop a voice that can attend to the condition of uprootedness.

The respective life trajectories of Derrida and Said were likewise indicative of variations in that type of displacement which, in the long run, results in death occurring far from one's birthplace. Both Derrida and Said led *extra-territorial* lives, to use a phrase coined by George Steiner. But I am not going to deal with their biographies beyond merely pointing out a possible correlation between their experiences of displacement and their interest in developing this concept metaphorically and theoretically. It is not inconceivable that the attraction toward the same subject on the part of Kirmen Uribe himself has also been encouraged by his continual trips here and there, although one would have to stop and think about the fact that his spirals are consciously focused on that native Ondarroa, where he always ends up returning. His literature implies a measured experience so that those who have not experienced the harshest aspects of displacement—as is the case of the author himself—may get some idea of what it implies.

Putting aside their many differences, the notions of displacement conceived by Derrida and Said share at root a vindication of interstitial spaces as especially propitious generative territories—once again that *baratzeartea*, that border between two worlds mentioned at the beginning of this chapter. Located there, movement does not necessarily imply a distressing uprootedness, but instead it presents an opportunity to rethink productively how our location conditions us in both existential and intellectual terms, if such a distinction is feasible. The fixed (the stable, the static) suggests a security; but also a limitation. This is far from meaning an escape from the world toward an ideal space. In contrast to what would be escape, displacement does not imply ignoring or forgetting one's origins. It is, rather, a question of inhabiting the space between the familiar (here understood as something like the home, or, in a less literal sense, the conventions of our thinking) and the never-rooted or the unknown, in order to be able to rethink it from a fresh perspective.

Our narrator achieves a difficult balance: writing on displacement focusing his fiction on topics and people with a strong connection to their native land (the Basque Country). Perhaps his insistence on this approach has something to do with the ethics associated with the nomadism mentioned above: that of a European subject "in transit with different identity-formations, but sufficiently anchored to a historical position to accept responsibility for it," as Braidotti suggests. We could say that Uribe's literature is a return trip in which it is acknowledged that the place one returns to is never the same as the place one left. His texts include memory flashes which comfort us and, at the same time, disconcert us. For the displaced person, what was once familiar is transformed into something disturbing.

Uribe's narrative makes his characters move, and that movement is a continual displacement of truth—or, more accurately, of certainty. I am not arguing here that Uribe's is a literature permeated by that which some call *moral relativism*. Rather, I believe that there is a truth at the base of his literature, a truth which refers to the unnegotiable existence of a dignity that should not be renounced. Not everything, therefore, is the result of a perspective that changes according to position. Writing offers us a persistently dynamic search which does not require finding anything, but which does foster continual encounters.

In *Bilbao-New York-Bilbao* the narrator tells a short story of two brothers from Mutriku who emigrated to Argentina. When one of them was blinded there in an accident, he decided to go back to his homeland. His brother accompanied him on the long journey but, right before arriving in their village, he turned around, leaving the blind sibling to his fate; some nuns picked him up and "brought him home" (19). Neither of the two, therefore, saw their birthplace again. The story can be read as a parable whose lesson could be related to perception, travel, and identity. There is no going back with displacement. Returning is impossible: the territory left behind will never appear again before the eyes of the displaced person, because both—the place and the person contemplating it—have changed irredeemably. Nostalgia is, meanwhile, a symptom of weakness, a hindrance. Discarding nostalgia, on the contrary, provides clarity of vision, which is one of the positive attributes of extra-territoriality or exile, as Said ("Reflections") and Claudio Guillén have pointed out. This does not mean that both opposing impulses cannot exist within the same person (split into two in Uribe's story of the two brothers): he who accepts the new situation and he who would like to revisit the past.

The same novel, the author's first, includes the diary of the young Ricardo Bastida which he kept on a trip to the United States in 1926. One of the first periods he registers is, precisely, that including the visit of the fourteen-year-old boy and his father to an eminent exile in Hendaye, no less than Miguel de Unamuno (59), exiled there due to his opposition to King Alfonso XIII and General Primo de Rivera. The narrator continues detailing his reading of the diary while he reveals the perceptions, exchanges, and thoughts that come into his mind during the journey to the United States. Among them are his thoughts about his chance traveling companion, included in the story about the *Dos Amigos* ship, which transported slaves from Africa to Cuba until one day, chased by a British boat, the captain opted to try and escape by making the Africans jump off into the water near the island of Fernando Póo (91–93). We come across a series of displacements which are connected thematically and which are also formally presented via a certain textual dispersion: they are stories of different kinds (from the lightness of the boy's journey to the humanitarian drama of slavery, or the exiled Unamuno's political commitment) which are barely outlined, and are presented as anecdotes. Their brevity serves to reiterate the topic well: juxtaposition shapes that mosaic of movements which illustrates the vital texture both of many individuals and the societies where they are inserted. As Said stated, the defining characteristic of our era is displacement and everything that surrounds it.

This frequent displacement from one source to another for the stories that the narrator includes favors a multiplicity of perspectives. This type of perspectivism implies an antidote against dogmatisms. One of the key questions is that besides coming up as a central theme, displacement also has a dimension in terms of *writing practice* to it. Both dimensions end up being indistinguishable even in critical language; hence Krupnick, for example, reviewing how post-structuralist writers have addressed it, refers to displacement as "an exile from older certitudes of meaning and selfhood" (5).

Uribe's writing includes and sometimes even celebrates displacement, in what it has about exploration and questioning static truths, dogmatisms, and some certainties which, more than liberating, trap one. In *Lo que mueve el mundo* we read that the "dark side" of heroism is, precisely, "having had such clear ideas," something which is associated with suffering (217) and is said about that fascinating character that is Mussche. Furthermore, like the good socialist he is, Mussche is likewise a convinced internationalist. He is not concerned where injustice is; humanity is one. For that reason, he goes to the Catalan front in the Spanish Civil War as a correspondent for the newspaper

Vooruit, and takes in the Basque girl Karmentxu. Just as certainty is questioned, in the same novel the inherent kindness of the original home is disputed and appears as a false notion: when the refugee children from Bilbao in Belgium had to go back home, the return was far from ideal.

> For them, their home was no longer that which they had left behind in Bilbao, but instead that in Belgium. Some returned with great sadness alongside their families, since there, post-war hunger was awaiting them. Nor were their parents lovers of culture like those they had met in Belgium, and they were stricter with their children. Abroad, they had had everything at hand. There were also those who returned to Belgium, seeing that there was no place for them in the Basque Country. (94–95)

Uribe places his characters in situations which lead precisely to putting a strain on those roots; they leave or are expelled from their land of origin, and that displacement—whether voluntary or forced—gives rise to a series of discoveries. Movement makes them think about who they are and how they have come to construct that identity, without taking the matter for granted. The question, instead, walks, flies, sails; and what they thought it was is in continual mutation, precisely as a consequence of that anti-static attitude, of that mobility. Although the original home has been destroyed, something different, yet perhaps similar, may emerge out of the ashes and the absence. The key to rebuild it, in Uribe's work, is love. He differs in this regard from Said's somewhat radical position when, in his essay on the artist Mona Hatoum, prefers "disparity and dislocation [over] reconciliation under duress of subject and object; better a lucid exile than sloppy, sentimental homecomings; better the logic of dissociation than an assembly of compliant dunces." Uribe proposes a more caring approach, emphasizing the multiple connections that displacement creates among the displaced. In geopolitical terms, those from that part of Europe which is native to a much wider context, which extends to the rest of the continent and the Americas. Uribe's literature offers a diverse, stimulating alternative to the agendas of institutional actors who, from above, advocate the idea of a more limited, closed, and static Europe. In contrast to this, our author combines a profound knowledge of a home of one's own while underscoring the importance of not getting too comfortable there. The need to explore alternative possibilities to those which customs and known spaces seem to determine seems contained in the etymology of the word *txekaria*, over which there is some debate in Uribe's *Mussche*:

> [. . .] I thought that it could be a word derived from etxe, "house."
> In my opinion it comes from *xerkaria*, a word used in the French Basque Country to say "the seeker."
> That would be a good definition of us—Karmele added—. Our whole lives seeking out new routes. (346)

Firmly rooted in a home, always seeking new departure routes—perhaps also an appropriate characterization of Kirmen Uribe's literature.

Bibliography

Braidotti, Rosi. 2006. *Transpositions: On Nomadic Ethics.* Cambridge: Polity Press.

Daisne, Johan. 1965. *Baratzeartea, een baskisch avontuur of de roman van een schrijver.* Brussels & The Hague: Manteau.

Derrida, Jacques. 1981. *Positions.* Itzulpena: Alan Bass. Chicago: The University of Chicago Press.

Guillén, Claudio. 1998. *Múltiples moradas. Ensayo de Literatura Comparada.* Barcelona: Tusquets.

Kortazar, Jon. 2013. *Contemporary Basque Literature: Kirmen Uribe's Proposal.* Trans. Cameron Watson. Madrid: Iberoamericana.

Krupnick, Mark (ed.). 1983. *Displacement: Derrida and After.* Bloomington: Indiana University Press.

Perret, Sally. 2014. Un nuevo tiempo espléndido. In Kirmen Uribe, *Vidas y ficciones*, 7–13. Iruñea: Pamiela.

Said, Edward. 2000. The Art of Displacement: Mona Hatoum's Logic of Irreconcilables. In *Mona Hatoum: The Entire World as a Foreign Land*, 7–17. London: Tate Gallery.

Said, Edward. 2000. Reflections on Exile. *Reflections on Exile and Other Essays*, 173–186. Cambridge: Harvard University Press.

Uribe, Kirmen. 2008. *Bilbao-New York-Bilbao.* Donostia: Elkar.

Uribe, Kirmen. 2012. *Mussche.* Zarautz: Susa.

Uribe, Kirmen. 2014. El idioma de la Virgen María de la playa. In *Vidas y ficciones*, 18–23. Iruñea: Pamiela.

Uribe, Kirmen. 2016. *Elkarrekin esnatzeko ordua.* Zarautz: Susa.

Uribe, Kirmen. 2017. La literatura es detenerse, es reflexión, es el territorio de la libertad y la belleza. *El Diario Montañés*, (uztailaren 12[a]). Mada Martínezek idatzitako berria.

Verstraete, Ginette. 2010. *Tracking Europe: Mobility, Diaspora, and the Politics of Location.* Durham: Duke University Press.

9

The construction of memory in Kirmen Uribe's narrative

María Jesús Nafría Fernández

In search of Basque identity

It is difficult to establish one single determining factor to define Basque literature. On the one hand, we may consider it to include all literature written in Basque, but it could also refer to where the authors come from or even the subject matter of the works. In spite of all the criteria that may be established, it would not reflect an obvious distinguishing factor, and the truth remains that it is a rapidly expanding body of literature. One of the reasons for this modern rebirth is the author and object of this study: Kirmen Uribe.

1 Language

In Uribe's work we find modernity and tradition, in a perfect symphony, written in the score of Basque. Or, as he writes in his novel *Bilbao-New York-Bilbao* (English language version, Seren 2014), on his first trip to New York, the writer Phillis Levin defines the language thus: " 'Your language looks like a treasure map' [. . .] 'if you just forget all the rest of the letters and focus in on the *x*, it looks as if you could find out where the treasure is' " (22). The similarity to a treasure, something to fight for and search out in good faith, is perhaps one of the most accurate images of Basque and its expansion throughout the world.

By means of language, Uribe's literary universe reveals a search for family and cultural identity, determined by a family past (the trigger for stories) and by the meta-literary present and future (the moment of the narration) (Martínez Rubio, 2015). While the subject of identity is present as a profound feature of his writing, we must not forget the style and the language with which he expresses it. Thus, the motifs which shape Uribe's universe and the fact that he should choose Euskara (Basque) as the language of his narrations leads us to the idea that underlies this whole narrative framework: the demand for the normalization of Basque as a literary language.

If we start from this cultural linguistic basis, it is necessary to offer a general clarification in this regard. It is essential for this research to turn to the ideas provided by Even-Zohar's "Polysystem Theory" (1979, 293), according to which, in societies in which two or more languages exist in a diglossic situation, one of these languages is configured as the main language while the rest survive in an unequal social and linguistic situation. These minority or minoritized languages, which we will term "small" here, occupy a decisive place within the configuration of a society's culture.

Furthermore, according to José Lambert, in a context such as that of the state, in which different small languages (Basque, Catalan, Galician) face up to the majoritarian one (Spanish), conflictive situations are established which give rise to links between identity and territory, and this diverse panorama is translated equally into literature.

Thus, in the case of *Bilbao-New York-Bilbao*, *Lo que mueve el mundo* (its title in Spanish, "What Moves the World"), and *La hora de despertarnos juntos* (its title in Spanish, "The Hour of Waking Together"), the choice of language is not something premeditated, but rather is a natural process.[67] However, it is impossible to deny that the use of Basque in this novel is associated with an intentional objective of cultural expansion beyond the borders of the Basque Country (Aitor Guenaga, 2018).

67 In an interview for the *Revista Contexto*, Uribe observes: "I consider Basque to be my literary language, I write novels in that language. Although I also like to write things in Spanish, short texts, mostly journalistic. I do so naturally . . ."

As Jone Miren Hernández points out in *Euskara, comunidad e identidad* (2007, 70–80), through a process like iconicity a direct relationship between the Basque language and a model of identity is established, without forgetting its condition as a small language and the historical circumstances derived thereof, since language served as a tool to construct Basque nationalism during the second half of the nineteenth century. Thus, it is not the message alone that is being communicated (the content) but also the means by which it is transmitted (the channel).

In this era of globalization and the free market, the objective of writing in Basque is not for its discourse to be transformed into a literary language (that had already been achieved by former literary groups) but instead to achieve the universalization of its message. The important thing is not the word in itself, but everything it implies.

In other words, the conscious use of a small language transcends the exclusively literary or linguistic environment, achieving historical, political, cultural, and familial significance. In this way, we create a map of literary interactions in order to recognize a collective identity.

2 Historical memory

The collective identity represented by language is related directly to the construction (or reconstruction) of a memory that allows for the completion of the identity process.

In Uribe's novelistic work up to this point, the starting point will always be Bilbao, from where a journey starts to New York, Ghent, or Venezuela, connecting different spaces (the personal, local, and globalized, between past and future), thereby shaping a concept of identity which goes beyond simple categorization, since it establishes a connection among different elements in different spaces, in a common fictional frame. In order to do so, various resources typical of current postmodern narrative are made use of, such as, for example, the inclusion of real documents within the history of different formats (represented differently in the text) or references to the very process of writing. In order to be able to explain the identity process which is constructed through continuous remembrance, there will first be a brief explanation of the reasons which led to the need to reconstruct the past, in the crisis of existent memory at the present time.

The first concept that must be clarified is that of identity, in the form in which the author here under study uses it. In recent years, there has been an increase in studies on calls for identity in its multiple expressions (geographical, sexual, ideological, etc.), which has provoked an excessive individualism and the loss of values such as community. As Daniel Bernabé explains in *La trampa de la diversidad. Cómo el neoliberalismo fragmentó la identidad de la clase trabajadora* (Akal 2018):

> In the late seventies [. . .], modernity, as a general identity of society, was foundering. A new generation appeared to begin to think in different terms to what had, to that time, been the guidelines of this period. The preoccupations centred on the struggle against state bureaucracy, the exploration of individuality, the rejection of the West as a reference point, philosophical diversity, ideological diversity. (42)

> Given that there no longer existed the capacity to explore subjects universally, nor was there room for broad demands, given that tastes could no longer be expressed in a unified form, we could only gain access to reality from fragmentation. (49)

In this sense, Uribe's work breaks with the current tendency toward excessive individualism, but without distancing itself from making its own demands, as something to share with the world and from which to enrich it. The concept of identity acquires a global value, since—as Sánchez Zapatero points out—although "recollections [about what underpins identity] are always personal, they only acquire their meaning when they are related to conceptual structures created by members of a community through culture, art, politics, the media and literature" (Sánchez Zapatero 2010, 25), becoming a shared memory, in what we could term "historical memory" or "cultural memory."

Having said that, in Spain a past with a single historical perspective has been constructed, thereby forgetting the different histories which inhabit the same space-time with that official version. Nevertheless, the concept of historical memory with which Uribe works overcomes those spatial and ideological limitations and recovers, through autofictional narrative, some remnants of stories that complement the narration of the recent past.

However, it is necessary to remember that the construction of identity in a society or community is related to the fears or concerns experienced. These remain impregnated in the individual and collective imagination, and both will constitute "memory." The images belonging to the past are constructed by recalled elements, as well as forgotten elements.[68]

In Spain, and the Basque Country, the construction of recent memory is determined by memory of the Spanish Civil War, as Olaziregi indicates.[69] Still today it continues to be a source of conflict, given that it is believed that the transition was not grounded in an assumption of responsibilities or forgiveness on the part of the dictatorial regime which preceded it, but instead has been used as a technique for "evasive forgetting" (Sevillano

68 "In this way, memory itself needs to forget the recent past to recover the remote past; a forgetting which takes the form of a 'return,' re-establishing a continuity with that more remote past," in Francisco Sevillano Calero, "La construcción de la memoria y el olvido en la España democrática," *Ayer* 52 (2003).

69 "In this sense, the growth in the number of novels which have chosen the Spanish Civil War not just as a setting of the stories narrated, but as their thematic and symbolic focus, is more than obvious among us," in Mari Jose Olaziregi, "La recuperación de la memoria histórica en la novela contemporánea vasca," *Trabajos y actas de la Real Academia de la Lengua Vasca* 54, 2, 2 (2009): 1038.

2003, 297), which implied silence in public life about the war and, above all, the Franco dictatorship.

With the arrival of democracy in 1977, Law 46/1977, of October 15, on Amnesty was passed,[70] in which all crimes committed to that date were annulled, including those by the authorities, public officials, and law enforcement officials. There was no condemnation of the anti-democratic acts which took place during the dictatorship, which implied the annulment of responsibility, without the existence of any kind of condemnation of everything that had happened during forty years of dictatorship. Thus, thanks to this officially imposed silence, nobody could denounce the crimes committed by state forces, and all the pending problems of the Second Republic remained unresolved—problems that currently are resurfacing, such as the territorial debate, secularity, monarchy, etc.

Thus, all the memories that came together simultaneously following the Civil War were excluded from the legal and political—the official—panorama. However, they should be brought to light in order to move forward and overcome all the conflicts of the past. That is why victims must take on the task of exercising memory: "The truth is that, for a long time, the victims have been invisible and not on their own account but because of the politics of memory" (Mate 2012, 79).

70 Article two. In any event, included in Amnesty are: a) The crimes of rebellion and sedition, as well as the crimes and offenses committed on their account, typified in the Code of Military Justice; b) Conscientious objection to the provision of military service, for ethical or religious reasons; c) The crimes of denial of aid to Justice for the refusal to reveal facts of a political nature, known in the exercise of professional practice; d) The acts of expression of opinion, carried out through the press, print, or any other means of communication; e) The crimes and offenses that could have been committed by the authorities, public officials, and law enforcement officials, in the event of the investigation and prosecution of the acts included in this Law; f) Crimes committed by law enforcement officials and agents against the exercise of people's rights.

3 How, then, should one construct a diverse memory, which resolves unresolved conflicts and which serves to reconstruct society?

So that reparation for this hurt may take place, the victims and their families and friends must be recognized, both on a personal level and on that of the state as responsible in a subsidiary way (Mate 2012, 86). Nevertheless, there would have to be a dual recuperation of memory: that of the victim and that of the perpetrator, in a process of internal change in which the concept of guilt is dealt with consciously. This internal change would consist of three phases: on the one hand, the presence of the victim (essential in elaborating the guilt); on the other, repentance; and finally, asking for forgiveness.

In the case of the Spanish Civil War, this act of reconciliation has never taken place, as Colmeiro explains:

> The reappearance of ghosts in post-Franco Spanish culture has a lot to do with repression in the past as an imposed prohibition during the dictatorship and as a political taboo derived from the "pact of forgetting" which happened during the political Transition. (Colmeiro 2011, 33)

The consequences of this pact of forgetting are still present today, and are seen in the numerous above-mentioned conflicts: the territorial problem, a questioning of the monarchy, etc. It is not surprising, then, that a redefinition of identity emerges, establishing a direct relationship between memory, identity, and the *locus* (the city typically being that place). The restoration of repressed memories, which is always far from the minds of the institutions, is opposed by official state policy, which consists of selective forgetting.

In the face of this panorama of disenchantment, extinguishing any possibility of restoration, society had two options: to fight (as was seen in places like the Basque Country) or melancholy.

> Memory played a fundamental role in the whole process of assigning new meanings to what had been experienced on the basis of two emotions that had remained deep inside the bodies of activists: euphoria in the face of the imminence of the longed-for horizon of liberation, and the resulting sadness of its dissipation during the transition. (Beorlegui 2017, 9)

Thus, while on the one hand memories of war and the dictatorship became a topic that nobody spoke about, a taboo, that pact of collective amnesia, that de-memory and disenchantment needed to express themselves in the cultural and literary field with the goal of redemption: "The task of history, therefore, would be different to the totalizing pretension of positivism, and would focus fundamentally on historicizing the 'memory boom' or the 'notion itself of memory itself' " (Beorlegui 2017, 29).

In this way, the engines were started that would activate historical memory, reaching different disciplines in order to establish a more complete discourse, which shed light on aspects forgotten by historiography.[71] We could frame Kirmen Uribe's work within this concept of historical memory, and it could be defined as the "memory novel."

Memory novels appear in an attempt to find answers to past events which have not been properly overcome, whether on account of ignorance, forced or voluntary forgetting, or because of losses. The context in which Uribe's novels take place is also marked by losses of identity references, caused by the Spanish Civil War and the Second World War.[72]

---

71 "The memory of the transition reveals some experiences which have passed by unnoticed for a historiography that tends to not give sufficient authority to oral sources because of their subjective nature," in David Beorlegui, *Transición y melancolía. La experiencia del desencanto en el País Vasco (1976-1986)*, (Madrid: Postmetrópolis Editorial, 2017), 43.

72 "I had not written anything for months–I told him–, and I did not even know what my next book was going to be like. The death of a great friend had left me completely devastated. That loss coincided with the arrival of our youngest daughter. I felt disoriented, on the one hand happy, on the other sad. Of course I knew some stories about the children of the war; their experiences had always attracted my attention, but it was very complicated to relate them as they should be," in Kirmen Uribe, *Mussche*

At this point, we arrive at element number three, which joins all the novels through one common thread: death.

4 Death

Through the individual memories of "small heroes"—as he points out in *Lo que mueve el mundo* (Seix Barral, 2013)[73]—Uribe constructs a past that is necessary to recall so that it is not repeated (Uribe 2013, 228) and which makes up a universal, collective, more equal and solidarity of memory.

There is always a trigger in Uribe's novels which provokes the exercise of remembering and narrating what is being remembered, whose story is completed through the labor of investigation which the author carries out with the goal of writing the novel in question. This trigger is the death of a loved one. This loss and the lack of information with regard to the life of his forebears plays a decisive role in all of his works.

Thus, in *Bilbao-New York-Bilbao*, in the conversation with Carmen Bastida, she says: "My life was changed by two events. The first blow was the war. The second was Papa's death" (Uribe 2014, 35).

Or, from the first chapter of the same work:

> And, as with the growth rings of fishes, terrible events stay on in our memory, mark our life, until they become a measure of time. Happy days go fast, on the other hand—too fast—and we forget them quickly.
>
> What winter is for fish, loss is for humans. Loss makes our time specific for us, the end of a relationship, the death of a person we love. (Uribe 2014, 7)

(Zarautz: Susa, 2012), 183–184.

73 "Then I shut up. Today I agree with him. The heroes are there, small heroes who from time to time pass away," in Kirmen Uribe, *Mussche* (Zarautz: Susa, 2012), 194.

These deaths provoke a series of question marks with regard to Uribe's past and that of his family, which he wants to uncover, and perhaps in this way to find his place in the world and in history, about which Bernabé spoke in the above-mentioned work: "Postmodernity is stupefaction and anguish made virtue and state; it is the total absence of places to go" (Bernabé 2018, 44). In *Lo que mueve el mundo*, it is the loss of his friend, Aitzol Aramaio, together with the birth of his daughter, which is simultaneously linked to the life of Robert Mussche, a Belgian intellectual who fought against fascism in Europe, and who became involved with the Basque Country when he adopted a "war child."

In the same way, in *La hora de despertarnos juntos*, it is the story of Karmele Urresti and the trumpeter and secret service member, Txomin Letamendi, as recounted to him by their daughter and about which he would have liked to remember more details: "If that visit is so vivid it's because now I regret not having looked into the extraordinary life of that woman with more curiosity and attention while she still maintained her full mental faculties" (Uribe 2016, 10).

Thus, it is by means of language and death that Uribe reveals the past of figures from history whose lives were marked by war and the fight for freedoms, and whose names do not appear in the history books. At the same time, he honors his loved ones at a more personal (and, lest we forget, autofictional) level (Nafría, 2014). In this way, he constructs a common, universal identity, breaking with the postmodern and liberal tradition of exclusivist individual identity.

5 Conclusion

By way of a summary of everything presented thus far, these three elements—language, memory, and death—serve to construct a memory novel at the individual as well as collective level (in uncovering situations which can be assimilated as one's own in any society in conflict) and they shape Uribe's literary universe, whose function is that of updating and (re)constructing a societal memory that makes for a more egalitarian future.

Bibliography

Beorlegui, David. 2017. *Transición y melancolía. La experiencia del desencanto en el País Vasco (1976-1986)*. Madrid: Postmetrópolis Editorial.

Bernabé, Daniel. 2018. *La trampa de la diversidad. Cómo el neoliberalismo fragmentó la identidad de la clase trabajadora*. Madrid: Akal.

Colmeiro, Jose. 2011. ¿Una nación de fantasmas?: Apariciones, memoria histórica y olvido en la España posfranquista, *452°F: Revista de teoría de la literatura y literatura comparada* [on-line], 4. http://www.raco.cat/index.php/452F/article/view/243538

Even-Zohar, Itamar. 1979. "Polysystem Theory". *Poetics Today* 1, 1-2: 287-310.

Guenaga, Aitor. 2018. Entrevista Kirmen Uribe, escritor. In *Eldiario.es* (martxoa).

Hernández, Jone Miren. 2007. *Euskara, comunidad e identidad.* Madrid: Kultura Ministerioa.

Lambert, José. 1999. Aproximaciones sistémicas y la literatura en las sociedades multilingües, *Teoría de los polisistemas.* Madrid: Arco/Libros.

Martínez Rubio, José. 2015. *Las formas de la verdad. Investigación, docuficción y memoria en la novela hispánica.* Barcelona: Anthropos.

Mate, M. Reyes. 2012. Sobre la reconciliación de la memoria al perdón. *Revista Internacional de Estudios Vascos*, 10: 70–93.

Nafría Fernández, María Jesús. 2014. *Bilbao- New York- Bilbao*: Un viaje por el universo literario de Kirmen Uribe. *Revista de lenguas y literaturas catalana, gallega y vasca* 19: 267– 287.

Olaziregi, Mari Jose. 2009. La recuperación de la memoria histórica en la novela contemporánea vasca, *Trabajos y actas de la Real Academia de la Lengua Vasca*, 54, 2, 2: 1027–1047. Online: https://dialnet.unirioja.es/servlet/articulo?codigo=3326410

Sánchez Zapatero, Javier. 2010. La cultura de la memoria. *Pliegos de Yuste: Revista de cultura y pensamiento europeos*: 25–30. Online: http://www.pliegosdeyuste.eu/n1112pliegos/pdfs/25-30.pdf

Sevillano Calero, Francisco. 2003. La construcción de la memoria y el olvido en la España democrática. *Ayer* 52: 297–320.

Uribe, Kirmen. 2008. *Bilbao-New York-Bilbao*. Donostia: Elkar.

Uribe, Kirmen. 2012. *Mussche*, Zarautz: Susa

Uribe, Kirmen. 2016. *Elkarrekin esnatzeko ordua*, Zarautz: Susa.

10

Kirmen Uribe's *Mussche*: A paper grave for Robert[74]

Mari Jose Olaziregi Alustiza

May this book be a tiny paper grave for Robert

*That grave which Carmen could not envisage (*Mussche*, 184)*

When Kirmen Uribe did the launch for his novel *Mussche* (M) in Donostia in 2012, he mentioned a request he had received from Carmen Mussche, the daughter of the Flemish writer, translator, and activist Robert Mussche, the protagonist of Uribe's novel: "Not a biography, please, I would like you to write a novel about my father. I want a creative work."[75] The request has something to do, as we will see ahead, with the function attributed to literature that seeks to recover a conflictive past; indeed, using the metaphor of the grave, as the narrator says in the novel (M, 184), the goal of this novel is to become the 'literary grave' of the tragically missing Robert Mussche, because it pays tribute to, and on some level replaces, the tortured body that his loved ones could not recover. This effort to write brings us face to face with one of the main goals of literature that recovers historical memory: to honor the memory of those who suffered cruelties

74 Paper prepared within the projects IT 1047-16 (Basque government) and FFI2017-84342-P (MINECO) developed by the level A consolidated research group MHLI (Memoria Historikoa Literatura Iberiarretan / Memoria Histórica en las Literaturas Ibéricas / Historical Memory in Iberian Literatures).

75 See the video at the Susa Publishing House link: https://www.youtube.com/watch?v=zrJ2LiR1tIc [December 16, 2019]. Uribe also speaks about Carmen Mussche's request in an article he published later on the problems he encountered in writing *Mussche*. See "Un héroe como nosotros" (*El País Semanal*, March 22, 2013).

in the past and to help make their grief more bearable. As is noted at one point in the novel, if one compares a diamond and a pencil (M, 142), the pencil is, without any doubt, the most durable, because in its fragility it possesses immense power and strength, it possesses the ability to give written testimony. In what follows, we will discuss, namely, how the novel *Mussche* arranges artifacts as a literary strategy to achieve those goals. *Mussche*, a forerunner of the historical memory that has achieved an increasingly obvious centrality in Uribe's work, also reflects on the role writers should play in politically conflictive settings and, underscoring the essential link between literature and memory, it additionally recovers the memory of Basque children that experienced a dramatic exile. Finally, we will suggest parallels between Uribe's novel and the works of W. G. Sebald as well as other works of Basque literature in recent years.

1 Narrative mosaic made up of pieces of memory

While most literary works possess memory as a raw material, some make that link more explicit. That is the case of the narrative mosaic arranged around the pieces of Robert Mussche's life that is *Mussche*. The novel is organized into three main parts. It begins with the exile of Karmentxu Cundin and her brother and continues with an account of the life of Robert Mussche, who takes them into his home. In order to undertake a literary construction of Robert's life, besides his own research (M, 62, 163, 186), the narrator makes use of the memories that Robert's daughter Carmen, the orphaned daughter who "has always gone around accumulating things" (M, 177) transmits orally to the narrator, to Uribe, the autofiction writer (M, 23, 104, . . .); family photographs (M, 44, 65, 102, . . .); letters; and Carmen's mother's everyday life (M, 129, . . .)—in order to guide the story that alternates unpredictably in the form of memory between different narrative planes. This is an example of what Marianne Hirsch termed *postmemory generation* (1997), because Uribe includes Carmen's memories of her father and the war throughout—not in a family setting, communicated orally, as would be the case of communicative memory (Assmann 1995), but through stories, images, behaviors, and other things. In Carmen's case, we see a powerful imaginary component made up of the memories of what Hirsch notes as the postmemory generation ("Postmemory is a powerful and very particular form of memory precisely because its connection to its object or source is mediated not through recollection but through an imaginative investment and creation," Hirsch 1997, 22).

The first part of the novel includes chapters 1–10, and covers the period between the Cundins' exile and the beginning of Robert's involvement in the Resistance. It narrates, among other things, Robert's bond of love-friendship with Herman Thiery (the Flemish writer who would use the pen name Johan Daisne), Robert's journey to the Catalan border, and Robert's involvement in the Belgian Socialist party.

The theme of the second part, comprising chapters 11–21, is Robert's clandestine political activity, which coincides with resistance against the Nazis. That activism develops alongside the most important years he will experience at the personal level, from the time he marries his wife, Vic, on July 15, 1941 to the point they become parents on August 16, 1942, with the birth of their daughter Carmen. However, happiness will be short lived, for just a few months, because once Robert enters the Resistance, he will be forced into a clandestine life. Far from his family, he will earn a living doing translations in Brussels, be arrested, and spend two months in Antwerp prison, until he is sent to Germany, to Neuengamme concentration camp, on December 27, 1944. On May 3, 1945 he will die, in the Bay of Lübeck, when the ship carrying him, the *Cap Arcona*, is bombed.

Lastly, we should mention the shortest part of the novel, which includes chapters 22–24. It involves us in the grief that Carmen Mussche experiences as the result of missing the father she never knew, but not just that, because this section presents the personal reasons that drove the autofictional author to write a novel. The basic theme in this section is friendship and, along those lines, the relationship between Robert and Herman is addressed, especially the suffering and regret experienced by Herman as a result of his dead friend, which can be found in Herman's works like *In memoriam Robert Mussche* (M, 193). The section ends with an offer to the autofictional author's friend Aitzol Aramaio, emphasizing that the story in *Mussche* is the "story of a hero" (M, 194). We could say that this concluding section, in in addition to clarifying from where the idea for the novel came ("I know that the journalist Julio Flor spoke to you about Karmentxu Cundin, and about Robert too, at the Medellin festival" M, 183), includes the objective ("May this book be a tiny paper grave for Robert" M, 184) and the real personal reason ("there's the story of a hero, my beloved friend" M, 194) behind the work.

2 Traveling memories

As noted, the novel *Mussche* begins with the journey of the sister and brother Karmentxu and Ramon Cundin, alongside 4,500 evacuated children, on board the ship *Habana*, in June 1937. The name of the ship, as is the case with several other elements in the novel—such as, for example, the bed that witnessed Vic and Robert's first encounter, "the Her bet von Napoleon bed" (M, 89)— is revealing of the mark that the passage of time leaves on spaces, symbols, or elements. As is well known, such elements connect us to the past of a nation, by becoming a site of memory (Nora 1997, 28). The ship called *Habana* is an important site of memory in the Basque collective consciousness, linked to the deplorable exile provoked by the War of 1935, as many Basque writers have demonstrated, such as Bernardo Atxaga in his novel *Soinujolearen semea* (2003; English translation, *The Accordionist's Son*, 2007) and Garazi Goia in the title *Txartel bat (des)herrira* (A Ticket to Exile, 2013). Uribe's novel makes it clear to us that the *Habana* was christened with the name *Alfonso XIII* (M, 13–14) and, during the time of the Second Spanish Republic, that it was rechristened with the name that would better reflect the sociohistorical context.

Eight-year-old Karmentxu Cundin and her brother Ramon became the bearers of the memory of the War of 1936 when they were taken into exile with 4,500 other children aboard the *Habana* in June 1937. Robert Mussche, a member of the Belgian Socialist Party, took the little girl Karmentxu into his home and the opportunity he was given to experience fatherhood was uplifting (M, 42). Karmentxu is defined as a happy little girl, and we could say that she plays quite a passive role in the novel, because the narrator underscores the fact that she is not very talkative and that she appears very pensive in photos (M, 44). The memory busts that the Mussches build when she is returned to the Basque Country, for example, seek to hold on to the sweet memory that she left (M, 82) as does the fact of Robert and Vic naming their own daughter Carmen.

The nature of memory—which recent memory studies have wanted to locate on the basis of their theoretical and methodological approaches—is actually roving and fluid, as Astrid Erll (2011) has stressed. If cultural memory was the key concept in early twentieth-century memory studies, through the well-known works of, among others, Maurice Halbwachs, Walter Benjamin, and Frederic Bartlett, then about half a century later, Pierre Nora's well-known *Les lieux de mémoire* (1984–1992) works placed national memory at the core of the research in the 1990s (Erll 2011, 6). For Erll, it is obvious that memory networks that transcend the borders of nation states are now conditioned by things like religion, diaspora, music, or consumer culture (Erll 2011, 8), and, therefore, that transcultural mobility also affects memory studies. In this sense, transcultural memory studies suggest a new way of observing, a specific point of view "which is directed toward mnemonic processes unfolding across and beyond cultures. It means transcending the borders of traditional 'cultural memory studies' by looking beyond established research assumptions, objects and methodologies" (2011, 9). Therefore, it is recognized that memory is completely fluid, that it has an itinerant nature, and that it supersedes space, human collectives, language, and political boundaries. Erll proposes turning to five dimensions in order to examine these traveling memories (2011, 12): media carriers, media, contents, practices, and forms.

We can find examples of all five in the novel *Mussche*. Thus, as well as the Cundin siblings who carry the memory of the War of 1936, we should point out the left-wing songs that they share with the Belgian socialist Mussche, such as *A las barricadas* (M, 50), the copy of a well-known song throughout early twentieth-century Europe. The bracelet that Robert wears with the colors of the Spanish Republic's flag in his Sunday meetings with the children in Ghent would be the same kind of thing (M, 52), as well as the demonstrations within the May Day celebrations (M, 67). The banner at the head of that demonstration that says "Fascism has killed 10,000 Spanish children" (M, 67) became, in fact, the main excuse for the international campaign started by the winning side in the War of 1936. As studies note (Pazos 2013, 387), the winning side classified the exile of thousands of children by the government of the Second Republic as propaganda (Pazos 2013, 388–389). The novel *Mussche* does not specifically explain the diplomatic issue that led to Basque children being exiled to Belgium (Pazos 2013, 411–415), but it mentions clearly that "the gestures to bring the children back once Bilbao fell" (M, 79) were set in motion and that the children's return was not, in any way, pleasant, because many of them could not find the homes and families they had left behind. And that is, precisely, the case of the siblings Karmentxu and Ramon Cundin (M, 80). They experienced in Belgium the peace, toys, cultural activities, and so on that they could not find at home (M, 26–27) and we could say that, with time, the surroundings and culture that were initially strange began to feel like *home* to them. This is indicated by references to the concert hall called Balzaal (M, 17), which is of symbolic importance in the novel. The exiled children are taken there when they arrive in Ghent and must be distributed among different families, and the stained-glass windows there, full of socialist symbolism, will appear striking to Karmentxu, who is suffering from alienation in the strange surroundings:

> In that colorful stained glass, a group of muscular men is trying to move a big wheel, using some big planks to get it out of the mud. There is a single woman in front pulling a cart, with a child in her arms, that woman also as spirited as the men. Behind them, in the middle of the composition, there is a proud red flag, blowing in the wind. (M, 17)

Displacements, the movements we make to unknown places, provoke anxiety and fear among us, and one notes traces of panic in the body (Ahmed 1999, 342). The journeys of the Cundin siblings, marked by the dramas of forced exile, had a huge effect on their childhood, and that is expressed in Karmentxu's case, because upon arriving at Balzaal, her body reacts violently in the face of the smiling Robert Mussche who is welcoming her, by being sick (M, 18). The well-known Ghent Arts Center, Vooruit ('forward' in Flemish), which became a symbol of the socialist movement between the wars, witnessed not just cultural activities but support and activities provided for cooperative workers. It was said that the meaningful stained glass in the Balzaal dance hall there symbolized "the wheel of the future, that of the coming freedom" (M, 28), in other words, what would in time be the wheel and the message of which Karmentxu would not be frightened.

As we can see, the novel mentions the dissemination and the extent of the Left in Europe during the early years of the twentieth century—the movement that spread initiatives, cultural activities, and symbols in favor of the proletariat. The members of that movement, like Robert Mussche himself, were inclined to support the Second Spanish Republic that had been called into question following the military uprising, together with many famous writers and intellectuals. Some of them are mentioned, specifically, as knowing Robert on his journey to

Granollers on the Eastern Front in late May 1938 (M, 67–69). Among others, there is mention that he knew to some extent Ernest Hemingway and André Malraux, but especially the artists Arturo Souto and Victorio Macho. The traumatic experiences he went through in Granollers, not being able to do anything for those he saw dying, would intensify Robert's commitment (M, 60) and he would proclaim that "in addition to creating, artists must liberate" (M, 69). As noted, on the front he discovered the plurinational and plurilinguistic reality of the state known as Spain, because he discovered Catalan, Galician, and Basque.

3 Literature and history

If anything stands out in Uribe's texts, it is the yearning to call into question the boundaries between literature and history. Authors embraced the narrative and discursive nature of the two fields as well as the cultural turn that has been acknowledged in contemporary historiography for some time, and some of them, such as Hayden White (1978, 41), called into question the authority, the supposed objectivity, of historiographical discourse itself. Contemporary literature, and especially fiction, has achieved a renewed legitimacy to speak about a traumatic past and many, moreover, contend that this literature facilitates *writing* trauma (LaCapra 2001, 142–144). Ultimately, efforts to recover the past also imply the acknowledgment that this past also affects the present, and that, from the present, we can make an effort to heal the pain and damage caused by that conflictive past. Following thesis 2 in Walter Benjamin's *Theses on the Philosophy of History*, Reyes Mate (2006, 69) states that "History is undertaken insofar as the present functions as a redemption of the past." And the desire to settle the debt with the past conditions, according to Mario Santana (2019), novel writing that addresses historical memory. This critic affirms that such novels *redeem* the past, they seek to settle past debts, and that they look back with that aim in mind.

That is, ultimately, what Uribe's *Mussche* seeks: to settle past debts by telling the rather unknown story of a committed figure like Robert Mussche. Invoking a literary model that is close to Uribe's narrative, that of W. G. Sebald, we could say that both authors assign literature the same purpose of recognizing and working on a traumatic past. Sebald made it clear that, if we were to compare writers and historians, the former are more appropriate when it comes to exploring the pain provoked by past carnages or, for example, in his own words, that they are "more capable of and responsible for producing accessible and authentic knowledge of the traumatic event" (Wilms 2004, 178). Hence, Sebald's works, such as the novels *Die Ausgewanderten. Vier lange Erzählungen* (1992) and *Austerlitz* (2001), demonstrate the hybridity genre, that of the blending of document and fiction: "I believe it is the junction between document and fiction where the most interesting things happen in literature" (Wolff 2009, 322). In order to overcome those genre boundaries, it is obvious that the same desire also conditions Uribe's work, which seeks to recover historical memory—especially the novels *Mussche* and *Elkarrekin esnatzeko ordua* (The Hour of Waking Together), both of which alternate continuously between historical and narrative tones.

In *Mussche*, the manipulation of narrative time is striking. The alternation of narrative planes that intensify the fragmentary structure is central in the chapters, and unremitting prolepses and analepses suggest movements of memory that come and go. Two narrative times are used to do this. First, that corresponding to a historical event or a specific story, in most cases summarizing events that have been well described by contemporary historiography and using the third person past or future. Second, events situated in the past, those told as if they were happening now or using the future, and those that narrators sprinkle with expressions like "I can imagine," emphazising that the past is recovered, that past is 'created.'

> Following the bombing of Gernika, the Lehendakari Jose Antonio Agirre reinforced the decision to place the children under protection. Between May and June that

> year of 1937, 19,000 children **left** the port of Bilbao en route to several European countries . . . (M, 13; emphasis added)

> And now, in light of the Mirantes' testimonies, **I can picture** Karmentxu Cundin on the ship *Habana*, just like the Mirante sisters, tying and untying her shoelaces, that little Karmentxu would later become a seamstress. Look, look, staring at her shoes, Karmentxu Cundin **won't be sick** on the entire journey. Her brother Ramon, though, will . . . They **will go** to sleep lying back-to-back . . . (M, 16–17; emphasis added)

Another striking example would be the stories of Robert's time at Neuengamme concentration camp. Chapter 15 recounts how he arrives there, his sufferings there, and the arrangement of these contents is truly remarkable. On the one hand, there are long passages told in the past (for example, pages 134–137 and 140–142) which offer specific information and data about the concentration camp (how the prisoners arrived and were classified, the techniques used by the soldiers to terrorize them, the cruel experiments of the physician Alfred Trzebinski, the numbers and deaths of prisoners, and so forth). Following those passages, we can find passages told in the present which portray Robert's experiences in present time (his feelings on the train, getting off the train, and what he does then . . .). It would appear as if the narrator is forcing us to be THERE, to relive what Mussche may have felt. As we can see from all of the examples, thanks to the story, the memory that has been denied to Carmen Mussche, of her father, is created by the narrator, and he offers that creation, 'the paper grave,' to the missing body. He provides a moving testimony for readers in the novel's most tragic passages, when he describes Robert's death in chapter 19: Uribe imagines that, as Robert is about to die, he imagines his daughter calling out "daddy, daddy," the same thing that his daughter Carmen, who never knew her father, said at the station to the prisoners that returned (M, 24):

> There will be no way out. In the very first attack, critically injured by a missile, he **will fall** to the ground, beside a picture that has fallen from the wall as a result of the explosion. A little girl **appears** in the picture, asleep. Robert **will close** his eyes and the little girl **will stroke** his cheek with her little hands, saying "Daddy, daddy." Robert's last gesture will be a smile.
>
> The day before, on May 2, the intelligence service of Great Britain **was informed**, through the Swedish Red Cross, that the bay ships were full of thousands of prisoners . . . (M, 162–163; emphasis added)

4 Art and politics

The central theme of the novel under study here is Robert Mussche's generosity, his sacrifice to the point of giving his life. We are presented with the perspective of Uribe, through his contrast with the behavior of Robert's friend, the writer Herman Thiery, because Robert gave everything in the fight against totalitarianism. Chapter 6 of the novel explains the epiphany-like events which would intensify Robert's commitment. On the one hand, what happened after a bomb fell at the Granollers front, namely, not doing anything to prevent the death of a man who would pass away in front of him and the feeling of guilt that would provoke (M, 59). On the other, the harrowing memory of his own father's death, after suffering for twenty long years, because his father died from extremely harsh living and work conditions (M, 59–60). Robert will never forgive himself for not making more of an effort to prevent those two deaths, and "kneeling, clenching his fists and looking up at the sky" (M, 60) he promises to do everything he can to make sure that something like that never happens again.

As we can see, the function that writers and creativity should have is under consideration here, and this is not at all a new topic in Uribe's work. We would contend that his work is full of metafictional passages which address that function, and questions like "what is writing for?" and "what is the political function of a writer's artistic creation?" traverse his work. There are multiple examples, beginning with his first novel *Bilbao-New York-Bilbao* (2008; English translation, 2014) (BNYB, page references taken from the English-language version), and up to and including his latest novel, *Elkarrekin esnatzeko ordua* (The Hour of Waking Together, 2016). In the former, he suggests the choice made by the Basque painter, Aurelio Arteta. As is well known, the legitimate government commissioned from him a painting of the bombing of Gernika and that request had a clear goal: to condemn the massacre that took place in Gernika before the rest of the world. Instead of doing the painting, "He explained that he was sick of the war; he would prefer to join his family in exile in Mexico. The commission later fell to Pablo Picasso" (BNYB, 12). The autofictional narrator undertakes a reflection; he asks himself what he would have done in that situation, whether he would choose "personal life or creation" (BNYB, 13), and he does not offer any answer, arguing that, "you have to live through the same situation in order to do so" (BNYB, 13). The novel *Elkarrekin esnatzeko ordua*, meanwhile, presents the case of the trumpeter Txomin Letamendi, a musician who said yes to Jose Antonio Agirre's request. He returned from exile in Venezuela and fought against fascism in the secret services, and like Robert Mussche, he paid dearly for doing so.

As is evident, the link between art and politics is multi-sided. On the one hand, it is known that a work of art can be evaluated in many different ways by society. Consider, for example, how the response to Picasso's *Guernica* was transformed from an initial lukewarm critical reception to being considered so politically significant, not just because it refers to Gernika, an indisputable symbol of Basque identity (Raento & Watson 2000, 707), and because it continues to be an indisputable presence in the Basque nationalist community (Bray 2015, 4–6), but because it has also been interpreted as a plea against suffering, against injustice, and for justice. That is precisely what Michel Foucault and Pierre Bordieu explored in their studies: how political and social value was given to art work, and on what levels such art work can be controlled and/or controlling (Bray 2015, 1). In the end, art work is a completely political activity, and just as politics can influence art, so art can influence politics, through ways of understanding and interpreting reality, and offering, as John Berger would say, 'new ways of seeing' (Bray 2015, 4).

There are evidently numerous examples of the political use of art, and we can find them in all ideologies, from the effort (thanks to the early 1950s vanguard) to give a more modern image in the world during the Franco era (Manterola 2018), to (continuing with the references in *Mussche*) the cultural diplomacy pursued abroad by the government of Lehendakari José Antonio Agirre (1904–1930). Indeed, we will find Robert and Karmentxu seated side by side at the Theatre Royale on February 22, 1938 at a performance of the Eresoinka choir, which had been created by the Basque Government (M, 60).

Whatever the case, if we were to give one example of the dependence of contemporary cultural politics on global market logic, we would have to cite the inauguration of the Guggenheim Museum in Bilbao in 1997. This initiative, sustained by the Basque nationalist government, besides halting the decline of postindustrial Bilbao and breathing new life into the city, put Bilbao on the world map "within the global culture of travel and consumerism, bridging transatlantic distances, linking New York with Bilbao and thereby facilitating traffic in modern art, museum franchises, tourism and reformulated urban images" (Douglass & Zulaika 2007, 344). Thereafter, Bilbao and the Basque Country would be associated more with the attraction of the remarkable museum than with the political conflict, and that is precisely the interpretation suggested by Katixa Agirre's novel *Atertu arte itxaron* (Wait Until It Clears Up, 2015) in an interesting literary dialogue it proposes with Kirmen Uribe's

Mussche (Olaziregi 2019, 353–354). This novel, which we might define as a *road novel*, is about a trip all over the Basque Country by the protagonist from Gasteiz, Ulia, with her fiancé Gustavo in the wake of the ETA ceasefire declaration. It is an interesting novel, not just because, like *Mussche*, it is an example of what M. Rothberg (2011) terms *multidirectional memory*, addressing the memories of different conflicts that have intersected. It includes, on the one hand, the memory of ETA terrorism, that of the March 11 Islamist attacks in Madrid, and that of the killings that took place in Gasteiz on March 3, 1976. Yet, this novel also reflects on the role and function that artists can fulfill in political conflicts, with the information Ulia is collecting for her doctoral thesis becoming a pretext for a biography of the well-known British composer Benjamin Britten. Britten, a friend of W.H. Auden, defended his position as a pacifist and conscientious objector in order to refuse to participate in the Second World War. Even so, he promised to adopt an exiled Basque child that he had taken in a year earlier, because of, on the one hand, his lifelong desire to be a father and, on the other, because he saw this as something he could do for those who had been punished dramatically by the war. The child chosen was Andoni Barrutia, a twelve-year-old Basque boy, like Karmentxu Cundin, a Basque child refugee, and he did not enjoy a great deal of luck with Britten, because in the end Britten only looked after him for two weeks at his home, arguing that he was impeding him from the solitude he needed to be creative. The novel transcribes precisely the lack of responsibility Britten demonstrated toward the exiled Basque child:

> That underground story written in lower case swallowed up forever the fate of Andoni Barrutia. How he got on, if he got on at all. Nor did Britten himself ever worry about this boy who he considered to be his son. Not at least in front of anyone else. Thereafter he would be deaf to the call of fatherhood. (*Atertu arte itxaron*, 112)

As we can see, Katixa Agirre's novel *Atertu arte itxaron* proposes an interesting dialogue with Uribe's *Mussche* by raising the case of an artist who gave priority to creative work in the context of Basque children who were exiled in the War of 1936.

5 Conclusions

Previously, we defined Kirmen Uribe's novel *Mussche* as a paper grave written for Robert Mussche, the missing Flemish writer, translator, and activist. As we saw, the novel shares the characteristics attributed to the 'postmemory generation,' because the recuperation of the memory of a traumatic past becomes a creative act, thanks to the images, stories, and other things Carmen Mussche collected throughout her life. At the same time, we underscored the fragmentary nature of the chapters in the novel and the story-document hybridity, thanks to the manipulation of narrative time, as well as the political goal of the novel, because recovering the past is rewriting the past, a testimony to the anonymous heroes that were left voiceless and unrepresented. Ultimately, we find in Uribe's *Mussche* a transcultural journey to the nature of memory in its entirety. And finally, we noted the dialogues that Uribe's *Mussche* has triggered with W. G. Sebald and the work of contemporary Basque writers.

Bibliography

Agirre, Katixa. 2015. *Atertu arte itxaron*. Donostia: Elkar.

Ahmed, Sara. 1999. Home and Away: Narratives of Migration and Estrangement. *International Journal of Cultural Studies*, 329–347. Volume: 2.3.

Assmann, Jan. 1995. Collective Memory and Cultural Identity. *New German Critique* 65: 125–133.

Atxaga, Bernardo. 2003. *Soinujolearen semea*. Iruñea: Pamiela.

Bray, Zoe (ed.). 2015. *Beyond Guernica and the Guggenheim. Art and Politics from a Comparative Perspective.* Reno: Center for Basque Studies.

Douglass, William & Zulaika, Joseba. 2007. *Basque Culture. Anthropological Perspectives.* Reno: Center for Basque Studies.

Erll, Astrid. 2011. Travelling Memory. *Parallax* 17.4: 4–18.

Fischer, Gerarhard (ed.). 2009. *W.G. Sebald. Expatriate Writing.* Amsterdam: Rodopi.

Goia, Garazi. 2013. *Txartel bat (des)herrira.* Donostia: Elkar.

Hirsch, Marianne. 1997. *Family Frames: Photography, Narrative and Postmemory.* Cambridge, MA: Harvard University Press.

LaCapra, Dominick. 2001. *Writing History, Writing Trauma.* John Hopkins U. Press.

Manterola, Ismael. 2018. Frankismoaren zentsura arte plastikoetan. *Euskera* 63, 2.2: 765–788.

Mate, Reyes. 2006. *Medianoche en la historia. Comentarios a las Tesis de Walter Benjamin "Sobre el concepto de la Historia."* Madrid: Trotta.

Nora, Pierre. 1997 [1984]. Entre Mémoire et Histoire. La problématique des lieux. *Les Lieux de Mémoire I*, 23–43. Paris: Gallimard.

Olaziregi, Mari Jose. 2019. "Narrativa vasca y memoria histórica: rememorar para convivir." *eHUMANISTA/ IVITRA* 15 (2019): 342– 361.

Pazos, Antón M. 2013. "La Santa Sede, la República y los niños vascos: una batalla diplomática dentro de la Guerra Civil española." *Hispania Sacra,* LXV, 131, January-June: 385–423.

Raento, Paulina & Watson, Cameron. 2000. Gernika, Guernica, *Guernica*? Contested Meanings of a Basque Place. *Political Geography* 19: 707–736.

Rothberg, Michael. 2011. From Gaza to Warsaw: Mapping Multidirectional Memory. *Criticism*, vol. 53, n 4, 2: 523–548.

Santana, Mario. 2019. Una poética de la redención. Historia y memoria en la ficción contemporánea. Talk given at the Université Bordeaux-Montaigne, May 13, 2019. Unpublished.

Uribe, Kirmen. 2008. *Bilbao-New York-Bilbao*. Donostia: Elkar.

Uribe, Kirmen. 2012. *Mussche.* Zarautz: Susa.

Uribe, Kirmen. 2016. *Elkarrekin esnatzeko ordua*. Zarautz: Susa.

White, Hayden. 1978. *Tropics of Discourse: Essays in Cultural Criticism*. Baltimore: The Johns Hopkins University Press.

Wilms, Wilfried. 2004. Taboo and Repression in W.G. Sebald's *On the Natural History of Destruction*. In *W.G. Sebald: A Critical Companion*, JJ. Long and Anne Whitehead (ed.), 175–189. Seattle, WA: University of Washington Press.

Wolff, Lynn L. 2009. "Literary Historiography: W.G. Sebald´s Fiction." In *W.G. Sebald: Schreiben ex patria / Expatriate Writing*, Gerhard Fischer ed.. Amsterdam/ New York: Rodopi, 317– 330.

POETRY

11

Gestural poetry

Estibalitz Ezkerra Vargas

As regards the recently published collection of poems *Meanwhile Take My Hand* (Graywolf Press, 2007),[76] Kirmen Uribe observed that the poems included therein were an exercise in overcoming the "discourses" and "social norms" that regulated people's lifestyles, the result of an effort to return to the "subject" and, in general, "real things." In the poet's own words, "the reader is fed up with empty words and wants to hear something, feel something" (Padrón 2002). In the prologue to the original edition in Basque (2001, 8), Rikardo Arregi Diaz de Heredia examines the matter of the *subject* and states that in Uribe's book of poems there are no "super human beings," that is, extraordinary individuals or those with divine characteristics. On the contrary, "in this book there are people of all ages, all origins, who live and die in specific places, people who own their bodies." In spite of that, Diaz de Heredia warns readers to proceed with caution when analyzing the themes and characters in the book of poems, and asks that they resist the temptation that one critical model has fallen into of mixing up, hiding, and, to some extent, falsifying what is the mundane—that which is an indicator and indicative of living in this world—with the expression "reflection of everyday life":

76 Kirmen Uribe, *Bitartean heldu eskutik* (Zarautz: Susa, 2001). This chapter is based on a previous online publication (no pagination): http://www.susa-literatura.eus/liburuak/poes33. The poems were translated into English from Basque by Elizabeth Macklin and published as: Kirmen Uribe, *Meanwhile Take My Hand* (Saint Paul, MN: Graywolf Press, 2007).

> We always have the sky over our heads, but . . . in this catastrophe of meanings of words which surrounds us, it seems as if the sky has lost its reality. For every one of us, our father will die once; that is not something which happens every day. Visiting hospitals or going to chemotherapy sessions, that yes, hospitals are full of people every day, and the motorways, and the supermarkets, and the parks. (2001, 9)

As Diaz de Heredia explains, in spite of the fact that tragedy is a part and expression of the human experience, it does not mean that it is routine or that it is expressed or felt in the same way. The latter notion—that is, presenting tragedy as if it were an everyday thing—ruins the singularity of the moment and its very meaning and, moreover, weakens the sentiments it produces.

Uribe's demand for a return to the subject goes against the everyday, precisely because it confronts the apathy and blindness which accompany the assiduousness of arriving at the essence of the subject. "Returning to the subject" means that we must be attentive to the mechanisms which transform the lives of human beings into something worthy of being lived. Those mechanisms are at the core of *Meanwhile Take My Hand*: the body, affect, and gesture.

1 The body

It is undeniable that technology and mass media have had a profound effect on human experience. In addition to carrying out the task of intermediation between us and reality, they condition the way in which we perceive that reality and even tell us what reality itself is. If we heed postmodern theories, as a consequence of the presence and hegemony of mass media in our lives, it no longer makes sense to ask what is real; because our experiences are so influenced, that is, so conditioned, any attempt to get at their core will be futile, because one referent will just lead us to another in a never-ending loop. The false simultaneity caused by the suppression of time and space which the media create, that empty homogeneous time (and space) which facilitates the birth of the modern nation-state according to Benedict Anderson (2006), reduces the distances as regards image and sound, leading to the sensation that what is "there" is actually "here." Yet, as has been noted, that is no more than an illusion. The bodies that populate the diverse geographies of the world continue in their place, perhaps further than ever away from one another and with a greater probability of perishing depending on where they are situated. The preferential place that postmodern theories grant figurative and verbal representation has some effect on the estrangement process with respect to the body and bodies, that is, to matter. The reality we experience will be a fiction, a fiction shaped by discourses and, insofar as we are corporal beings, we will inevitably die.

Having a body totally conditions human existence: having a body makes us vulnerable, fragile in the face of misfortune. We are matter that at some point dies and disintegrates. That is a fact. The poems included in *Meanwhile Take My Hand* confront that fundamental feature of the human condition and, alongside life, show us death, alongside achievement show us loss, without forgetting at any moment the materiality of the body. In the celebrated poem "Visit," for example, the sick woman equates the process of her decaying body to the deterioration to which drug addiction has condemned her, to remaining in her hospital bed. All organic things spoil, rot, disintegrate, decompose. In the case of the poem, it is particularly tough: "the needles hurt" in that weakened body and "the serum sends the cold through every one of [her] veins." But matter does not rot immediately; on the contrary, it is a process which occurs gradually, little by little. In that sense, the verb "rot," unlike the verb "die," adds a special emphasis as regards time. On the one hand, it is a preamble and a sign of death and, on the other, it makes the death process perceptible. In the context of the poem, the process of her decaying body marks the sick woman's presence and also her approaching absence—she is still alive but death is inevitable. That fact, in addition to underscoring the transcendence of the moment—she is still alive—transforms the reader into a witness of what is inevitable: the sick woman is fading away before our eyes.

Nevertheless, not all bodies suffer the same vulnerability. As Judith Butler states in her *Frames of War* (2009), some bodies are more prone than others to being wounded. Yet that is not a characteristic particular to the body in general. On the contrary, the way we perceive some bodies, in particular, will condition their life: a life will be exhilarating, or it will be precarious (in other words, take place in bad conditions and with a short life expectancy), whether losing that life leads to grief or not. In *Frames of War*, Butler critiques the so-called War on Terror carried out by the US government in the wake of the attack on the Twin Towers in New York on September 11, 2001. She analyzes lives condemned to uncertainty; that is, she examines the bodies that, as a consequence of that war, are more vulnerable and are at greater risk of dying: those of Arabs, Muslims, and, in general, dark-skinned people. In the attack on the Twin Towers, both in the buildings and in the planes that crashed into them, there were Arabs, Muslims, and dark-skinned people. Many of them were even US citizens. Their death, however, did not catch the attention of the media; the authorities did not ask people to pray for them; their loss did not cause widespread sorrow. The existence of those bodies was not worth anything and, therefore, their death was not perceived as a loss.

One need not go far to find bodies that are not deserving of grief. There are, knocking at our doors, those people converted into refugees and migrants as a consequence of political and economic conflicts. Thus, war takes up a lot of space in *Meanwhile Take My Hand*. However, in a search to question the hegemonic discourse of Europe and North America in recent decades, war does not appear as a distant phenomenon which does not have any connection to "us." In the poem "Bad Dream," for example, the vague nature of the context (there is no information to clarify which war the narrator is talking about) facilitates the negotiation of distance between what is being narrated in the poem and the reader, and it also makes possible all kinds of connections and "domesticating" options. Readers in the Basque Country perhaps connect what is said in the poem to the Spanish Civil War, and those in English possibly to Syria or somewhere else. Nevertheless, the singularity of the poem "Bad Dream" does not consist of its capacity to suggest a common space that some would consider characteristic of universal literature, but rather in its ability to present a fact that can be considered universal, the experience of war, in a specific way: the poem speaks from a point of view that is not usually employed in official histories, that of children. The children in the poem are fleeing in a car: ". . . longing to take advantage / of the last chance their fate had left them," in order to try and ". . . cross the border, without any grown-ups / alone, when they just barely know how to drive." This could be understood as an act of bravery—the children leave of their account without any adult supervision in a car they can hardly drive—but their parents' desperation, which is noted immediately thereafter, adds another nuance: they "preferred their children to die on the highway / than in the city the bombs daily ripped apart." It is significant that one form of death, in this case dying in a car crash, is presented as if it were better than another (dying as a result of war), because the form in which one's body comes to an end is not just any old occurrence. The way a person dies can be revealing of what kind of life they have had. If a child were to die in a traffic accident it would be a tragedy, of course, but children will still be children, and the traffic accident, an accident. War, however, is a more complex phenomenon, because the dead that have not participated in it directly disappear from the discourse of war itself, transformed into civilians. It is not important who they were before the conflict started, what kind of life they led, what their dreams were. From the moment in which they become dead civilians they become a statistic. As Didier Fassin explains, statistics are not a mere abstraction; they reflect how we perceive specific lives and specific deaths. Death statistics are insubstantial, distant, opaque.[77] In the media, the civilian deaths in war are the spectacle of the body that demonstrates the traces of violence in the conflict: it is easy to recognize a victim in these disfigured bodies, but it will give us no information about the bodies these corpses once were. That will be lost in the mists of time, to the benefit of the triumph of statistical data. The poem titled "Bad Dream," in contrast, confronts that statistical vision, presenting the children as children, in a car they barely know how to drive, without any kind of protection, fleeing from the disaster.

Likewise, the poem "Soldadu mongoliarrak" ("Mongolian soldiers")[78] addresses the subject of war, in this case in order to highlight deconstructed geographies and bodies intermingled with concepts of distance and proximity. The subject matter of the poem is that of Mongolian soldiers who during the Second World War were on the side of the Allied or the Axis powers. Once the war was over, both sides abandoned them and they escaped in a lorry. But it is a futile escape since they do not know where to go. "It will not be easy to return to their home / across a continent. It's impossible / For those who have lost they are no more than slaves; / for those who have won, traitors." After having risked their lives for the European and North American powers, nobody now wants them; their bodies were valuable on the battlefields, but outside them they are worth nothing. In the end, they drive the lorry into the River Po and they all drown. In spite of the non-Western soldiers' important actions (both in WWI and WWII), they —like the Mongolian soldiers— shine by their absence in Western historiography; their deaths do not even take up a sentence. At the end of the day, there can be no grief for the death of a body that has not even existed.

The poem titled "Mohammed" takes another step in that direction when it comes to explaining the involvement

77 Didier Fassin. "What Is (a) Life Worth? Biolegitimacy and Inequality" (paper presented at the Critical Inequalities Conference, University of Illinois, Urbana-Champaign, USA, May 9–10, 2014).

78 Translator's note: This poem does not appear in the English-language edition of the book.

between Europe and the bodies it does not want, in exploring more deeply the relationship between past and present. The narrator, Mohammed, tells us that, "I thought of father's story as we crossed from Tangiers to Cádiz. / Father lost his arm in a European war," but he could not stay there, most likely because of the mistrust of bodies from the same place as his father. Such mistrust is nothing new but, rather, something very old, as is obvious in the story Mohammed's father tells him about the tower in Toledo: there is a long history of hatred toward Arabs, in spite of the fact that the explanations usually given to justify this have changed. His father's warnings falling on deaf ears; the son, some decades later, at night, takes the same route that his father did, because for bodies like his it is impossible to cross the border by day. In the prison yard he recalls his homeland, the stories his father told him as a child, the scam pulled by a trafficker who was going to help him on the journey and the load of money he lost because of him, the beauty of Western European cities, the police harassment, and the death of his friend. Unlike his father, Mohammed has not lost his arm, but his fate is not much better than that of his father: that of Mohammed is another body consumed by Europe.

2 Affect

One of the original qualities of the poem "Visit" is that the events are not told from the sick woman's point of view, but from her brother's perspective. He reminds us of the things his sister, who has not yet woken up after her operation, told him—her fears, what she requested each time her family came to visit. Similarly, "Bad Dream," "Soldadu mongoliarrak," and "Mohammed" are poems based on memories: they do not just relate events; through the process of narration they rescue what has been forgotten from oblivion and encourage the reader to remember them. Memory is not called into action in just any way, but something must activate it. That something must have a certain value for whoever is remembering, it must make them feel something that it is worth being recalled. In order to understand the nexus of the object-affect-memory chain, Sara Ahmed's (2006) words can be of use. According to Ahmed, affect is specific because it is always aimed at an object: "So when we feel fear, we feel fear *of* something" and we feel happy because something makes us so. Ahmed terms the relationship between object and affect "emotional intentionality" and, according to this relationship, it links affect with contact; we are affected by that which we come into contact with:

> In other words, emotions are directed to what we come into contact with: they move us "toward" and "away" from such objects. So, we might fear an object that approaches us. The approach is not simply about the arrival of an object: it is also how we turn toward that object. The feeling of fear is directed toward that object, while it also apprehends the object in a certain way, as being fearsome. (2006, 2–4)

According to Ahmed, the affective response of the subject in regard to the object will depend on the way in which the former orients itself in relation to the latter (if it perceives it as "near" or "far" and the meaning of distance for the subject). In the same way, the orientation of the subject in relation to the object may collapse the distance between what the former feels and the latter expresses: being afraid of the other may turn one into that fearsome other. The process which leads from the object of fear to the subject of fear is the result of exercising epistemological violence: the subject refuses to let the object project on it its desires and fears. In the poem "Soldadu mongoliarrak" we can see a clear example of this exercise, since the countries that have made use of those soldiers in the title of the poem define them as "slaves" and "traitors" because their bodies are no longer useful/desirable. That extension of the distance between the two of them will condition the fact that, later, the bodies of the Mongolian soldiers are or are not perceptible.

Specifically, emotional intentionality or the possibility that an object might provoke a certain effect is related to past histories or, as Ahmed explains, "impressions on the skin" (2–4). In that sense, it will be difficult for something that we have forgotten in the present to excite or mobilize us. Therefore, poems like "Bad Dream," "Soldadu mongoliarrak," and "Mohammed" are, as well as an exercise in memory, affective exercises; at the same time we recover forgotten events and the bodies involved therein, this suggests an affective map on which distances are reduced, the involvement of bodies is acknowledged, and the possibilities of a collective "we" are expanded.

3 Gesture

The poem "The River," which begins *Meanwhile Take My Hand*, speaks about an absence: we can no longer see the river that at one time was in plain sight. In the place where it once was there are now "benches and pavement"; the narrator tells us that "Now it's a square in the workers' quarter." Later we are told that the river cannot be seen but that it has not disappeared entirely: three poplars are a sign that the river keeps running, below the earth. Like the poplars, the oldest people there retain a memory of the river and say that a dozen more rivers like the "disappeared" one lie underneath the city. The narrator compares the covered river to the feelings people hide within but that are perceptible from the outside: "If they are not fears, they're contritions. / If they are not doubts, inabilities." But how to bring them to the surface? What must one do to recognize and overcome the fears, the contritions, the doubts, and the inabilities? In the next scene, there is a woman throwing articles of clothing from her window, among them her wedding dress, which gets stuck in one of the poplars. Would they perhaps be her fears and contritions, her doubts and inabilities? The poem does not clarify this. Instead, we are immediately told that the wind has uprooted the poplar tree from which the dress was hanging, and that its roots "could be an older woman's hand / awaiting any other husband's caressing." Before her last operation, the sick woman in the poem "Visit" asks for a similar gesture from her relatives—that they take her hand: "I don't want promises, I don't want repentance, / just some sign of love is all." In the other poems examined here—"Bad Dream," "Soldadu mongoliarrak," and "Mohammed"—the gesture offered to another is present in memory.

In the face of disaster, there is little that a caress, taking someone's hand, or recalling a specific event can do. In that kind of small gesture, however, there is a declaration: it is a sign that we are attentive to someone else and that we feel close to them. Their presence touches us and mobilizes us and, in the face of what is causing them anguish, we offer them consolation and express our sympathy. That is the activism suggested by the poems in *Meanwhile Take My Hand*: the revolution that a small gesture can mean in order to convert life into something exhilarating and make bodies worthy of grief.

Bibliography

Ahmed, Sara. 2006. *Queer Phenomenology: Orientations, Objects, Others*. Durham: Duke UP.

Anderson, Benedict. 2006. *Imagined Communities: Reflections on the Origins and Spread of Nationalism*. London: Verso.

Butler, Judith. 2009. *Frames of War: When Is Life Grievable?* New York: Verso.

Fassin, Didier. What Is (a) Life Worth? Biolegitimacy and Inequality. ("Critical Inequalities" conference, May 9–10, 2014, University of Illinois, Urbana-Champaign, Illinois, USA.

Padron, Jose Luis. 2002. Hitzaren esanahietan sakontzea. *Bilbao*, April.

Uribe, Kirmen. 2007. *Meanwhile Take My Hand*. Translated from Basque by Elizabeth Macklin. Saint Paul, MN: Graywolf [2001. *Bitartean heldu eskutik*. Zarautz: Susa].

12

Kirmen Uribe's work and an interpretation of *Bar Puerto*

Lourdes Otaegi

1 *Bar Puerto*, Uribe's seminal work

It is widely accepted that *Bitartean heldu eskutik* (2001; *Meanwhile Take My Hand*, 2007), which Kirmen Uribe published in 2001, is, next to *Harri eta Herri* (Stone and Town/Country) by Gabriel Aresti and *Etiopia* by Bernardo Atxaga, the most successful poetry book among the Basque-speaking readership.[79] The book attracted critical attention because of this success and on account of its deserved acceptance at the international level, given that it has gone through two editions in Spanish, via the Visor publishing house, and has been published in Catalan, French, English, Russian, and Georgian.

We will discuss *Bar Puerto. Bazterreko ahotsak* (*Bar Puerto: Voices from the Edge*), a project that saw the light of day that same year, with the aim of making some small contribution to Uribe's poetical work. *Bar Puerto* was published by the record label Gaztelupeko ahotsak and is based on a multimedia performance taken to the stage in different places in the year 2000 by Mikel Urdangarin and Bingen Mendizabal together with Kirmen Uribe. In fact, in Kirmen Uribe's two creations *Bitartean heldu eskutik* (the book of poetry) and *Bar Puerto* (the C.D.), two of his literary contributions come together—so much so that the success of the book is due, according to different experts and in addition to its quality, to the impact

79 From the beginning, Jon Kortazar linked Uribe's novelty and success to his communication in performances. As evidence of that, see, among other things, "Cuerpos y voces: postmodernidad y poesía en la obra de Kirmen Uribe," *Bulletin of Hispanic Studies* (2008): 111–142.

resulting from the festivals and recitals which are at the base of the compact disc. Jon Kortazar (2009, 2011) specifies that Uribe made a name for himself thanks to the shows he put on as part of the Korrika cultural festival in the year 2000, together with Urdangarin and Mendizabal, the resulting press reports were well received and enhanced his reputation.

Here, seeking to go beyond the nexus between the book of poems and the compact disc, we would like to formulate a new hypothesis: that the "first seed" of Uribe's later work is also to be found in the poems and narrative of *Bar Puerto*. On the one hand, the short story in *Bar Puerto* relates a journey taken by someone going through a crisis, from the big city to their hometown. But, as the text reveals, it is also a trip to the heart of oneself, and this dual journey would become a constant element in Uribe's later works: the author carries out the task of a search or an internal quest, in order to do so making use of a journalist's strategies (archives, letters, diaries, interviews) and, simultaneously, he searches for and questions himself, and reflects on how to fit into the world. Furthermore, there is a second constant element in his works: the need to collect the testimony of marginal voices. The reflection on the testimonies of the silenced is a permanent element in Uribe's work.

Our goal is to demonstrate that the short story of *Bar Puerto* is the seminal creative work of Uribe's literary identity, and that the originality one can perceive in this work is significant in so far as it implies the initial development of a spirit that would pervade the author's later works. Although the objective of this chapter is to demonstrate all this, we must also mention other multimedia performances by Uribe: on the one hand, *Zaharregia, txikiegia agian* (Too Old, Too Small, Maybe, 2003); and on the other, a sung recital which he offered on the annual poetry day held in Madrid, titled *La noche en blanco* (Sleepless Night) and in which a Madrid-based musician, Quique González, also took part, to great acclaim, at the Fine Arts Circle hall in Madrid; subsequently, this recital was also given in Barcelona. In July 2011 he took part in the Medellín Poetry Festival in Colombia, the largest poetry festival in the world, although this time with a Colombian musician, Oriol Caro. Put succinctly, Uribe has taken part in many collaborations and shows, the most recent of which took place in 2018 with pianist Vim Mertens in the performance titled *Mussche*. Here, as in his novel, the protagonist is Robert Mussche, a Flemish writer who shelters the Basque child Karmentxu Cundin and, as a member of the Resistance against the Nazis during the Second World War, even spends time in concentration camps. Kirmen Uribe published this book, based on Mussche's life, in 2012, and he conceived this special concert with the same narrative thread in mind. Mertens put the book to music in the form of a soundtrack. Uribe, meanwhile, read out passages from the book as well as unpublished poems related to the subject matter.

The second project which most resembles the topic of study here is *Zaharregia, txikiegia agian*, given that as regards its content, we can find the same spirit in both. While the former came in the form of a compact disc and the performance was accompanied by a visual complement in the form of cinematographic images by Josu Izagirre, the latter led directly to a film: Arkaitz Basterra created the documentary *Agian* on the basis of Kirmen Uribe's multimedia show, and Basterra's feature film was presented at Zinemaldia, the San Sebastián International Film Festival. It included Kirmen Uribe's poetry, music by Mikel Urdangarin, Bingen Mendizabal, and Rafa Rueda, and Mikel Valverde's illustrations, all in a joint creative process. The title of the documentary was taken from one of Uribe's poems which concerns the contribution of culture produced in the Basque language. Specifically, the members of the group ask themselves how they can contribute to international culture, but, besides that, they also question the fundamental basis of what it means to be human. Those five people have something to contribute through their identity, creativity, and work.

One particular aspect of the documentary's narrative thread is interesting for our purposes here. To reiterate, the documentary, titled *Agian*, focuses on the show *Zaharregia, txikiegia agian*, a multimedia project created out of Uribe's poetry in 2003, and a project created in New York out of the experience of a recital offered by the poet and the musicians. It was also published in the form of a CD-book, and the documentary was filmed in the context of a worldwide tour of the multimedia show. In Basterra's opinion, at the end of the day, the essence of the film is that everyone has dimensions that they share with all other humans and that Basques are no exception to this, that being an old and small culture is no impediment to that. In a minute-long presentation of the video *Agian*,[80] Uribe says the following: the core of his discourse is "love for human beings who are hidden in their most intimate corners." Herein, clearly and concisely, are words that are the starting point of our hypothesis: love for the marginalized and an effort to give them protagonism, one of the two basic ingredients of the *Bar Puerto* performance, which is the legitimation of the contribution of Basque speakers. Let us examine, then, section by section, the steps taken in this argument.

Beforehand, however, we should offer some introductory words about the success of Uribe's lyrical work and opinions about the influence on this achievement of the characteristics of his poetry and the multimedia methods used to disseminate it.

2 A bad moment for lyrical poetry?

Poesia hilda al dago? (Has poetry died?) asks Joseba Sarrionandia on the cover of his latest collection of poems. And before answering the question, in the poem of the same name, he tells us straight away yes, that it is dead, but that poetry is not the guilty party. In the prologue to this work, Sarrionandia says that in his opinion poetry probably died in the nineteenth century alongside God, starting with that famous "*Gott ist tot*" of the philosopher Friedrich Nietzsche. And this affirmation saw God as linked to a cosmic consciousness. That loss brought with it a freedom of the spirit, a freedom from the obsolete forms that

80 See http://www.sonoraestudios.es/films/works_view.php?id=15

came down to us from antiquity, and from the connections established by the hierarchy of myth and theocracy or by the determined forms and rules of poetry that were left behind.[81] According to Sarrionandia, from that moment on, in the same way that modern humans reflect on their identity, so poetry is reinventing its essence continually. Perhaps that is why poetry has been so metapoetic during the last century, because it must re-establish its own essence: one perceives that poets are continually reflecting on its essence, its function, and its place, especially poets like Sarrionandia.

Sarrionandia, in asking if poetry is dead, raises the question of the durability of this genre. News of the death of poetry leads us inevitably to inquire into the vitality of the genre: what usefulness or functionality does this prestigious genre have nowadays?

The interaction between poetry and society was a preoccupation throughout the twentieth century for Basque writers. Actually, although we could extend this as far as we want in reflecting at the theoretical level on the crisis of poetry, it is clear that statistics reveal the first clues as to the decline in the number of readers of this genre. The systematic data collection carried out by Joan Mari Torrealdai (1997, 332–335) highlights the fact that, during the 1990s, the number of readers, poets, and literary products declined, and the gap between narrative and poetry grew. According to the statistics, growth came to a halt in the 1980s and fell noticeably in the 1990s. The number of poetry books sold did not reach half that of novels. Moreover, poetry books are hardly ever reprinted. A print run of a thousand copies fully meets the demand of readers. Translations, meanwhile, make up only 13.3 percent of poetry books. After carrying out the survey, Torrealdai's

81 Nietzsche's *Die fröhliche Wissenschaft* also addresses the subject, and that is where Sarrionandia's joke comes from: "God is dead. God remains dead. And we have killed him. How shall we comfort ourselves, the murderers of all murderers? What was holiest and mightiest of all that the world has yet owned has bled to death under our knives: who will wipe this blood off us? What water is there for us to clean ourselves?" (Nietzsche, *The Gay Science*, section 125).

conclusions state clearly that publishing houses consider the market for Basque poetry to be too small and such a small print run does not justify publication.[82] As Torrealdai says succinctly, publishers contend that if a book of poems sells more than 500 copies, it can be considered a bestseller. Yet the situation is the same, too, in other languages. According to the data of J.M. Mondelo (*L'auteur multimedia*, 1991), one can see that poetry print runs are extremely small: in France, too, a poetry book is a bestseller if it sells more than 1,000 copies.

Torrealdai, the Basque sociologist states that poetry functions better, however, in the magazine sector, and asks whether this would not be better refuge for the genre in the Basque case as well. Having arrived at this point, I think we should look for the parameters which might clarify the paradox of the success of Uribe's *Bitartean heldu eskutik*, given that the first edition published in 2001 sold out in a month and a half. We could say that, in the field of poetry, it has been the bestseller of our times, both according to Basque and French standards.

Experts have reflected on the crisis of poetry in the context of Basque literature. According to the data, the historiography affirms that both at the time of the Spanish Second Republic and during the long post-civil war era, until 1975, poetry was the hegemonic and canonical genre. Jon Kortazar, speaking about poetry published in the 1980s (1997), described both the weakening of vanguard poetry and the notable arrival of the poetry of experience and the poetry of commitment. From the Spanish transition to democracy onwards, in his opinion, it was obvious that the centrality achieved by narrative, and the health of this modern genre, was an expression of the maturity of Basque literature, coinciding with the coming of literary autonomy in place of the canonical nature of poetry. For her part, Mari Jose Olaziregi (1998), after considering the findings of surveys on the habits of readers of Basque literature, suggested

82 Writers, however, point out that the quality of poetry has decreased and, specifically, Koldo Izagirre suggests it is perfect poetry but it does not "express anything" (Torrealdai, 336).

another important reason for this change in the canonical nature of the genres: she argued that Basque literature demonstrated a great dependency on teaching and that, seeing as how narrative texts made up the majority of obligatory readings in school, it came as no surprise that poetry sales were small in comparison to the rest.[83]

Hasier Etxeberria collected authors' opinions about the crisis of poetry in his collection of interviews *Bost idazle* (2002). In one of these, Bernardo Atxaga would suggest the need to respond positively to the crisis of poetry, contending that literature has no limits and that authors should not limit themselves to typical or everyday topics, but should instead be ambitious and bold with new methods and subject matter. He believed that, in order to do so, writers should get closer to readers: "They should be a desert preacher" (Etxeberria 2002, 33).

In line with this collection of opinions, among Torrealdai's suggestions there is one especially interesting way of exploring the crisis in poetic production. In his opinion, book production must compete with multimedia products and, therefore, Basque literature is changing rapidly: in post-transition products there was a strengthening of the tendency to publish in a joint book and multimedia way (both on diskette and CD). In Torrealdai's words, multimedia products have not replaced books, but they have changed them radically:

83 Drawing on the conclusions of Harkaitz Zubiri's work, in which he examines the number and profile of readers of current Basque literature (2013: 51), there are around 15,000–20,000 enthusiastic habitual readers of Basque literature, around 40,000 moderate habitual readers, and some 100,000–150,000 sporadic or specifically momentary readers (including the former). Of those, "the vast majority live in Gipuzkoa and Bizkaia, mainly in the former, and there are certainly more women readers; most are in the 25–54 age range, and, perhaps, most have been to university." Based, then, on this profile of Basque literature readers, we would also need up-to-date studies on poetry readers, since Zubiri's interesting work does not offer any information about readers' preferences as regards literary genres. Zubiri, Harkaitz (2013) "Euskal literaturaren irakurleak zenbat eta nolakoak diren aztergai. Soziolinguistikako datuetatik eta irakurketa ohiturei buruzko ikerketetatik abiatuta," *Uztaro*, 87, 51–68.

> As well as blending genres together, the writer must invent new creative universes, using new technologies; they have the text to hand, a fixed and living image, sound and so on. Nowadays, texts are not prisoners of their material support. (1997, 551)

In this vein, we could say that, for forty years, multimedia platforms helped Basque poetry to forge ahead between the pages of poetry books and the ears of readers. Indeed, given that literature in Basque, and especially the lyrical genre, has an extensive oral tradition in oral transmission, from the 1960s to the present, public performances and recorded versions (record, diskette, compact disc, and online) have, in Basque culture, become a valuable resource for contemporary Basque poets to reach their readers.

On being questioned about the crisis of Basque poetry, Uribe said that poetry took too much shelter in books and that it should seek out new ways of reaching recipients (Asurmendi 2003). He believed, however, that this search demanded a modernizing process and knowing how to adapt to the needs of society. The poetic voice and the demands of readers should encounter one another naturally. Continuing with these opinions, the poetry of authors who have chosen the multimedia path has been dynamic and successful when it has been set to music. When an unknown poem shut away in a book has been set to music and presented in public performances, it has often become very well known, whether the poem has been sung by the author or whether poets' texts chosen by singer-songwriters have been combined with music or used in recitals. But perhaps one cannot cite the undeniable impact of multimedia composition as the only reason for the success of Uribe's poetry, since we have also seen how other similar projects have failed or have had little effect. Context is also important. One should recall, for example, that *Bar Puerto* became known as part of the Korrika cultural festival celebrations, and that among its elements, besides poetry and music, there was a complex performance of light, images, and theatrical props.

As noted already, *Bar Puerto* was not the first such performance to be done in Basque, so what made it special?

The first people to incorporate performance into Basque literature were the members of the group Ez dok amairu (They are not thirteen). In 1965, as well as reviving and playing popular songs in a modern way, they began to set poetic texts in Basque to music in order to communicate Basque cultural heritage to people. Seeking to unite tradition and vanguard, Joxan Artze and Mikel Laboa made the most significant contributions and, after the group split up, Laboa continued to present performances both with Atxaga and the texts of Sarrionandia. In previous works I analyzed the dramatic force of Laboa's *lekeitiokoak*, for example the short pieces titled "Gernika" and "Komunikazioa-inkomunikazioa."[84] Furthermore, certain dramatic elements that Xabier Lete incorporated into his song recitals, such as the communications, explanations, and confessions he made between texts, also had an important function in reaching the public, and his later songs were aided by well-known dramatized interpretation, using the communication of body language better than any other singer-songwriter. For we should not forget that Lete acted between the 1960s and 1980s with the groups Jarrai and Intxisu.

The shows by Ez dok amairu and by Laboa combined elements of such performances by integrating the characteristics of an artistic rite. The performers, despite not acting in the strictest sense, did so in some way as actors "conferred" with an artistic rite: they offered their expression transformed into something intensely emotional, and made the audience feel like a participant in the collective, a participant in a live dynamic experience.[85]

84 See, among others, "Mikel Laboaren *lekeitioak*: Esanezina oihu bilakatua," in *Oroimenaren lekuak eta lekukoak*, I.Arroita & L. Otaegi (ed.) (Bilbao: University of the Basque Country, 2015), 147–170.

85 Johan Huizinga defined performance as: "A free activity standing quite consciously outside ordinary life as being 'not serious' but at the same time absorbing the player intensely and utterly" (Marvin Carlson,

The poet members of the Pott Banda group also made use of live performance in order to make their poetry accessible to readers. We should not forget the records of Ruper Ordorika, since LPs like *Hautsi da anfora* (The amphora is broken), icons of the early 1980s, drew readers' attention to the books of Atxaga and Sarrionandia, and made them into symbols of the contemporary counterculture. But live performance incorporated resources that reached the group's audience more directly, and in this terrain special mention should be made of the show *Henry Bengoa Inventarium*, which Pott Banda performed between 1986 and 1987. In comparison to the previous performances of Ez dok amairu or Laboa and Artze, the distinctiveness of *Henry Bengoa Inventarium* resided in the presence of a narrative thread. Recalling its plot, Henry Bengoa has disappeared and the people who are out looking for him carry out an inventory of the objects found in his home, at the request of the owner of the house. His friends try to guess how and why Henry has disappeared. In Atxaga's words, that show was a "hybrid," given that it implied a fusion of different literary genres (narration, poetry, epistles, and theatrical dialogues) and songs. As well as voices modulating in the different genres cited, there were gestures, sounds, onomatopoeias, lights, smoke, and a basic ritualized choreography which brought the performance close to drama. One should recall that within this narrative thread, the text and other elements changed from one performance to another as they were adapted to the place, audience, and other variables (as Laboa used to do in his shows) to the point of making each one unique. The group which dominated public performances in the following decade (the 1990s) was the Lubaki ensemble, whose principal members were Harkaitz Cano and Asier Serrano, and subsequently both have participated in performances in which poetry and music are combined.

Kirmen Uribe arrived in the same vein, and he has been the most active poet to use the technique of multimedia performance

---

Performance: A Critical Introduction (London and New York: Routledge, 1996), 13.

in the twenty-first century, gaining much renown with the shows *Bar Puerto* and *Zaharregia, txikiegia agian* (Too Old, Too Small, Maybe). In this regard, Joseba Gabilondo (2009), taking as his starting point the existent relationship between Basque poetry and orality, and reflecting on the reasons why Uribe's first book of poems was so successful, rejects the idea that it was because of the quality of the poetry or his affective approach. In Gabilondo's opinion, the reason for the success of Uribe's book is the appeal of his performances in taking his poetry to a wider audience. In his opinion, the success of Uribe's book can be explained thanks to another argument: "The history of Basque poetry is a postmodern history which is situated *wholly*[86] within the setting of orality and performance" (2009, 37). Both Gabilondo and Kortazar argue that his public image has been popularized by his articles in the press, and that his poetic performances in the form of song, recital, and lecture made him famous, even before the publication of his first book. Gabilondo's hypothesis, however, goes even further and in this regard he states:

> The 'meaning,' 'quality' and 'success' of Uribe's book can *only*[87] be interpreted on the basis of this complex and widely deployed performance, not as a text, but as a poetic performance. (2009, 39)

In Gabilondo's view, then, Uribe's poetry and literature are "revolutionary"[88] because he has understood how to use, in a very fitting way, the "importance and opportunity of literary performance" (2009) and because he has succeeded in convincing those close to him of how productive this direction is. In this same vein, following various poetry and music recitals during the early years of the twenty-first century—such as *Ibiltarixanak* (2001,

86 Emphasis in the original.
87 Emphasis in the original.
88 This is an allusion to the "quiet revolution" of Uribe's poetics. See, among others, Kortazar, Jon, *Bitartean New York: Kirmen Uriberen literaturgintza* (Donostia: Utriusque Vasconiae, 2011) (in English: *Contemporary Basque Literature: Kirmen Uribe's Proposal*, Madrid: Iberoamericana/Vervuert, 2013).

Iñigo Aranbarri and Jose Luis Otamendi)[89] and *Mugarri Estaliak* ("Covered Limits," 2008, Castillo Suarez, Juan Migel Arzelus, and Koldo Arrantz)—Gabilondo speaks about the *Katamalo* (Mask) phenomenon, which has been especially important, and cites the words of the researcher Iratxe Retolaza.[90] Speaking about the success of *Katamalo*, which emerged out of a collaboration between Gorka Arbizu, the singer-guitarist from the group Berri Txarrak, and Gotzon Barandiaran, Retolaza coined the term "Katamalo phenomenon" to describe the fascination among listeners with this collaboration. The poetic-musical experiment included, moreover, poems by Barandiaran and texts by Joseba Sarrionandia and Jose Luis Otamendi in the shows put on between 2004 and 2008. After two years performing under the name Katamalo, they recorded the CD *Erantzi. Katamalo zuzenean* (Undress. Katamalo Live) with a repertoire of 21 poems accompanied by the music of the violin, piano, guitar, and accordion.

We can also define the "Katamalo phenomenon" as poetry that is performed and transformed into song, and Gabilondo considers it a continuation of the trail blazed by Uribe. Looking at these phenomena dating from this decade together, one should perhaps recall the influence of a factor that has been often overlooked by researchers to date: namely, that the skill and sensibility of musicians as well as the contribution of other generally overlooked elements like projections, lights, videos, props, and so on are fundamental to the success of the performance, to the success of the collaboration between musicians and poets, as well as to that of the writers' texts.

89 *Ibiltarixanak* was a demonstration of a 50-year-long journey through poetry, undertaken with the help of song, music, poetry, and language. Taking its title from a book of the same name by Toribio Etxebarria, a writer from Eibar, a show was created in which texts were sung and read out by the following authors: Orixe, Nemesio Etxaniz, Gabriel Aresti, Joxe Azurmendi, Koldo Izagirre, Joseba Sarrionandia, Itxaro Borda, Rikardo Arregi Diaz De Heredia, Jose Luis Otamendi, Miren Agur Meabe, Juanjo Olasagarre, and Iñigo Aranbarri. The musicians were Imanol Ubeda, Jon Ander Ubeda, and Karlos Arantzegi.

90 Iratxe Retolaza "Literatur taldeak eta emenaldiak" (2008), talk following the end of the *Katamalo* shows (place unknown).

There is no doubt that these elements have been decisive, among other reasons, due to the memorable collaborations between Laboa and Artze, between Atxaga and Ordorika, and between Sarrionandia and Ordorika. And this was the case, likewise, in the collaboration between Uribe and Urdangarin and between Barandiaran and Urbizu.

The reason for the success of the multimedia shows is also to be found in the music, something that is clearly appealing to recipients, and also in the aesthetics adapted from images. In the case under study here, in Uribe's poetic performance, the involvement of the popular singer Mikel Urdangarin and his group was decisive; likewise, Josu Izagirre's video contribution was essential when it came to situating the texts and the music within the multimedia aesthetic. As Jon Kortazar suggests, Uribe's script and texts were very suited to carrying out the kinds of performances which also had been undertaken previously by Markuleta, Zaldua, Aranbarri, Otamendi, Aristi, and others in order to "take poetry into the streets, to make those who do not read poetry taste the delicacy of the genre, yet taking care of the materials, enriched by the dialogue among the arts, looking after and improving the conditions of poetic communication" (Kortazar 2011, 15).

One must acknowledge the influence of Urdangarin's voice, of the group's music, and of Izagirre's video on the aesthetic result of the performance, but the script and text were Uribe's, and in my opinion, contrary to Gabilondo's argument, Uribe's personal poetics were decisive in the success of the show and the book; the authenticity and proximity that his method of communication transmits are well-known qualities of Uribe's gaze, as is the aesthetic-affective perspective which he chooses in order to explore his subject matter. In the next section we will analyze and reveal these poetics on the basis of a detailed interpretation of the structure of and texts in the performance *Bar Puerto*.

3 *Bar Puerto*: A shared space

Uribe offered an interesting clue about the poetics of his first book of poems and his multimedia shows when he was asked about the key to these personal literary poetics, which entails his conception of poetry. For him, it is a main priority for the text to be as "close" as possible to the readers-spectators. He believes that, even though one may use familiar references, poems can still end up being too complex. And, as in the Bauhaus style, while a concept may be complex, it can still be expressed in direct and subtle outlines:

> I wanted to achieve that dark-to-light change. Straight lines at all times. A house is made with just a few lines. That doesn't mean that it's easy. Simple yes, easy no (. . .) In order to achieve it, one must use familiar references and not clichés.[91]

Uribe thinks it is artificial to narrate the fruits of one's imagination instead of things that listeners understand or know, and he believes that recipients consider this strange, distant from their experience: "The story can be a fiction, but the emotions must be true. True emotions manage to transmit. There must be an emotional truth."[92]

Specifically, in order to explain the originality of the *Bar Puerto* performance, we propose the theory that Uribe's contribution implied an innovative narrative step in relation to the work *Henry Bengoa Inventarium* (1987). Atxaga introduced a novelesque narrative thread into the script; that is, it was organized in the form of a chronicle of the vicissitudes of those who are looking for their friend Henry Bengoa, introducing elements of suspense, while Henry's friends are constructing, piece by piece, a profile of the missing person by means of a collective "we." In Uribe's *Bar Puerto*, we discover innovative

91 Enbeita, Zihara, "Mundua begiratzeko era." *Argia* March 4, 2007. Online: http://www.argia.eus/argia-astekaria/2078/mundua-begiratzeko-moduak [October 14, 2018]

92 Ibid.

characteristics. On the one hand, it speaks about a character who writes in the first person, and the autofictional character based on the poet himself makes a conversation topic out of his intimate crisis. Therefore, the narrator's emotional truth is shown in full bloom. By means of the journey undertaken by this broken character in order to reconstruct himself, in one section he is looking for a physical collective space; Uribe wants to speak about the island of communication which emerged with the testimonies of castaways who have met in a specific stopping place on the itinerary of individual options.[93]

From Atxaga's poetic "chronicle" in the disappearance of Henry Bengoa we go to the generic mold chosen by Uribe, the public reading of a "diary." In sentences composed as an introduction to the narration titled "Ipuin bat eta hamaika istorio" (One short story and many stories), we are told that this man has decided to return to his hometown, seeking to leave behind the sadness of a broken relationship in the city, because of the need to reconstruct himself as a person. In the town he finds out that his childhood neighborhood will be demolished in order to build a new highway. This awakens echoes of the past, songs and memories of couples, and also concentrates his attention on the voices of those others who are on the verge of losing that place, and he begins to collect his testimonies. Bear in mind that in the *Bar Puerto* project the true focus is a place in which people meet: *Bar Puerto* is a physical and psychic space in which spectators will listen to different marginal voices besides the author's voice. These are, therefore, two important elements in this short narrative: on the one hand, the autodiegetic narrative voice, created daily in the form of a diary, and, on the other, the voices of the rest, the testimonies of the witnesses in

93 Although it is beyond the scope of this chapter to undertake such comparative work, it would be interesting likewise to compare Uribe's performances with the structures and methods of enunciation in performances like *Ibiltarixanak* by Mikel Urdangairn or *Katamalo* by Katamalo. In any case, in those performances the central focus, when it comes to choosing the texts, is a critical message aimed at Basque society, and not a narrative thread, as in the case of the two performances—*Bar Puerto* and *Henry Bengoa Inventarium*—under analysis here.

situ. In a lyrical interaction, the testimonies open up the focal point of the poetic self, finding the voices and experiences of other people within the crisis of the self and in search of their roots.

Let us now return to analyzing the title of the CD and the written text:

> In all coastal towns there's a tavern called Bar Puerto.
> The fishermen and port workers get together there to take a break.
> Gathering the stories there, a longtime intention.
> Because there are a lot of stories in the world and we're aware of only very few of them.
> Everybody has a good story.
> Bar Puerto. Voices from the edge.
> To gather up the weird portside locutions. (96)

The first part of this paratext, which coincides with the title, *Bar Puerto*, situates us in a mythical sea, that is, in a special place which is the limit between life and death, and that puts us into contact with a broad imaginary world constructed by literature. That imaginary world in Uribe's text produces an echo among readers because he does not "exploit" it in endless intertextuality. On the contrary, the port is presented as a biographical space of the real author and the lyrical self. Moreover, left in its Spanish formulation it also has the effect of dislocation: this place may be an impersonal tavern in a port in any town, but, in reality, it is the "Basque" sea and the "Basque" port, put in communication at the same time with the literary and biographical sea. In this sense, the text, as regards the imaginary, is clearly linked to his 2006 book *Portukoplak* (Port songs); here, Uribe's literary imaginary emerges and is extended from the realm of popular literature to that of contemporary poetry, but both the "old" texts as well as those of the written and oral tradition stand out. This is what he says in the prologue: "I have given preference to the unity of the book over arbitrary poems and songs. I have given preference to songs over poems, and to classic poems over contemporary poems." And thus, there is a poem or song of reflection surrounding every text.

The treatment of this sea/port, according to Gabilondo, is Uribe's typical use of a "*neocostumbrista*" gaze on the Basque physical and human landscape, given that the focus of his poems is the melancholic recollection of times gone by (2009, 43); he describes Uribe's poetry as a "melancholic and ahistoricist fondness of *neocostumbrismo*" (2009, 49). In the opinion of this critic, in these texts Uribe has fallen into the anti-modern "sin" that anyone would have deplored as the greatest taboo in literature during the 1970s and 1980s, which is that of avoiding the gaze shaped by *costumbrismo* (2009, 43–44). The excessive forcefulness of this argument, rather than demonstrating the *costumbrista* gaze which many Basque writers have been accused of employing, perhaps highlights more this critic's own obsessions. Whatever the case, he presents literary representations of a non-urban Basque Country as if they were all in Txomin Agirre's shadow, transforming the Ondarroa priest's canon into an insurmountable obstacle and, as Harold Bloom would say, perceiving all Basque writers to have given in to the great "anxiety of his influence" (1973). In this sense, however, instead of rejecting or "prohibiting" the literary worlds and methods that Agirre worked with, branding them as a "sin" or "taboo," it would have been a rewarding contribution on the part of the critic to analyze seriously how Basque writers have attempted to overcome that anxiety of Agirre's influence, interpreting incorrectly the works of canonical writers and opening up spaces to the imagination when constructing their own work.

Sticking to the text of Uribe's *Bar Puerto*, let us recall that the trip to the seaport by the author of the diary is presented as an external journey: he arrives by train and, upon finishing his stay, leaves to return to the big city. We know that it is a significant internal journey too because, in reality, revisiting his roots is about collecting local voices and signs of identity of his broken self, to heal his feelings and move on. That, inevitably, is where an important part of the text made up of local voices, is situated: the voices of the port are resources making up Uribe's effort to get himself back on track. He therefore spends ten days adapting to the place, calming his inner emotions, and preparing his plan to write a feature. From December 22 on, for fifteen days he will make recordings and, finally, on February 15, he writes the epilogue which includes later notes, thereby drawing the diary to a close.

The method of expression in the narration titled "Ipuin" (Short Story), as noted earlier, has an autobiographical style: it possesses the structure of a journal and an obvious narrative style in the form of an intimate diary. It begins on December 12, 1999 and ends on January 15, 2000. It is situated on the verge of a temporal axis, as well as on the threshold of a century, at the limits of the author's inner crisis, in a change of direction. Specifically, one notes a time of fundamental change when he contends that "Time doesn't always stay the same size" and "one morning we get out of bed and suddenly realize that not one day alone but ten years have passed and we don't, as we did last night, see our whole life stretching out before us" (91).

At the intimate level, the end of a romantic relationship is hinted at: "That thing of ours had nowhere to go. That thing of ours ended the way the fruit is going to fall from an apple tree" (93). In *Bar Puerto* he reflects the melancholic gaze of a way of life that is about to disappear; and perhaps because of that, in the face of the news that the neighborhood is deteriorating, he adopts the attitude of clinging to the memory and ephemeral nature of the moment, and decides to collect the local voices. In the entry for December 16 he says he wants "to go back to the town I was born in and make something like a documentary" (96).

Why this plan? Is Uribe perhaps fascinated by the characteristics of the voice? Perhaps, as happened with Mikel Laboa himself, the folds of the voice of the port have cast a spell on him? Clearly, both would like to capture the essence of that special atmosphere which is on the point of disappearing and make it last, but for different reasons and in different ways. In his memory, Laboa linked those voices to his dramatic time in Lekeitio in his childhood when, during the Spanish Civil War, he had to flee Donostia-San Sebastián (Otaegi 2016). They were for him mysterious and attractive voices, and became the germ of an idea to create the *lekeitiokoak* (The People and the Things of Lekeitio) following an inescapable intuition. In Uribe's case, however, the voices of Ondarroa are linked inexorably to his identity, and they are a kind of soundtrack to his sensibility and aesthetic identity. Besides that, we must underscore the fact that, among the differences between Laboa and Uribe, the latter does not give voice to unknown or anonymous townsfolk and does not convert them into an "essential yell" as Laboa did. The owners of the voices collected by Uribe are real people whose names and surnames appear on the CD, and throughout the performance one hears recordings of these voices. With their words they tell the story of an ever-changing world; they are witnesses of a time without any direction; they are marginal, yet they are real, made of flesh and bone, and are introduced by name and surname; they are not archetypes and they do not serve some representative function.

Behind the intentions of the compiler of the diary, as explained in the entry for December 16, is what the filmmaker Luis Buñuel did in *Los olvidados*. In that dramatized report, Buñuel collected testimonies over the course of 21 days in the shantytowns of Mexico City. Like Buñuel, the writer of Uribe's diary is interested in small stories linked to a bigger story of a place, and the collection is also undertaken with all the physical-acoustic minutiae, with the realism of the testimonies. Buñuel dedicated 21 days (a space of time similar to the two months the diary in *Bar Puerto* lasts) to filming the project: his collection began on November 16 and finished on December 5.

What the witnesses' voices tell is the story of the forgotten, the voice of the marginalized. This collection of voices leads to a contemporary historical awareness and, for that reason, is a factor which especially deserves to be taken into account. We can think of it as the first ear of wheat to characterize the harvest that we find in the author's later works. The testimonies of the marginalized express an awareness of the contribution made to the current historical point of view. In effect, in postcolonial studies, in subaltern studies, and in memory studies there has been a fundamental change in contemporary history: that produced by what is termed the "emotional turn." In addition to leaders and ideologues, anyone can legitimately take the floor and tell their "story." We are living in a period which has been christened "the era of the witness" by Annette Wieviorka (1998) and, following the expression of the Holocaust expert Elie Wiesel (1977), we are all witnesses to life, and it is worth us bearing witness to our experience.

Paul Ricoeur (2003, 210)[94] was the theoretician that spoke more precisely about the specificities of the discourse of the witness. According to his conclusions, the characteristics of witnesses' speech are reliability and emotivity, given that when witnesses speak about events and emotions that affected them, that implies credibility. Furthermore, witnesses' narrative is dialogic and constructs, alongside listeners, trust-based relationships. Yet in Ricoeur's opinion, witnesses' speech improves the network of intersubjectivity which accompanies social solidarity; we believe each other and, empathizing with those nearby, we build emotional support that society can offer individuals; it constructs the collective memory of society, and even more so if the circumstance suffered by witnesses has provoked great suffering among more victims. Only during a time when human rights are a reference point is it possible for witnesses to achieve that importance, insofar as these rights have generated recognition of the collective experiences and respect for the identity of minorities. The culture of intimacy prevails in public institutions and in the media and, in that way, what was a private emotion is

94 Ricoeur, Paul. *La Mémoire, l'histoire, l'oubli*, (Paris: Le Seuil, 2000) / *La Memoria, la historia, el olvido*. (Madrid: Trotta, 2003) and *Memory, History, Forgetting*, trans. Kathleen Blamey & David Pellauer, (Chicago: University of Chicago Press, 2004).

demonstrated in public culture, in the opinion of Bain Attwood (2008, 75–95), also transforming the arts into witnesses of that private emotion.

Uribe has been very intuitive in blending in with that contemporary spirit, and he has offered, through fiction, by means of simple language, that change in perspective when it comes to looking at reality: everyone has a good story within, and the manner of expressing that good story is the short narrative method, which has clear features of subjectivity because above all else it seeks the empathy of listeners. From here stems the emotional truth of testimony. Those voices move the author of the diary in *Bar Puerto*, and the testimonies become communicative events which help him to get back on track; for that reason, he also grants permission to enter into the intimacy of the author of the diary about his "story." Likewise, in the book *Portukoplak* (Port Songs), the reflections that the literary texts chosen stimulate in Uribe are testimony to an emotivity and not to mere literary or philological comments; they are channels to blend together with the authenticity of the texts.

4 The marginalized

The voices in *Bar Puerto* form part of a heterogeneous group, both as regards their origins and their ages and genders. The first voice is that of Omar Sampoo, from Guinea-Conakry, and the core of his narration is the suffering and discrimination endured by his father as a soldier in the Second World War. The second and third witnesses are Josu Urresti and Eli Ituarte, two elderly people. The *gudari* (Basque soldier in the Spanish Civil War) Josu Urresti narrates his avatars during the war and the details of his time in prison, both in Larrañaga and in San Cristóbal. Eli is slightly younger, and speaks about her parents and her childhood illnesses: she was born during the war and her mother was in prison at the time; her father, however, was in hiding, and the family spent several years separated. The voices of the fourth recording are those of sailors: the brothers Emilio and Agustín López and Maximino Fontán. All three include events that occurred in crossings on Basque boats in the Great Sole Bank. Echoes of the Second World War also appear slowly: disappeared submarines, the old remains of planes that crashed into the sea . . . Voices five and six transport us back to the 1970s: on the one hand, Marian Etxabe, who suffered from the wave of the hippy generation and music; and Unai Badiola, on the other, a sailor with a lively personality who resisted the alternating rhythms of a life at sea and the onslaught of solitude.

In Uribe's narrative thread, those voices acquire meaning and interact, above all because the "matters" of the rest intertwine with the poems and with the notes the author of the diary makes about their inner state and impressions. That is the reason for the personal incidents and memories which trigger the narrator's thread, the echoes of the songs that we hear from the voice of Urdangarin ("Txatxamatxalinatxu," "Ene mutilik txipiena," (My tinniest boy) "Zeruak eta lurrak," (Skies and Earths) "Ene maitea" (My beloved one), the meetings (Omar's initial narration and the Africans who ask him for help at the end of the narration), the interpretations of the brave sailors and the adventures of writers (of Pellot, the corsair from Hendaia, and of Tusitala, that is, Stevenson), and the emigrant in Paris who returns to his town to spend Christmas there and the narration of the German girl he meets. They are all elements of narrative matter formed by echoes. They all finish off an emotional, polyphonic, and harmonious amalgam, full of intimate echoes.

The essential thing is the narrative voice of a subjective self that collects testimonies. He demonstrates several symptoms of a personal crisis: it is shown in a journey carried out at a moment of crisis in search of identity, while various dimensions of his life are unstable; he appears to be searching, especially among friends and relatives, for ways to cure himself of lost affections. For that reason, the emotions of the wound of his inner crisis envelop the witnesses' short testimonies and, in this project, are expressed in six poems, recited and offered in the form of song: "Biluzik," (Naked) "Oraindik goiz da," (It's Still Early) "Lehenago bezala," (As Before) "Urriko poema,"

(Poem of October) "Bisita," and "Bar Puerto." They are poems shaped by the poetic self through the words of witnesses and as the outcome of their emotions, a reflection of the influence of place and the witnesses' words. Toward the end of the diary, however, he adds introspection in order to assume the painful expression of a lack of love; for that reason, the significant symbolic dream of the dump as a hole suggests the closing of the cycle. The nightmare signals the place that is his navel and the core of his crisis; the hole is only a disturbing metaphor. The text closes like this: renewing strenght in order to face up to solitude, given that, when he goes home to the big city, "As I open the door an immense hole opens up where my navel used to be" (121).

The stories, however, focus on different elements of the collective. In this narration we can perceive three points of interest:

First, with these six voices—arranging them according to the temporal axis of the events captured in the war which marks family memory and experience itself—the chronological order of the story is attained. The leading character's interest is, above all, in the historical memory of Basque society. But Uribe also establishes his gaze on small stories, on the history that marginal people recount. He is not trying to test a thesis and those voices are not just proof of an argument. The text suggests the importance of the past in the consciousness of the current subject, and throughout subsequent narratives Uribe will reflect the development of this initial seed: the Spanish Civil War and post-war period predominate in *Bilbao-New York-Bilbao* and in *Elkarrekin esnatzeko ordua* (The Hour of Waking Together); in *Mussche*, however, it is the Second World War and, in spite of that, the suffering stands out above the narrative, since its goal is to reflect how the war affected the lives of people.

Second, ideas are important throughout all of the narrations, and comings and goings are essential elements in their evolution, and they imbue *Bar Puerto* with their different contributions. Immigrants of all kinds live in the Basque Country, and the journeys that locals make around the world for work and other goals highlight the migratory dynamic of human beings these days; he takes the *roving identity* of contemporary human beings into consideration, exploring in tandem the journeys undertaken now and then by people from here and elsewhere.

Third, he also takes into consideration the voices of marginal societies that cannot fit into the traditional Basque Country: the testimony of those who have to leave the town is important, especially testimonies such as that expressed in the words of Marian Etxabe, given that, in spite of the fact that she had to flee the limitations of a closed fishing town, she managed to return and settle there again. That is her achievement. It is worth mentioning that several characters in this short narration show ambivalence toward their fathers. In *Bar Puerto* the narrator alludes in one way or another to a problematic affection for an absent father; the father is a mythical and admired sailor, but it is difficult to show any affection for him. An image of the father is outlined in the book which leaves a lot of major gaps. The Galician sailors demonstrate an intermittent unknown father, but not even they knew that when the skipper addressed them as "sons," he was showing them affection.[95] Along the same lines, in the story narrator's friend tells him about the father of the German girl, who went to war and would never return. Nor did Eli Ituarte know her father until she was grown up, because he had to flee as a result of the civil war. And, finally, nor does the father in the poem "Visit" know how to speak about his ill daughter and he is incapable of approaching her, remaining in the doorway, silent. Although in an indirect way, the author of the diary aims at the reconciliation of Marian Etxabe, a reconciliation with her family and with her hometown. The message of hope at the end of her testimony is significant:

95 In regard to this, the words of the poet from Ondarroa, Leire Bilbao, in her poem "Aita" (Father) in the book *Scanner* (2011), are significant when she speaks about the difficulties of children when it comes to developing affection for their father: "Umetan gorroto nuen etxera etortzen zen gizon hura:/ bizarra egin gabe, Old Spice usainaz" ("As a child I hated that man who came home:/ without shaving, and smelling of Old Spice").

"I had never, ever thought I would feel so comfortable in my hometown" (115).

These testimonies and the "story" we listen to out of the protagonist's mouth shape a reality that is situated on the axes of space and time, a reality which the author wants to collect as a document; but the first indications of autofiction in this narration are interesting, since he offers it as a kind of seed for the novels that would follow. The author's intention, in the opinion of experts, was to collect a testimony of suffering and undertake a life eulogy, and that intention, moreover, in the way it was expressed, led to a particular style: we can hear in Uribe's narrations and narrative poems the declarations of several hidden heroes, conveyed in line with the aspirations of an autofictional voice, and emitted in an innovative hybrid genre, in the style of a novel-report. It is perhaps worth underscoring that, with this autofictional voice, with the help of other voices, he managed to create a polyphony and characteristic interlocution, implying a dialogic communication which constitutes the main complement of social cohesion, giving rise to the fact that, by means of the voices of different people, the values of reality and different forms of looking at the world are made known and accepted.

What emotive experiences does Uribe include in *Bar Puerto*? On the one hand, "nearby memory" (Josu Urresti and Eli Ituarte) reveals the suffering of war (Omar and his father who was a soldier in the Second World War) and remote memories (through the remains of planes and submarines from the Second World War found by the Galician fishermen in the Great Sole Bank). Uribe wants us to hear how long war wounds last in human identity; he shows us the mirror of their influence in the Basque collective memory. On the other hand, the witnesses transmit a testimony of how harsh life is for those who work at sea; he talks to us about distance, solitude, and the pain of uprooting. The sailors who give testimony of the unbearable loneliness create an echo in the writer of the diary because he is also suffering the specter of solitude and because he grew up in an environment of the harshness of a life at sea. Lastly, Marian Etxabe's narration, which reveals the experience of feeling excluded and strange, an outsider, also gives emotive witness to suffering, perhaps that of the very narrator's alter ego, suggesting a dissidence toward the social patriarchy that distanced her from the town. There appear to be echoes of this in poems like "It is Still Early" in which "The new world as yet unmade" (113) hurts him. However, the poem "Bar Puerto," which closes the book, implies refuge— "Believe me, that land's another world. / Down there, no need at all to run away"—since it is "the island of shipwrecked souls" (122).

Put another way, the narrator, like the human being he is, shares with the witnesses different dimensions: he speaks of the place that collective memory has in the memory and identity of the Basque Country; moreover, the intermittence and severity of a fisherman's family life influences the narrative self as well as the very narrator; finally, the destiny of human collectives who live like solitary castaways in society evokes the distancing of the author himself, as well as the joy of return and reconciliation. The voice of the witnesses is subjective, and we should not, therefore, transform it into an instrument to formulate a general hypothesis. Yet the witnesses demonstrate a capacity to fulfill Uribe's objective: they inhabit that "island" or microcosm, and it is worth preserving their memory, since everyone has a good story to tell. Furthermore, the voices in *Bar Puerto* are voices which facilitate the self-awareness of the "I" narrator, given that he shares the witnesses' emotions: the burden of suffering from a conflictive past, the loss of feelings, uprootedness, solitude, communication difficulties, and the need for others' acceptance.

The expression of the witnesses' memory is full of legitimacy and has been located at the core of numerous contemporary aesthetic projects, and this was also the case here. The legitimacy of intimate "tales" and "stories" does not necessarily stem from contributing reliable historical data, or from carrying out profound philosophical reflections, or from the fact of being valid to scrutinize the anthropological or sociological truth of society. This work of the memory and expression of testimonies is important because it is bathed in affectivity, and because both the witness and the listener or reader are affected by strong emotions, it has a quality which nourishes the communicative network of society. It is precisely there that we can find the first seed of the essence of adhesion which the narrator achieves in *Bar Puerto* and *Meanwhile Take My Hand*: the literary authenticity of the emotional communication which the credibility of testimonial language archives is a talent that would be developed in Uribe's later works.

Bibliography

Attwood, Bain. 2008. In the Age of Testimony: The Stolen Generations Narrative, "Distance," and Public History. *Public Culture* 20, 1: 75–95. Online: https://read.dukeupress.edu/public-culture/article-abstract/20/1/75/31914/In-the-Age-of-Testimony-The-Stolen-Generations?redirectedFrom=fulltext [October 14, 2018]

Asurmendi, Mikel. 2003. XXI mendeko poesiaz hausnartzen: Rikardo Arregi, Juanjo Olasagarre, Kimen Uribe. *Argia*, 2003/10/05. Online: https://www.argia.eus/argia-astekaria/1914/xxi-menderako-poesiaz-hausnartzen-rikardo-arregi-diaz-de-heredia-juanjo-olasagarre-kirmen-uribe [October 30, 2018]

Bloom, Harold. 2009 [1993]. *La ansiedad de la influencia. Una teoría de la poesía*. Madrid: Minima Trotta.

Carlson, Marvin. 1996. *Performance: A critical introduction*. London: Routledge.

Etxeberria, Hasier. 2002. *Bost idazle*. Irun: Alberdania.

Gabilondo, Joseba. 2009. Euskal poesiaren historia postmoderno baterantz: ahozkotasunaz eta performantzeaz (Gerra karlistetako bertso paperetatik rock erradikalera eta K. Uriberen poesiara). *Egan* 3-4: 5–52.

Kortazar, Jon. 1997. *Luma eta lurra*. Bilbao: Labayru.

Kortazar, Jon. 2008. Cuerpos y voces: postmodernidad y poesía en la obra de Kirmen Uribe, *Bulletin of Hispanic Studies* 85, 1: 111–142.

Kortazar, Jon. 2009. Eugngo euskal poesiaren historia. Bilbao: Euskal Herriko Unibertsitatearen Argitalpen Zerbitzua.

Kortazar, Jon. 2011. *Bitartean New York: Kirmen Uriberen literaturgintza*. Donostia: Utriusque Vasconiae.

Mondelo, J. M. 1991. L'auteur multimédia. M. Pratiques.

Nietzsche, Friedrich. 1974. *The Gay Science: With a Prelude in Rhymes and an Appendix in Songs*. London: Vintage.

Olaziregi, Mari Jose. 1998. *Euskal gazteen irakurzaletasuna. Azterketa soziologikoa*. Bergara: Bergarako Udala.

Otaegi, Lourdes. 2016. Mikel Laboaren lekeitioak: Esanezina oihu bilakatua. In *Oroimenaren lekuak eta lekukoak*, Izaro Arroita & Lourdes Otaegi (ed.), 147–170. Bilbao: Euskal Herriko Unibertsitateko Argitalpen Zerbitzua.

Ricoeur, Paul. 2003. *La Mémoire, l'histoire, l'oubli*. Paris: Le Seuil. (*La Memoria, la Historia, el Olvido*. Madrid: Trotta).

Torrealdai, Joan Mari. 1997. *Euskal kultura gaur*. Donostia: Jakin – Caja Laboral Popular – Elkarlanean.

Uribe, Kirmen. 2010. *Bar Puerto: Voices from the Edge* (trans. Elizabeth Macklin). Donostia: Elkar. (Original work published in 2010).

Wiesel, Elie. 1997 [1977]. The Holocaust as a Literary Inspiration. In *Dimensions of the Holocaust*. Evanston: Northwestern University Press.

Wieviorka, Annette. 1998. *L'ère du témoin*. Paris: Plon.

Zubiri, Harkaitz. 2013. Euskal literaturaren irakurleak zenbat eta nolakoak diren aztergai. Soziolinguistikako datuetatik eta irakurketa ohiturei buruzko ikerketetatik abiatuta. *Uztaro* 87: 51–68.

CHILDREN'S AND YOUNG ADULT LITERATURE

13

Stories of a Basque sheepherder turned gunslinger: Kirmen Uribe's *Garmendia* series[96]

Mari Jose Olaziregi Alustiza

It is hard to believe that a certain Garmendia was a gunslinger in the Far West "at least as famous as Billy the Kid, Jesse James, or Wyatt Earp" (Uribe 2015, 15).[97] This is how the writer Kirmen Uribe (1970) introduces the protagonist of his series of adventures for readers aged nine and older. I will allude to this series, at the center of which is the gunslinger Garmendia in the Far West,[98] and I will start from the hypothesis that it offers a counter narrative, in the form of an adventure novel, to those Basque narrations that have represented Basque emigration to the Far West. Following some brief considerations of the particularities of Uribe's work, I will move on to an analysis of the Garmendia series in order to explore more fully both its representation of a Basque sheepherder turned gunslinger and the intertextual nexuses presented by the stories, as well as the novelty it offers within the corpus as a whole of Basque works that represent the Basque diaspora in the United States.

---

96 Paper prepared within the projects IT 1047-16 (Basque government) and FFI2017-84342-P (MINECO) developed by the level A consolidated research group MHLI (Memoria Historikoa Literatura Iberiarretan / Memoria Histórica en las Literaturas Ibéricas / Historical Memory in Iberian Literatures).

97 "Billi Mutikoa, Jesse James eta Wiatt Earp-en adinakoa, gutxienez" (*Garmendia eta zaldun beltza*, 2003, 15).

98 I will use for my analysis the first edition in English of *Garmendia and the Black Rider* (2015), and the Basque editions of *Garmendia errege* (King Garmendia, 2004) and *Garmendia eta Fannyren sekretua* (Garmendia and Fanny's Secret, 2006). The initials GBR, GE, and GFS will serve as references, respectively, for each book analyzed.

1 Kirmen Uribe, a frontier writer

Uribe's trajectory of children's and young adult literature texts includes, to date, six works: *Ekidazu, lehoiek ez dakite biolina jotzen* (Ekidazu, Lions Don't Know How to Play the Violin, 2003), in collaboration with the children's theater company Kukubiltxo and the music group Oskorri; *Ez naiz ilehoria, eta zer?* (I'm Not Blonde, So What? 2004), published by the Editores Asociados and translated into Catalan, Galician, Asturian, and Spanish; *Guti* (2005); and the aforementioned series based on the "feared" Basque gunslinger Garmendia: *Garmendia eta zaldun beltza* (2003); *Garmendia and the Black Rider*, 2015); *Garmendia errege* (King Garmendia, 2004); and *Garmendia eta Fannyren sekretua* (Garmendia and Fanny's Secret, 2006). It is not an especially extensive trajectory, yet it is clearly, as one would expect, dominated by the spirit of renewal that runs through the work of the writer from Ondarroa.

In effect, this is a writer whose trajectory includes important poetry collections such as the winner of the Critics' Prize *Bitartean heldu eskutik* (2001; *Meanwhile Take My Hand*, 2007) and *17 segundo* (17 seconds, 2019); innovative novels, such as the winner of Spain's National Prize for Narrative in 2009, *Bilbao-New York-Bilbao* (2008; English-language version, 2014), *Mussche* (2012), and *Elkarrekin esnatzeko ordua* (The Hour of Waking Together, 2016); multimedia projects that combine literature and music, such as *Zaharregia, txikiegia agian* (Too Old, Too Small, Maybe, 2003), *Bar Puerto. Bazterreko ahotsak* (*Bar Puerto: Voices from the Edge*, 2010), and *Jainko txiki eta jostalari hura* (That Tiny Playful God, 2013); essays like *Lizardi eta erotismoa* (Lizardi and Eroticism, 1996) and *ABC: Bilbao Museoaren Alfabetoa* (ABC: The Alphabet of the Museum of Bilbao, 2018); and so on. It is an eclectic trajectory that endorses a call to creative disobedience and that seeks to question the *established* norms that govern different literary traditions. That is why Uribe's writing flees the linear narration of events and embraces what he terms "composite novels" or narrations that encompass diverse narrative planes, points of view, and contexts. Uribe loves to search for and explore new forms and he believes, as he contends in his most recent autopoetic text (Olaziregi & Elizalde 2020, 17–20), that Basque literature may contribute creatively to the renovation of world literature. In the same vein as the Italian Claudio Magris, Uribe has defined himself as a "frontier" writer (Uribe 2014) who likes to give voice to those who have not had one, to those invisible beings in the eyes of society who inhabit his narratives and poems. Whether it is a question of emigrants or exiles, of any kinds of people who suffer exclusion, these are "non-grieved bodies" (bodies that don't matter) as Estibalitz Ezkerra terms them in her analysis of his book of poems *Meanwhile Take My Hand* (Ezkerra 2020, 58), given that their loss rarely generates compassion or grief. That is the case of Amira, the Moroccan protagonist of *Ez naiz ilehoria, eta zer* (I'm Not Blonde, So What?), an immigrant in Vitoria-Gasteiz who has to contend with those (racial, cultural, and social) labels that "betray" her. Amira is a foreigner, a being who, as Julia Kristeva would say (1991, 3–4), forces us to show the secret way in which we face the world.

In any event, if there is a key notion that runs through Kirmen Uribe's literary trajectory, it is, in effect, that of displacement. Luis Martín Estudillo (2020) analyzes this in the Basque author's first three novels in order to underscore, on the one hand, his ethical and historical dimension insofar as Uribe has a clear preference for focusing on characters on the move due to political and economic pressures. Yet, on the other hand, such displacement is also expressed in the formal preferences (fragmentation, polyphony, and so on) of Uribe's texts, preferences that match an anti-dogmatic idea of literature and that have influenced a lot of western fiction in the last quarter of a century (Estudillo 2020, 115–132). The Garmendia series that I will examine in the following sections is located clearly in a reality, that of the Basque diaspora in the United States in the nineteenth century. And he locates it precisely by situating his focus on a Basque emigrant who, like thousands of Basques, migrated to the

Americas in order to herd sheep, but for whom destiny reserved a profession that he certainly never imagined.

2 Basque diaspora

Elsewhere, I reflect on the specificities of Basque migration to the United States and how this has been represented in the literature written in Basque (Olaziregi 2014, 2015). I confirm the importance of the development of postcolonial criticism since the 1970s in order to conceptualize terms like *diaspora*, *exile*, *multiculturalism*, *frontiers*, and *transnationality*, and in order to trace the specificities of a world cartography that has been conditioned clearly by the constant displacement of its inhabitants. Authors like Edward Said, for example, did not hesitate in classifying our era as "the age of migrants, curfews, identity cards, refugees, exiles, massacres, camps and fleeing civilians" (Said 2000, 17), an era, in sum, shaped by collective stories of rootedness-uprootedness and alienation.

Behind the chronicle of Basque migration to the Americas there are centuries of history, although this was intensified clearly by the vicissitudes experienced in the Basque Country during the nineteenth century (Olaziregi 2014, 108–109; 2015, 323–326). Among the sociopolitical factors that have been put forward to explain the reasons behind these migratory flows, I would mention, without doubt, the growing nineteenth-century industrialization in the Basque Country and the subsequent shift from a rural-agricultural to an industrial society, demographic pressure, the Carlist wars, and compulsory military service following the abolition of the *fueros* (traditional charters that guaranteed a measure of Basque self-government) by Spanish Prime Minister Antonio Cánovas del Castillo in 1876, as well as the prevailing inheritance system of primogeniture. All of this influenced an increasingly large wave of Basque emigration throughout the nineteenth century. The initial destination for Basque migrants was Latin America (experts state, for example, that 10 percent of the current Argentinian population is of Basque extraction) but, from 1850 on, as a result of the so-called Gold Rush in California, this migratory flow diverted toward the American West. There, in the absence of gold and silver mines to exploit, Basques reverted to the work for which they were originally in demand in Latin America: herding. This was a profession marked by little social prestige, but it did constitute one of the few work options for migrants such as Basques, with little formal education and no English. Such hard mountain work and the terrible loneliness it implied were only alleviated by their occasional stays in a network of Basque boarding houses, places that Jeronima Echeverria (1998) defines as making up true homes away from home for the sheepherders. These were places to stay when they were sick, places in which they socialized, and places in which they shared hardships and dreams with their compatriots.

Canonical studies such as *Amerikanuak: Basques in the New World* (1975) by William A. Douglass and Jon Bilbao examine rigorously the vicissitudes of Basque migration to the United States, a presence that also left its imprint in literature in Basque through the character of the *indianua* (Indian), the Basque emigrant who returned home from his American odyssey a rich man (or not). His negative representation in literature written in Basque until well into the twentieth century (with such telling titles as *Ameriketan galduak* (Lost in the Americas, 1967) by Nemesio Etxaniz) is especially striking. And, as I contend in the abovementioned articles (Olaziregi 2014, 2015), this negative representation of Basque emigration and the Americas was created by canonical Basque authors, almost all of whom had not migrated themselves. Having been transformed into the Basque nation's "Other," the Americas became, as well-known authors such as J. Hiriart Urruti, R. M. Azkue, J.M. Etxeita, and even the best exponent of Basque *costumbrista* prose, Domingo Agirre, argued, a good place for the body, but not for the soul. The French Basque writer and journalist J. Hiriart Urruti stated this in an article published in the weekly *Eskualdun Ona*: "bizitzeko, bego Amerika: haatik hiltzeko, Eskual Herria. Erran nahi: gorphutzarentzat, sakelarentzat, abere, . . . han, han hobe. Bainan arimarentzat lekhu hotzak hek, eta murritzak" (In order to live, the Americas are better; but to die, the Basque Country. In other words: for one's body, pocket, fortune . . . there, better there. But for the soul, the American lands are cold, and limited) (Jean Hiriart Urruti, *Eskualdun Ona* 1905-3/10). This emigration by Basque compatriots, a migration that, in the case of Iparralde (the northern continental Basque Country), was truly striking, compelled Basque nationalism and the Basque Church to form an alliance against the exodus to the Americas. They feared that the migrants would not return, and that they would lose their faith and the traditional customs that they had learned at home. As such, any news referring to the 400,000 Basque emigrants already in the Americas by the first third of the twentieth century was framed by this ideology (Alvarez & Tapiz 1996), of which pastorals by the bishops of Pamplona, Bayonne, and Vitoria-Gasteiz in 1852, 1855, and 1867 against such emigration were good examples (Alvarez 1999). The sheepherders who appear in Basque-language novels like *Jayoterri maitia* (Beloved Homeland, 1910) by José Manuel Etxeita, although they return as rich *indianuak*, suffer all kinds of hardships in their American travels. In contrast, Joanes, the sheepherder protagonist of the canonical *costumbrista* novel *Garoa* (Fern, 1912) by Domingo Agirre, exemplifies the "good Basque." He is a Catholic, loves the traditions, and defends the Basque nationalism of Sabino Arana. Joanes is the spiritual guide of his flock and his offspring, an "authentic" Basque who rejects emigration and the urban centers at the very moment of demographic and industrial transformation.

We have to focus on another type of corpus to feel the suffering and nostalgia of thousands of Basque immigrants: a corpus of texts made up of other kinds of texts—testimonies, *bertsos* (improvised verses), and so on—which are not usually included in the canonical Basque literary works on immigration. Some of them were included in weeklies that were published entirely in Basque in Los Angeles, like *California´ko Eskual-Herria* (1893–1897) and *Escualdun Gazeta* (1885–1886). Some of them are published in *Far Western Basque Country* (2017) by Asun Garikano. They are the testimonies of thousands of migrants who narrate their journeys through the likes of letters, chronicles, news items, and so forth. The vast majority of those migrants ended up working as sheepherders, a job that enjoyed little prestige in western culture (Garikano 2009, 243). Other expressions, such as the tree carvings made by sheepherders in the mountain forests, also served to convey their experiences. There are stories with unknown and often anonymous protagonists, like those of the *bertsolaris* (oral improvisers), which do not belong to the so-called canonical literature but instead to its peripheral polysystem, that which is commonly termed oral literature. Some of those improvised *bertsos* are analyzed by Pio Pérez (2016), who concludes that "the improvisation of verses has served as a catalyst, a constructor, and transmitter of information and emotion in the migratory project" (Pérez 2016, 412).

3 The Basque sheepherder, archetype

Thus far I have offered a very brief account of the negative representation of the Americas and emigration within the literature written in Basque. This was the case until well into the twentieth century, at which point essential works, such as *Itzulera baten historia* (Story of a Return, 1990) by Martin Ugalde, opted for another kind of representation that was more in keeping with the reality of many migrants who adopted the homeland that took them in as their own and made a show of their hybrid identity. Moreover, current novels, like *Soinujolearen semea* (2003; *The Accordionist's Son*, 2007) by Bernardo Atxaga, have updated this new representation in suggesting that the Americas have also been constructed for some Basques as the new paradise in which to self-exile and flee terrorist violence (Olaziregi 2015, 328–330). But the truth is that it was another of the Basques' literatures (Lasagabaster 2005)—that written in English—which offered the first novel that attested to identity hybridity of a Basque sheepherder who had emigrated to the lands of Nevada, thereby dispelling any nostalgia for the homeland left behind, a nostalgia that had been present throughout most of twentieth-century Basque-language narrative. I am referring to the essential *Sweet Promised Land* (1957) by Robert Laxalt. Previous publications, like *White Stars of Freedom: A Basque Shepherd Boy Becomes an American* (1942) by Mirim Isasi, did not manage to convey as Laxalt did the complex reality of the Basque migrant. The identity of his main protagonist, the sheepherder Dominique Laxalt, would not thereafter be tied necessarily to a yearned-for land, the Basque Country, nor assimilated entirely into the new American landscape, but rather linked to a third "in-between" (cf. Bhabha 1994) space, an intermediate space that he makes hybrid and permeable. It could be contended that the novel served to dignify the image of the Basque migrant, to give him visibility, and initiated a whole series of works set in the American West that used the figure of the Basque sheepherder as an archetype (Río 2000). Accordingly, Laxalt's next novels, *The Basque Hotel* (1989) and *The Governor's Mansion* (1994), also gave a prominent place to the figure of the Basque sheepherder. As David Río (2000) points out, this is literature about Basque sheepherders but not pastoral romance, given that it does not portray them in an idyllic or bucolic setting, but often presents realistic stories centered on their difficult adaptation to a hostile physical environment. Likewise, one should mention Basque-American writers like Frank Bergon, author of the historical novel *Shoshone Mike* (1989), and Martin Etchart, whose debut novel was titled *Aritzona* (2014; *The Good Oak*, 2012), both of whom continued to recreate the figure of the Basque sheepherder in the United States. Furthermore, as Río (2000) emphasizes, the image of the Basque sheepherder has been transformed into an attractive literary archetype for American authors who are not of Basque descent, such as, for example, Ann N. Clark, Richard Stookey, Michael Thomas, and Annie Proulx. Whatever the case, the aforementioned works, alongside interesting novels like *Deep Blue Memory* (1993) by Monique Laxalt Urza, which offers a guide to understanding the gender politics that governed

Basque migration to the United States, have enriched markedly the representation of Basque migration to the American West.

4 Garmendia, from sheepherder to gunslinger

Garmendia, the protagonist of Kirmen Uribe's series, joins the corpus of children's and young adult literature in Basque that recounts the stories of Basque sheepherders who migrated to the Americas. I am referring to *Bi letter jaso nituen oso denbora gutxian* (1984; "Two Letters All at Once" in *Two Basque Stories*, 2009) by Bernardo Atxaga, whose protagonist, Old Martin, narrates in his own "Basquenglish" the personal difficulties that led him to Boise, Idaho. This was a city to which many Basques from Bizkaia gravitated in the 1890s, initially on account of its silver mines, and around which they later consolidated their presence by providing food for the silver miners and in sheepherding (Totoricagüena 2005, 212–213). Today, Boise is clearly the US city in which the Basque legacy is most visible. Other stories for young people, like *Indianua* (The Indian, 1993) by "Txiliku" and, above all, *Lur Zabaletan* (On the Wide-Open Plains, 1994) by Aingeru Epaltza, also constitute attractive adventure narrations about Basque sheepherders in the United States (Olaziregi 2014, 112–114).

The novelty of the Garmendia series with respect to previous works consists not only in the fact that it is aimed at the youngest readers (nine years old) but also in that it presents a Basque sheepherder who, without wanting to, becomes an outlaw gunslinger who will experience some amazing situations, just like in the famous Westerns.[99] The books' illustrations by Mikel Valverde remind us, beginning with the first volume *Garmendia eta zaldun beltza* (*Garmendia and the Black Rider*), that we are in the Far West. We see on the front cover an image that

99 It is a fact that well-known Hollywood Westerns included Basque immigrants in secondary roles as part of their storylines. I am referring to movies like *Thunder in the Sun* (1959), directed by Russell Rouse. Indeed, Oscar Álvarez Gila and Iker Arranz Otaegui examine the representation of Basque immigrants in film in "La imagen del inmigrante vasco en el cine: ¿Reflejo, construcción o refuerzo de los estereotipos sociales?" in *Revista de Letras y ficciones audiovisuales* 4 (2014): 68–96.

could be Monument Valley, located between Utah and Arizona. Therein appears the protagonist of the series, Garmendia, whose physiognomy and appearance (a fat man with a surprised/shocked look on his face on horseback) is far removed, clearly, from the stereotyped Hollywood bloodthirsty gunslinger. The narrator will remark later that Garmendia weighed more than two hundred and forty pounds, had a round face and fair eyes, soft hair like that of a baby, and that he was quiet and shy (GBR, 16). Another element common to the three volumes in the series is their peritextual dimension: a narrator, speaking in the first person, presents Garmendia's story as real and states, moreover, that he heard it from his uncle (GBR, 7–9). Therefore, through this well-known recourse, this compiler or transmitter of Garmendia's story, in addition to stressing the real underlying layer of the character, manages to emphasize the origin of the series: the stories that his uncle told Uribe himself and that the Basque writer confirmed during the presentations of the book.[100] In *Garmendia eta zaldun beltza*, Uribe, who is well-known for the constant recourse to autofiction in his work through striking examples such as the prize-winning *Bilbao-New York-Bilbao*, tells the story of the Basque gunslinger Garmendia's persecution on account of having been falsely accused of the murder of Wild Rose's husband (GBR,13). Recounted by a heterodiegetic, extradiegetic narrator in the third person, past tense, the text presents a frenetic rhythm, full of adventures, with constant calls to the narratee thanks to expressions like "I assure you" (GBR, 15) and "As I mentioned before" (GBR, 33), calls that seek to attract the reader's attention. Yet what is truly noteworthy is the "encyclopedic" dimension of the work, which is full of references to famous Hollywood Westerns, nineteenth-century American figureheads (writers, adventurers, and tycoons), Basque sayings and songs that define Garmendia's cultural foundations

100 Cf. Marin, Maribel, "Kirmen Uribe convierte 'Garmendia Errege' en un canto a la amistad. El escritor prolonga las aventuras inspiradas en un personaje real," *El País*, 10/12/2004. Online: https://elpais.com/diario/2004/12/10/paisvasco/1102711215_850215.html?prm=enviar_email [August 17, 2020].

(GBR, 40), and authors and works of nineteenth-century world literature. These intertextual references do not hide the author's wish to establish a story or, more accurately, a counternarrative that dignifies and grants an adventurous halo to the unvalued profession of sheepherder and Basque migration in general. In effect, the leader of the town in which the action takes place, Clean City, is called Tidy Harry in a clear allusion to the well-known Clint Eastwood movie *Dirty Harry* (1971). Moreover, Garmendia's co-protagonist and friend, Amalio Juárez, is of Mexican descent and his portrayal matches the Mexican stereotype in the United States: he has a dark complexion, a mustache and beard stubble from not shaving for a few days, is thin, and arrived in the US by crossing the Rio Grande, the well-known river that marks the natural American-Mexican border, illegally (GBR, 23). Yet *Rio Grande* (1950) is also a famous Western starring John Wayne and Maureen O'Hara. Moreover, the line Amalio repeats constantly—"No mames buey" (GBR, 27)—in addition to revealing his origins, gives color to the text; as do the pair of gunslingers, Rat and Bat, one fat and the other thin (GBR, 32), who evoke celebrated comic double acts in film and who repeat constantly an absurd dialog that clearly gives rhythm and color to the text:

> -Zer uste duzu, Bat? -galdetu zion Ratek Bati.
> ["What do you think, Bat?" Rat asked Bat.]
>
> -Zuk uste duzuna, Rat-erantun zion Batek.
> ["The same as you, Rat," Bat answered.] (GBR, 41)

The cast of historical characters to whom the story pays homage is completed on the one hand by Buffalo Bill and his traveling show, in a clear allusion to William Frederic Cody (1846–1917), an explorer, buffalo hunter, and showman. Amalio is clearly critical of him (GBR, 60) due to the fact that he displays Native Americans whom he himself defeated in battle in his show. On the other hand, there is also mention of the oil tycoon Rockefeller

(GBR, 70–71), in reference to John Davison Rockefeller (1839–1937). Garmendia and Amalio run into him on a train, and he is portrayed as being especially avaricious. The heterotypical space of the Sirena Saloon, which is run by the character Fanny and located outside the town, is also interesting:

> It was Fanny, the owner of the Sirena Saloon. She was a robust woman, blonde, and blue-eyed. She was strong, a straight shooter, and could seduce any man.
> Tidy Harry thought that the Sirena Saloon was a den of sinners. In his opinion, only varmints and drunks frequented the place. (GBR, 45)

This brave and active woman, who will fall in love with Garmendia and is capable of shooting and saving him from the gallows in GBR, could be an allusion to Frances Matilda Van de Grift Osbourne Stevenson, better known as Fanny Stevenson (1840–1914). She was the wife of writer Robert Louis Stevenson, and was a strong, free-spirited woman who handled a Colt, prospected for gold in the Nevada desert, traversed the mountains of California, and traveled across the United States in order to rescue her first husband. She served as a true muse for the author of *Treasure Island* and what is more, Uribe's text displays the courage that also seduced the Scottish writer. Statements such as "Often, it's best to hide in plain sight. They'll look right past you" (GBR, 52), remind one of the well-known strategy revealed masterfully by E. A. Poe in *The Purloined Letter* (1844). That is because Uribe's Fanny is a fan of literature and she demonstrates this in her choice of poem to decorate her saloon (GBR, 47), the first strophe of *I Started Early – Took My Dog* by the famous American writer Emily Dickinson (1830–1886).

I started Early – Took my Dog—
And visited the Sea—
The Mermaids in the Basement
Came out to look at me— (GBR, 47)

It will be Fanny who leads, alongside her friends, the liberating of Garmendia and Amalio from the gallows; she will be the one to take them in at the saloon so they can escape, somewhat bizarrely, from Clean City. The train that they will take illegally will take them toward the book's final surprise, a fortuitous encounter, in the last chapter, with the Black Rider—Zaldun Beltza—an outlaw who, in reality, will turn out to be Garmendia's cousin. He is an inoffensive sort but, fueled by the tabloid press of the time, by the "spectacle" (GBR, 81), he will experience his own mythologizing in flesh and blood.

In short, GBR is an attractive adventure story with all the ingredients befitting of the genre: persecutions, premonitory dreams (GBR, 22–25), betrayals, and so on. And all of that is embellished with large doses of humor in order to introduce a Basque sheepherder whose coyness has a lot to do with the isolated life that sheepherders led in the United States, and whose habits, such as building small cabins in the mountains, making tree carvings, and the fact that his best friend is a small wren whom he calls lovingly Gilda (GBR, 17) in honor of a sacristan he had known in his home town, add to the rationale of his shyness and isolation: the fact that he does not speak English (GBR, 16). Such unfamiliarity, as theorists of postcolonial criticism have pointed out repeatedly, places immigrants in a situation of inferiority and subalternity.

The second volume in the series, *Garmendia errege* (King Garmendia, 2004), is, as the author himself observed, a song to friendship. It narrates Garmendia's and Amalio's experiences when they go to take part in Buffalo Bill's show, a very successful traveling spectacle that was in reality established in 1883. There, they coincide with familiar couples like Rat and Bat, and with Chief Sitting Bull (GE, 39), who has been transformed into an exotic attraction in the show. As in *Garmendia eta zaldun beltza*, Uribe once more deploys an attractive intertextuality and offers a very rigorous sociohistorical contextualization. As such, he mentions restaurants such as the Occidental in San Francisco, part of the celebrated Occidental Hotel that existed between 1861 and 1906 (GE, 61). Furthermore, Garmendia ends up acting at the famous Jenny Lind Theater, which is today San Francisco City Hall. There is also mention of well-known nineteenth-century fantasy tales such as *Dracula* and *Frankenstein* (GE, 63). And the guests at a dinner in the Occidental delight in the fantastic and ghostly stories told by a mysterious old sailor, stories of gigantic creatures along the lines of *Gulliver's Travels* (1729), and so forth. In Chapter 4, a well-known Chinese traditional tale about the origin of the universe is even included.

This is an attractive intertextual work that, in reality, concludes its storyline with the disagreements that emerge between the two main protagonists, Garmendia and Amalio, on account of the Basque's "success" in the show. In effect, his strength, which, as the narrator states, is demonstrated in traditional Basque sports such as stonelifting (GE, 34), makes Garmendia the most important attraction in Buffalo Bill's show. Indeed, strength, which is termed *indarra* in Basque, constitutes a central quality of the Basque rural worldview. It is a quality that flourishes in many rural sports and that functions, primarily, as a metaphor of masculinity (Zulaika & Douglass 2007, 262). Garmendia's show of strength will be a key element that contributes to his exoticizing, and this takes place via his change of name to Orson (cf. Orson Wells), because the Basque surname "Garmendia" is "strange" and not "modern" enough in the eyes of the boss, Buffalo Bill (GE, 35). The show christens Garmendia as "the king of strength," "Indartsuen errege" (GE, 43), and he is portrayed with clothing in the style of European kings (GE, 43), crown and cape included. It is easy to deduce the colonial reading of what Garmendia signifies before the eyes of Buffalo Bill and the spectators who attend the shows. Garmendia is, in reality, that beast, that exotic animal like Sitting Bull (GE, 39–40) that has been domesticated and is displayed like a trophy of domination. Hence, it hurts Garmendia's good friend Amalio to see what his pal has been transformed into, and he leaves Garmendia to fend for himself, just like when he was a sheepherder in the mountains of the West and had to wait weeks for the supply wagon to arrive (GE, 49). It will be his good friends from the Sirena Saloon, the cook Xi, accompanied by Fanny and Janet, who will rescue Garmendia from the "curse" (GE, 81) of the traveling show.

The third and last work in the series, *Garmendia eta Fannyren sekretua* (Garmendia and Fanny's Secret, 2006), focuses its plot on Fanny's disappearance after her visit to Italy. Already as part of the introductory text authored by an autofictional Uribe that precedes all of the books in the series, he speaks about the presence of the composer Giacomo Puccini in the United States, right at the same time as Garmendia. This coincided with Puccini's composition of *La fanciulla del West* (The Girl of the West), in which, by all accounts, there is a Basque character, Nina Mitxeltorena, a woman with a somewhat disorderly lifestyle (GFS, 6) like Fanny, who, at the start of the story has already been missing for three or four months (GFS, 13), to the despair of her beloved Garmendia. Alongside Amalio, he will embark on an impassioned search for her. The use of synopses and ellipses accelerates the rhythm of narrating the preparations for the journey (GFS, 17), as well as the arrival of the two men in New York, from where they will embark as stowaways on the *Valeria* (GFS, 4). The reader will feel the bustle of the Brooklyn harbor (GFS, 19) in its vibrant bars, and the presence of the Statue of Liberty, in 1886, gives a potential time-frame to the events narrated. The comments of the implicit author about the dangers of Garmendia's haughty attitude at the Bar Inn are especially striking (GFS, 22), as well as the comical scenes on the ship when the Basque needs to relieve himself (GFS, 28).

Venice will be the city in which the search for Fanny becomes more intense, during a journey full of suspense and palace intrigues. In order to carry out the search, Garmendia and Amalio will count on the help of a besotted gondolier nicknamed *Michelle Amore* (GFS, 34), who will tell them tales of adultery and deceit (GFS, 36), stories that Garmendia will compare to others he has heard about, like that of Pernando Amezketarra (1764–1823), a popular *bertsolari* and rogue that Gregorio Muxika transformed into a literary character in his 1927 bestseller, *Pernando Amezketarra*. Yet the gondolier will also function as a guide to the fascinating city of Venice, in which seducers like Giacomo Casanova (GFS, 42) will go to prison for their amorous adventures, and who will pass, sadly, the Bridge of Sighs (GFS, 41), on their journey to incarceration. Inevitably, misunderstandings and mysterious adventures will lead to a masked ball in which Garmendia and Amalio, with the aid of the triplets Prima, Seconda, and Terza, all dressed in flowing gowns of the era, will find Fanny (GFS, 71). The happy ending will have all the ingredients of an Italian celebration: poems, a table full of food, and Margherita pizza, like that which Raffaele Esposito made for his love (GFS, 86).

4 A short conclusion

I have analyzed above the novelty implied for young readers by Kirmen Uribe's Garmendia series. As I argue, the three volumes in the series constitute a counternarrative within the narrations that have represented the Basque diaspora and migration to the United States. Uribe deconstructs the stereotype of the Basque sheepherder and offers stories based on a real character, the sheepherder Garmendia from Bizkaia, set in a Far West full of gunslingers and miscreants, in the purest style of Hollywood Westerns. Yet beyond offering attractive adventure stories, Uribe succeeds in demonstrating the contradictions and tensions of a late nineteenth-century American society in which immigrants and Native Americans attempt to resist being subjected to exoticization.

Bibliography

Agirre, Domingo. 1907-1912. *Garoa*. RIEV.

Alvarez Gila, Oscar. 1999. Clero vasco y nacionalismo: del exilio al liderazgo de la emigración (1900-1940). *Studi Emigrazioni*, 133: 101–18.

Alvarez Gila, Oscar & Tapiz Fernández, José María. 1996. Prensa nacionalista vasca y emigración a América (1900-1936). *Anuario de Estudios americanos* 53, 1: 233–260.

Atxaga, Bernardo. 1984. *Bi letter jaso nituen oso denbora gutxian*. Donostia: Erein. Spanish: *Dos letters*. Translated by Arantxa Sabán. Barcelona: Ediciones B, 1990. English: "Two Letters All at Once" in *Two Basque Stories*. Translated from Basque by Nere Lete. Reno: Center for Basque Studies, University of Nevada, Reno, 2009.

Atxaga, Bernardo. 2004. *El hijo del acordeonista*. Translated by Bernardo Atxaga and Asun Garikano. Madrid: Alfaguara. (Originally published in 2003). English: *The Accordionist's Son*. Translated from the Spanish by Margaret Jull Costa. London: Harvill Secker, 2007.

Bhabha, Homi. 1994. *The Location of Culture*. London: Routledge

Douglass, William A. & Bilbao, Jon. 1975. *Amerikanuak: Basques in the New World*. Reno: University of Nevada Press.

Echeverria, Jeronima. 1998. *Home Away from Home: History of Basque Boardinghouses, Hotels and Communities*. Reno: University of Nevada Press.

Epaltza, Aingeru. 1994. *Lur zabaletan*. Pamplona: Pamiela.

Estudillo, Luis Martin. 2020. Literatura eta desplazamendua: Kirmen Uribe. In Mari Jose Olaziregi Alustiza and Amaia Elizalde Estenaga (eds.) *Kirmen Uribe: bizitza, fikzioa*, 115-132. Bilbo: Euskal Herriko Unibertsitateko Argitalpen Zerbitzua, Mikel Laboa Katedra.

Etxeita, José Manuel. 1988 [1910]. *Jaioterri maitia*. Bilbao: Labayru.

Ezkerra, Estibalitz. 2020. Keinuen poesia. In Mari Jose Olaziregi Alustiza and Amaia Elizalde Estenaga (eds.) *Kirmen Uribe: bizitza, fikzioa*, 55-64. Bilbo: Euskal Herriko Unibertsitateko Argitalpen Zerbitzua, Mikel Laboa Katedra.

Garikano, Asun. 2009. *Far Westeko Euskal Herria*. Pamplona: Pamiela. English: *Far Western Basque Country*. Reno: Center for Basque Studies, University of Nevada, Reno, 2017.

Isasi, Mirim. 1942. *White Stars of Freedom: A Basque Shepherd Boy Becomes an American*. Chicago: Whitman &Cía.

Kristeva, Julia. 1991, *Strangers to Ourselves*. New York: Columbia University Press.

Lasagabaster, Jesús María. 2005. *Las literaturas de los vascos*. Bilbao: Universidad de Deusto.

Laxalt, Robert. 1957. *Sweet Promised Land*. New York: Harper.

Olaizola, Jesus Mari, "Txiliku." 1993. *Indianua*. Donostia: Elkar.

Olaziregi, María José. 2014. De vascos y migrantes. Breves consideraciones sobre las representaciones de la emigración en la literatura vasca. In *Inmigración/Emigración na LIX*, Blanca Ana Roig-Rechou et al. (coord.), 105–118. Vigo: Xerais.

Olaziregi, María José. 2015. Literatura vasca y emigración: la representación de América en la narrativa vasca. In *La memoria novelada III. Memoria transnacional y anhelos de justicia*, Juan Carlos Cruz Suárez et al. (ed.), 319–332. Berna: Peter Lang.

Pérez, Pio. 2016. El canto del pastor no espanta las ovejas: memoria y nostalgia en los versos improvisados de los emigrantes vascos. *Disparidades. Revista de Antropología* 71, 2: 389–414.

Río, David. 2000. Presencia de los vascos en la literatura norteamericana contemporánea. *Euskonews & Media* 91: 15–22.

Said, Edward. 2000. The Art of Displacement: Mona Hatoum's Logic of Irreconcilables. In *Mona Hatoum: The Entire World as a Foreign Land*, 7–17. London: Tate Gallery.

Totoricagüena, G. 2005. *Basque Diaspora: Migration and Transnational Identity*. Reno: Center for Basque Studies, University of Nevada, Reno.

Ugalde, Martin. 1990. *Itzulera baten historia*. Donostia: Elkar. Spanish: *Historia de un regreso*. Translated by Koldo Izagirre. Hondarribia: Hiru, 1995.

Uribe, Kirmen. 2001. *Bitartean heldu eskutik*. Zarautz: Susa. Spanish: *Mientras tanto, cógeme la mano*. Translated by Gerardo Markuleta and Ana Arregi. Madrid: Visor, 2004. English: *Meanwhile Take My Hand*. Translated from the Basque by Elizabeth Macklin. Saint Paul, MN: Graywolf, 2007.

Uribe, Kirmen. 2003. *Ekidazu, lehoiek ez dakite biolina jotzen*. Donostia: Elkar.

Uribe, Kirmen. 2003. *Garmendia eta zaldun beltza*. Donostia: Elkar. English: *Garmendia and the Black Rider*. Translated by Nere Lete. Reno: Center for Basque Studies, University of Nevada, Reno, 2015.

Uribe, Kirmen. 2004. *Ez naiz ilehoria, eta zer?* Donostia: Editores Asociados.

Uribe, Kirmen. 2004. *Garmendia errege*. Donostia: Elkar.

Uribe, Kirmen. 2005. *Guti*. Donostia: Elkar.

Uribe, Kirmen. 2006. *Garmendia eta Fannyren sekretua*. Donostia: Elkar.

Uribe, Kirmen. 2008. *Bilbao-New York-Bilbao*, Zarautz: Susa. Spanish: *Bilbao-New York-Bilbao*. Translated by Ana Arregi. Barcelona: Seix Barral, 2009. English: *Bilbao-New York-Bilbao*. Translated from the Basque by Elizabeth Macklin. Bridgend, Wales: Seren, 2014.

Uribe, Kirmen. 2010. *Bar puerto*. Donostia: Elkar.

Uribe, Kirmen. 2012. *Mussche*. Zarautz: Susa. Spanish: *Lo que mueve el mundo*. Translated by Gerardo Markuleta. Barcelona: Seix Barral, 2013.

Uribe, Kirmen. 2013. *Jainko txiki eta jostalari hura*. Donostia: Elkar.

Uribe, Kirmen. 2014. El idioma de la Virgen María de la playa. In *Vidas y ficciones*. Pamplona-Iruña: Pamiela, 18–23.

Uribe, Kirmen. 2016. *Elkarrekin esnatzeko ordua*. Zarautz: Susa.

Uribe, Kirmen. 2020. Desobedientzia gidaliburua. In Mari Jose Olaziregi Alustiza and Amaia Elizalde Estenaga (eds.) *Kirmen Uribe: bizitza, fikzioa*, 17-20. Bilbo: Euskal Herriko Unibertsitateko Argitalpen Zerbitzua, Mikel Laboa Katedra.

Zavala, Antonio. 1984. *Ameriketako bertsoak*. Tolosa: Auspoa.

Zulaika, Joseba & Douglass, W. 2007. *Basque Culture: Anthropological Perspectives*. Reno: Center for Basque Studies, University of Nevada.

BIBLIOGRAPHY

Kirmen Uribe[101]

Uribe has a BA in Basque philology from the University of the Basque Country (UPV-EHU) and he studied comparative literature at the University of Trento, Italy. Among contemporary young Basque writers, he is the most internationally renowned. Uribe's work has been widely recognized, having won several prizes at the Basque, European, and international levels.

Uribe currently resides in New York, where, through "She Writes" project, he was awarded one of the Cullman Fellowships from the NYC public library in order to write his next novel during the period 2018–2019. He recently released that novel, called *The Past Life of Dolphins* (2021). Uribe currently lectures at NYU and gave his latest seminar at Barnard College (Columbia University) as a guest international writer.

Kirmen Uribe has written in different genres, such as novels, poetry, children's and young adult literature, and essays. Below is a bibliography of his works:

Novels

Bilbao-New York-Bilbao. 2014. Bridgend: Seren Books (translated by Elizabeth Macklin). Original in Basque: *Bilbao-New York-Bilbao*. 2008. Donostia: Elkar.

Mussche. 2012. Zarautz: Susa. Spanish: *Lo que mueve el mundo* (translated by Gerardo Markuleta). Barcelona: Seix Barral, 2013.

Elkarrekin esnatzeko ordua. 2016. Zarautz: Susa. Spanish: La hora de despertarnos juntos (translated by J.M. Isasi). Barcelona: Seix Barral.

101 For more information on the writer and his work, see http://kirmenuribe.eus/en/.

Izurdeen aurreko bizitza. 2021. Zarautz: Susa. Spanish: *La vida anterior de los delfines* (translated by J.M. Isasi). Barcelona: Seix Barral, 2022.

Poetry

Meanwhile Take My Hand. 2007. Minneapolis: Graywolf Press (translated by Elizabeth Macklin). Original in Basque: *Bitartean heldu eskutik*. 2001. Zarautz: Susa.

17 segundo. 2018. Zarautz: Susa. Spanish: *17 segundos*. Madrid: Visor, 2020.

Children's and Young Adult Literature

Garmendia and the Black Rider. 2015. Reno: Center for Basque Studies, University of Nevada (translated by Nerea Lete). Original in Basque: *Garmendia eta zaldun beltza*. 2003. Donostia: Elkar.

Ekidazu, lehoiek ez dakite biolina jotzen. 2003. Donostia: Elkar.

Ez naiz ilehoria, eta zer? 2004. Donostia: Elkar.

Garmendia errege. 2004. Donostia: Elkar.

Garmendia eta Fannyren sekretua. 2006. Donostia: Elkar.

Guti. 2005. Donostia: Elkar.

Essays

Lizardi eta erotismoa. 1996. Irun: Alberdania.

Recompilations

Portukoplak. 2006. Donostia: Elkar.

Multimedia

Zaharregia, txikiegia agian. 2003. Soraluze: Gaztelupeko Hotsak.

Bar Puerto: Voices from the Edge. 2010. Donostia: Elkar (translated by Elizabeth Macklin). Original in Basque: *Bar Puerto: Bazterreko ahotsak*. 2010. Donostia: Elkar.

Jainko txiki eta jostalari hura. 2014. Donostia: Elkar.

The authors who have contributed to this collection

Hasier Arraiz

Arraiz has a BA in Hispanic philology (University of the Basque Country). He is currently studying for a master's in teaching literature in secondary education.

In the meantime, Arraiz has also been active mostly in politics, always in the sociopolitical field for the left-wing Basque nationalist movement. He was incarcerated in several prisons outside the Basque Country for being part of the leadership of the Batasuna political party. He learned a lot during his time in prison. In 2013, he was the first president of the recently created political party, Sortu. He was also a member of the Basque Parliament for one term (from 2012 to 2016) for the EH Bildu coalition.

Without renouncing political activity and, ultimately, his political identity, in July 2016 he decided to put aside his professional political work. Since then, he has published a work on the new generation of contemporary Basque narrative and on the effect and importance of Kirmen Uribe's work on that generation: *Maitasun keinu bat besterik ez* (Just a Gesture of Love, Erein, 2019).

Leyre Arrieta Alberdi

Arrieta holds a PhD in contemporary history and is an associate professor at the University of Deusto. She teaches courses specifically within the communication degree. She has carried out research, both individually and as part of a group, on Basque nationalism, Basque exile, and European identity. Her other research areas of interest include music symbolism, the role of the media, and, in general, contemporary Basque history.

Arrieta has published numerous articles in scholarly journals and has collaborated in many collective books. Among her most important works are: *Radio Euskadi, la voz de la libertad*

(1998, with J. A. Rodríguez Ranz), *Diputación y modernización. Gipuzkoa 1940-1975* (2003, with M. Barandiaran), *Estación Europa. La política europeísta del PNV en el exilio (1945-1977)* (2007), *La historia de Radio Euskadi (Guerra, Resistencia, Exilio, Democracia)* (2009), *Fondo Gobierno de Euzkadi: historia y contenido* (2011), and, with other authors, *Diccionario ilustrado de símbolos del nacionalismo vasco* (2012) and *El primer Gobierno Vasco. En pie sobre la tierra vasca* (2016). Her latest work is a critical edition of *La causa del pueblo vasco* by F. J. Landaburu (2017), a politician whose biography she is currently researching.

Amaia Elizalde Estenaga

Elizalde Estenaga is Assistant Professor in the Faculty of Education and Sports (Department of Language Education and Literature) at the University of the Basque Country and a member of the MHLI research group (www.mhli.net). She carried out her doctorate under the joint supervision of the University of the Basque Country (UPV-EHU) and the Université Bordeaux-Montaigne (UBM), financed by a predoctoral contract from the UPV-EHU. In 2018, she defended her dissertation, "Jon Miranderen *Haur besoetakoa* (1970), modernitate ukatua," and she has taught university courses on literature in the Faculty of Arts at the UPV-EHU and within the master's program in Basque studies at the UBM. She has presented papers at several international conferences and published various academic articles about Basque literature, cultural studies, memory, and censorship.

Estibalitz Ezkerra Vegas

Ezkerra is a lecturer of Basque studies at the University of California, Santa Barbara. In 2019, she received a doctorate in comparative literature from the University of Illinois, Urbana-Champaign and in 2010 her master's in English literature from the University of Nevada, Reno. Likewise, she holds bachelor's degrees in art history and journalism from the University of the

Basque Country. Her research work focuses on the comparative interdisciplinary analysis of memory, politics, and history in literature and cultural production in post-conflict countries. She is the author of the informational booklet *Basque Literature in the Twentieth Century* (2012), published by the Etxepare Basque Institute, and she has written about Basque literature in Basque and other languages in the collection of essays *Basque Literary History* (2013).

Miren Ibarluzea Santisteban

An Assistant Professor in the Faculty of Education at the Bilbao campus of the University of the Basque Country (UPV-EHU) and member of the MHLI research group (www.mhli.net), Ibarluzea earned a doctorate from the UPV-EHU in 2017 with the international dissertation titled "Itzulpengintzaren errepresentazioak euskal literatura garaikidean: eremuaren autonomizazioa, literatur historiografiak eta itzultzaileak fikzioan" (Representations of translation in contemporary Basque literature: autonomization of the field, historiographies of literature and translators in fiction) and she was awarded the special doctoral prize for the 2018–2019 academic year and the Sixth Koldo Mitxelena Prize for a doctoral thesis in Basque in 2018. Ibarluzea researches issues related to Basque translation studies, Basque literature, and language and literature didactics. She was a lecturer at the Michel de Montaigne-Bordeaux 3 (Department of Basque Studies) and Sorbonne Nouvelle-Paris 3 (Department of Iberian and Latin American Studies) Universities between 2011 and 2015 and taught classes in translation at the Department of Philology and Basque Studies, Faculty of Humanities, at the UPV-EHU (2015–2016).

Jon Kortazar

Kortazar is a professor of Basque literature at the University of the Basque Country (UPV-EHU). He is the head of the LAIDA (Literature and Identity) research group that published *Egungo Euskal Literaturaren Historia* (2007–2017) in eight volumes. It was published in English as *Contemporary Basque Literature* (Center for Basque Studies, Reno, 2016). His most important works are: *Literatura vasca. Siglo XX* (1990, seven reprints), *La pluma y la tierra. Poesía vasca de los años 80* (1999), and *Montañas en la niebla. Poesía vasca de los años 90* (2006). With Iberoamericana/Vervuert he published *Contemporary Basque Literature: Kirmen Uribe's Proposal* (2013), and edited *Autonomía e ideología. Tensiones en el campo cultural vasco* (2016) and *Bridge/Zubia. Imágenes de la relación cultural entre el País Vasco y Estados Unidos* (2019). He has coordinated several monographs on Basque literature in the journal Ínsula.

Luis Martín Estudillo

Martín Estudillo is a professor in the Department of Spanish Studies at the University of Iowa and an affiliate researcher at the Universities of Minnesota and Groningen (Netherlands). He is the executive editor of the journals *Hispanic Issues* and *Hispanic Issues Online*. He received the Collegiate Teaching Award as part of the Dean's Scholar Award and the Collegiate Award from the University of Iowa, as well as two awards from the National Endowment for the Humanities. His latest books are *The Rise of Euroskepticism: Europe and Its Critics in Spanish Culture* (Vanderbilt University Press, 2018) and *Despertarse de Europa. Arte, literatura y euroescepticismo* (Ediciones Cátedra, 2019). Currently, he is finishing a monograph that explores the work of Francisco de Goya.

José Martínez Rubio

Martínez Rubio holds a PhD in Spanish literature (Universitat de València). His field of specialization is the contemporary novel linked to Spanish and Latin American historical memory (narrative forms of representation, integrational debates about traumatic processes, African decolonization processes, and representations of and conflicts over queer identities). His most recent works are *El futuro era esto. Crisis y rematerialización de la Modernidad* (Orbis Tertius, 2014), *Identidades inestables. Avatares, evoluciones y teorías de la subjetividad en la narrativa española actual* (Indigo, 2016, ed.), and *Las formas de la verdad. Investigación, docuficción y memoria en la novela hispánica* (Anthropos, 2015).

María Jesús Nafría Fernández

Nafría Fernández holds a BA in Spanish philology from the Universidad Complutense of Madrid and, with a master's in both literary studies and publishing studies, she has always been linked professionally to the sphere of culture. She is an editor specializing in the fields of academic texts and independent publishing.

She is currently preparing a dissertation about Basque literature, analyzing aspects related to memory construction, cultural identity, and the influence of violence on Basque literature and Basque society. Several of her works specialize in Kirmen Uribe, the main object of her dissertation. At the same time, she has participated in international conferences and published several articles in specialized journals.

By way of alternative cultural activities, she collaborates on *El café de la lluvia*, a website in which she publishes articles in her own section, "El anillo de los peces," on subjects linked to the literature of yesterday and today, forgotten authors, as well as rediscovered works, combined with social topicality.

Mari Jose Olaziregi Alustiza

Olaziregi holds a PhD in Basque philology and is an associate professor in the Department of Linguistics and Basque Studies at the University of the Basque Country (UPV-EHU). She has been a visiting professor and taught at the Center for Basque Studies (University of Nevada, Reno), Universität Konstanz (Germany), the University of Chicago, and the City University of New York Graduate Center. She directed and designed the Network of Readerships and Chairs in the Basque Language and Culture of the Etxepare Basque Institute (Department of Culture in the

Basque Government) in the period 2010–2016, and since 2004 she has been the editor of the Basque Literature Series by the Center for Basque Studies at the University of Nevada, Reno. Moreover, she is an associate member of Euskaltzaindia, the Basque Language Academy. A specialist in contemporary Basque literature, she has published works such as *Euskal eleberriaren historia* (History of the Basque Novel, 2002) and *Waking the Hedgehog: The Literary Universe of Bernardo Atxaga* (2005). Her edited works include *Six Basque Poets* (2006), *Writers in Between Languages: Minority Literatures in the Global Scene* (2009), and *Basque Literary History* (2012). Since 2013, she has directed the Consolidated Research Group MHLI, Memorias Históricas en las Literaturas Ibéricas (Historical Memories in Iberian Literatures), at UPV/EHU, as well as projects IT 1047-16 (2016–2021, Basque Government) and FFI2017-84342-P (2017–2021, Mineco).

Lourdes Otaegi

Otaegi holds a PhD in Basque literature (University of Deusto, Bilbao), and is currently an associate professor in the Department of Linguistics and Basque Studies (Faculty of Humanities, EHU-UPV, Vitoria-Gasteiz). She is part of the "Memoria Histórica en las Literaturas Ibéricas" research project (Mineco 2016–2019) and participates in different research projects related to gender studies (Vanacem 2016–2019), as well as projects about Basque literary theory and historiography (Mineco 2016–2021). Her main research area is the study of the lyrical genre, and her dissertation focused on the poetic ideas of Xabier Lizardi and what was termed the "Euskal Pizkundea" or Basque literary renaissance (1879–1936). She later extended her studies to contemporary writers and she describes the evolution of the genre through the twentieth century in "Modern Basque Poetry" (*Basque Literary History*, 2012). She has been an associate member of Euskaltzaindia, the Basque Language Academy, since 2003, and as secretary of its literary studies committee (2000–2010) she coordinated the work that culminated in the first *Diccionario de términos literarios* in Basque (2008).

Sally Perret

Perret is an associate professor in the Modern Languages Department at Salisbury University (United States) and director of the Global Languages Education Program in the Department of Secondary Education. She received the Most Outstanding Supervisor Award for her work with education candidates. Perret specializes in cultural studies, particularly in the field of new methods of literary production. She has published her work in the *Hispanic Review*, *Hispanic Research Journal*, and *Journal of Spanish Cultural Studies*, and is an affiliate researcher in the LAIDA (Literatura eta Identitatea Ikerketa Taldea) research group.

www.ingramcontent.com/pod-product-compliance
Lightning Source LLC
LaVergne TN
LVHW010053110826
845155LV00028B/312

* 9 7 8 1 9 4 9 8 0 5 7 1 0 *